A BASIC READER FOR COLLEGE WRITERS

A BASIC READER FOR COLLEGE WRITERS

DAVID I. DANIELS
CAMDEN COUNTY COLLEGE

JANET M. GOLDSTEIN

CHRISTOPHER G. HAYES
UNIVERSITY OF GEORGIA

TOWNSEND PRESS   Marlton, NJ 08053

Books in the Townsend Press Writing Series:

BASIC ENGLISH BRUSHUP
BASIC ENGLISH BRUSHUP, SHORT VERSION
ENGLISH BRUSHUP
BASIC WRITING SKILLS WITH READINGS
WRITING SKILLS WITH READINGS
A BASIC READER FOR COLLEGE WRITERS
THE TOWNSEND THEMATIC READER

Copyright © 1989, 1995 by Townsend Press, Inc.
Printed in the United States of America
ISBN 0-944210-75-9

All rights reserved. No part of this work may be
reproduced in any form without permission in writing
from the publisher. Send requests to:
Townsend Press, Inc.
Pavilions at Greentree–408
Marlton, New Jersey 08053

Send book orders and requests for desk copies or supplements to:

**Townsend Press
1038 Industrial Drive
Berlin, New Jersey 08009**

**For even faster service, call us at our toll-free number:
1-800-772-6410**

**Or FAX your request to:
1-609-753-0649**

ISBN 0-944210-75-9

Contents

Alternate Table of Contents   ix

Preface to the Instructor   xv

How to Become a Better Reader and Writer   xx

Personal Memories

1. Bird Girl (with Answer Key)   *Clark DeLeon*   2
2. Being a Boy   *Julius Lester*   14
3. The Back of the Bus   *Mary E. Mebane*   21
4. To Get a Story, I Flimflammed a Dead Man's Mother   *Bob Teague*   32
5. Back from Death?   *Susan Seliger*   43

Families and Children

6. Batter Up   *Bill Cosby*   56
7. What Do Children Owe Their Parents?   *Ann Landers*   64
8. Students in Shock   *John Kellmayer*   75
9. When My Brother Was Slain   *Ben Fong-Torres*   83
10. Living the Simple Life   *Carolyn Lewis*   93

Sports and Leisure

11 Fun. Oh Boy, Fun. You Could Die from It
    Suzanne Britt Jordan   102
12 Rudeness at the Movies *Bill Wine*   109
13 Strike Out Little League *Robin Roberts*   117
14 Television Addiction *Marie Winn*   125
15 Boxing Is a Barbarism Civilization Can Do Without
    H. Bruce Miller   132

Understanding Ourselves

16 What Is Intelligence, Anyway? *Isaac Asimov*   142
17 Funerals Are Good for People
    William M. Lamers, Jr.   149
18 The Urge to Conform *Vincent Ryan Ruggiero*   158
19 "Learning" to Give Up *Albert Rosenfeld*   167
20 Don't Let Stereotypes Warp Your Judgments
    Robert L. Heilbroner   176

Social Issues

21 A Crime of Compassion *Barbara Huttmann*   186
22 How About Low-Cost Drugs for Addicts?
    Louis Nizer   194
23 Why We Throw Food Away *William Rathje*   202
24 Escape Valve *Gregg Easterbrook*   210
25 What We Can Learn from Japan's Prisons
    James Webb   217
26 Turning On Turned-Off Workers *Michael LeBoeuf*   227

Survival Skills

27 The Smart Way to Buy a New Car
    Luella Fern Sanders   240
28 Classroom Note-Taking *Clarissa White*   250

29 Owning a Pet Can Have Therapeutic Value
    Jane Brody   259

30 Face Up to Your Fears *Lois B. Morris*   268

31 Specific Details *David Sqwire and
    Frances Chitwood*   278

32 Problems and Pain *M. Scott Peck*   286

Partial Answer Key

Batter Up   293

Fun. Oh Boy, Fun. You Could Die from It   295

What Is Intelligence, Anyway?   298

A Crime of Compassion   299

The Smart Way to Buy a New Car   301

Acknowledgments   304

Glossary   307

Index   317

Reading Performance Chart   321

Alternate Table of Contents

Narration

Bird Girl *Clark DeLeon* 2
The Back of the Bus *Mary E. Mebane* 21
Batter Up *Bill Cosby* 56
When My Brother Was Slain *Ben Fong-Torres* 83
A Crime of Compassion *Barbara Huttmann* 186

Description

The Back of the Bus *Mary E. Mebane* 21
Back from Death? *Susan Seliger* 43
Rudeness at the Movies *Bill Wine* 109
A Crime of Compassion *Barbara Huttmann* 186

Examples

Being a Boy *Julius Lester* 14
To Get a Story, I Flimflammed a Dead Man's Mother *Bob Teague* 32

Back from Death? *Susan Seliger*   43

What Do Children Owe Their Parents?
Ann Landers   64

Living the Simple Life *Carolyn Lewis*   93

Rudeness at the Movies *Bill Wine*   109

Funerals Are Good for People
William M. Lamers, Jr.   149

The Urge to Conform *Vincent Ryan Ruggiero*   158

"Learning" to Give Up *Albert Rosenfeld*   167

Don't Let Stereotypes Warp Your Judgments
Robert L. Heilbroner   176

Why We Throw Food Away *William Rathje*   202

Owning a Pet Can Have Therapeutic Value
Jane Brody   259

Face Up to Your Fears *Lois B. Morris*   268

Specific Details *David Sqwire and
Frances Chitwood*   278

Process

The Smart Way to Buy a New Car
Luella Fern Sanders   240

Classroom Note-Taking *Clarissa White*   250

Face Up to Your Fears *Lois B. Morris*   268

Specific Details *David Sqwire and
Frances Chitwood*   278

Problems and Pain *M. Scott Peck*   286

Definition

Being a Boy *Julius Lester*   14

Students in Shock *John Kellmayer*   75

Fun. Oh Boy, Fun. You Could Die from It
Suzanne Britt Jordan   102

ALTERNATE TABLE OF CONTENTS xi

Television Addiction *Marie Winn*   125
What Is Intelligence, Anyway? *Isaac Asimov*   142

Classification

What Do Children Owe Their Parents?
Ann Landers   64
Owning a Pet Can Have Therapeutic Value
Jane Brody   259

Comparison and Contrast

Living the Simple Life *Carolyn Lewis*   93
Television Addiction *Marie Winn*   125
What We Can Learn from Japan's Prisons
James Webb   217
Turning On Turned-Off Workers *Michael LeBoeuf*   227
Specific Details *David Sqwire and
Frances Chitwood*   278

Cause and Effect

Students in Shock *John Kellmayer*   75
When My Brother Was Slain *Ben Fong-Torres*   83
Rudeness at the Movies *Bill Wine*   109
Television Addiction *Marie Winn*   125
Funerals Are Good for People
William M. Lamers, Jr.   149
The Urge to Conform *Vincent Ryan Ruggiero*   158
"Learning" to Give Up *Albert Rosenfeld*   167
Don't Let Stereotypes Warp Your Judgments
Robert L. Heilbroner   176
How About Low-Cost Drugs for Addicts?
Louis Nizer   194

Why We Throw Food Away *William Rathje*   202

Escape Valve *Gregg Easterbrook*   210

What We Can Learn from Japan's Prisons
James Webb   217

Turning On Turned-Off Workers *Michael LeBoeuf*   227

Owning a Pet Can Have Therapeutic Value
Jane Brody   259

Face Up to Your Fears *Lois B. Morris*   268

Problems and Pain *M. Scott Peck*   286

Argumentation and Persuasion

Bird Girl *Clark DeLeon*   2

Being a Boy *Julius Lester*   14

Batter Up *Bill Cosby*   56

What Do Children Owe Their Parents?
Ann Landers   64

Living the Simple Life *Carolyn Lewis*   93

Fun. Oh Boy, Fun. You Could Die from It
Suzanne Britt Jordan   102

Rudeness at the Movies *Bill Wine*   109

Strike Out Little League *Robin Roberts*   117

Television Addiction *Marie Winn*   125

Boxing Is a Barbarism Civilization Can Do Without
H. Bruce Miller   132

What Is Intelligence, Anyway? *Isaac Asimov*   142

Funerals Are Good for People
William M. Lamers, Jr.   149

"Learning" to Give Up *Albert Rosenfeld*   167

A Crime of Compassion *Barbara Huttmann*   186

How About Low-Cost Drugs for Addicts?
Louis Nizer   194

Escape Valve *Gregg Easterbrook*   210

What We Can Learn from Japan's Prisons
James Webb   217

Owning a Pet Can Have Therapeutic Value
Jane Brody   259

Problems and Pain   *M. Scott Peck*   286

Preface to the Instructor

The number of college students who need work in basic skills is now very large—and growing rapidly. These students present a special challenge to those of us who teach them. On the one hand, they enter college expecting to think about and discuss issues at a serious intellectual level. On the other, they need to improve their basic writing and reading skills. Addressing these two equally important requirements demands of us a balancing act worthy of a tightrope walker.

A Basic Reader for College Writers is designed to help meet both the skill needs and intellectual needs of today's students. The book provides a series of thirty-two lively and thought-provoking essays, each accompanied by an extensive set of activities to help students read, understand, and write about the essays. In particular, by providing instruction and practice in the skills necessary for close and thoughtful reading, the text will help all those teachers whose students say, "I read it, but I didn't understand it."

The most important and distinguishing feature of the book is our emphasis on an *essential principle* that students must learn and practice. The principle is that any thoughtful communication of ideas has two basic parts: (1) a **point** is made and (2) that point is **supported**. Students learn to apply this principle to become better readers, writers, and thinkers. They are encouraged when *reading* an essay to look for a central idea as well as for the reasons, facts, examples, and details that support that idea. They are reminded when *writing* to follow the same basic principle: that is, to make a point and then provide support for that point. And they discover that *thinking* (which they also do when actively reading or writing) involves testing the worth of ideas by deciding whether there is solid support for those ideas.

Here are other important features of the book:

High Interest Level

At the heart of the book are the thirty-two selections, grouped into six thematic units. We believe that it is crucial for such reading selections to be of high appeal. Students will not begin to enjoy reading if the material is dull. Also, a teacher's enthusiasm for a compelling essay can be infectious. We have thus spent a great deal of time locating and class-testing selections that will truly capture the interest of students and teachers. All of the readings are clearly and logically written; all present intriguing ideas, helpful practical information, or revealing insights into human nature.

Frequent Skills Practice

Complementing the high-interest selections is a series of high-quality activities that truly help students improve their reading and writing. The book assumes that reading and writing are interrelated skills. Work on reading can improve writing; work on writing can improve reading. Practice in reading and writing follows each of the thirty-two selections. Here is the sequence of activities:

First Impressions Following each reading is a freewriting activity titled "First Impressions" that encourages students to come to terms with what they have read. The activity consists of three questions that permit students to respond on different levels of feeling and opinion. For example, the first question is always "Did you enjoy reading this selection? Why or why not?" The two other questions focus on particular issues raised by the essay—issues about which every sudent should have something to say.

The "First Impressions" activity provides at least two additional benefits. First, it lays the groundwork for oral participation; many more students can contribute intelligently to classroom discussion after they have colllected their thoughts on paper in advance. Second, as an integral step in the writing process, freewriting can supply students with raw material for one or more of the paragraph and essay assignments that follow the selections.

Words to Watch and Vocabulary Check Basic students need to strengthen their vocabularies in order to succeed in college—and they know it. *A Basic Reader for College Writers* builds vocabulary in the most research-proven and interesting way, by providing hundreds of useful words in context. Up to fifteen of a selection's words and phrases are defined in the "Words to Watch'" section that comes before each reading. Other words that may be unfamiliar to students appear as part of the "Vocabulary Check" activity that follows each reading. Stduents thus have frequent opportunities to sharpen their skill at deriving meaning from context. A convenient glossary of words at the back of the book supplies the definitions and pronunciations for all of the "Words to Watch."

Reading Check Practice in reading skills is provided through an activity titled "Reading Check," a series of comprehension questions that follow the

"Vocabulary Check." The questions involve four key skills: finding the central point and main ideas, recognizing key supporting details, drawing inferences, and understanding the writer's craft. The craft questions include such elements as transitions, types of support, introduction and conclusion strategies, tone, purpose, and patterns of organization.

Outlining Activity or Summarizing Activity The treatment of outlining and summarizing is a unique feature of this book. While teachers agree that these skills are an important part of thoughtful reading and writing, they are all too seldom taught. From a practical standpoint, it is hardly possible for a teacher to respond individually to entire collections of class outlines or summaries. We have tried, then, to create activities of increasing difficulty that truly involve students in outlining and summarizing—in other words, that truly make students *think*—yet also make it possible for a teacher to give realistic feedback. It is through continued practice *and* feedback on challenging material that a student becomes a more effective reader and thinker. The first outlining activity can be seen on page 30; the first summarizing activity appears on page 11.

Paragraph Assignments and Essay Assignments Four writing assignments—two paragraphs and two essays—conclude the activities for each selection. The assignments emphasize the basic principle of clear communication: that a student make a point and support it. Numerous sample topic sentences and thesis statements as well as specific suggestions for supporting these points help students to succeed on these assignments. At the same time that it provides these guided opportunities for writing, the book remains, as its title indicates, a basic reader. Rather than attempting to teach the art of writing, *A Basic Reader for College Writers* focuses on teaching students to do the careful reading and sound thinking that effective writing requires.

Ease of Use

The book is designed to be simple for both teachers and students to use. The activities already listed are easy to present in class and convenient to correct. Answers to the activities appear in three places:

- ***A glossed selection*** Comments and answers accompany the first selection, "Bird Girl." Students thus learn right at the start how to complete the activities and questions that follow each reading selection.
- ***A partial answer key*** Answers and explanations are given at the back of the book for the first selection in each of the remaining five units. The five glossed selections are: "Batter Up"; "Fun. Oh Boy, Fun. You Could Die from It"; "What Is Intelligence, Anyway?"; "A Crime of Compassion"; and "The

Smart Way to Buy a New Car." The answer key helps those students who benefit from self-checking. It also helps ensure that students understand the issues that they will then be asked to write about. Students are likely to use the partial answer key in an honest and positive way to improve their reading skills if they know that they may be checked on the many selections for which answers are not provided.

- *A complete answer key in the Instructor's Manual* Complete answers for all the activities are provided on letter-sized sheets in a separate Instructor's Manual. At the teacher's option, these sheets can easily be duplicated and distributed to students so they can check their own answers. The manual also contains additional writing assignments for each of the six units, as well as a model syllabus that can be used as a guide in planning a course.

Other features or supplements of the book allow for ease of use as well. A *preview* that accompanies each selection provides helpful background information and stimulates student interest. The activities are designed for *quick checking and grading*, either by the student or by the teacher. The *perforated pages* in the book add to the ease of grading. And many of the writing assignments are *interchangeable*: paragraph topics may be used for essays and vice versa.

Finally, a *computer disk* is available to help students work through the vocabulary and reading questions that accompany ten of the selections. The disk is a helpful motivational tool that will enable students to work at their own pace towards a basic understanding of any of the ten selections. Teachers will then have more time available to deepen that understanding while preparing students for writing activities.

In short, *A Basic Reader for College Writers* contains an appealing collection of readings and an exceptional series of activities that will give students extensive guided practice in reading and writing. We believe the book's value lies in the quality of the selections, the activities that follow, and the integrated approach to reading and writing that is maintained throughout.

Acknowledgments

We are grateful for the advice and suggestions provided by the following reviewers:

France Conroy, Burlington County College
Ann Dobie, University of Southwestern Louisiana
Toni Empringham, El Camino College
Yvonne Frye, Community College of Denver
Helen Gordon, Bakersfield College
Roslyn J. Harper, Trident Technical College

Paul Hauser, Kirkwood Community College
Brian Huot, Syracuse University
Peggy Jolly, University of Alabama at Birmingham
Nancy Martinez, University of New Mexico
Joseph G. R. Martinez, University of New Mexico
Jerry Olsen, Middlesex Community College
Kathleen Schatzberg-Smith, Rockland Community College
Jill L. Sessoms, USC-Coastal Carolina College.

In addition, we owe thanks to a number of people who helped make this book possible. Dot Carroll, Virginia H. Kerrick, and Elaine J. Lessig each made significant contributions to the initial stages of the manuscript. Our gratitude also goes to Carole Mohr, Executive Editor at Townsend Press. Her insightful editing work, especially in the early and middle stages of the project, made the book much better than it would have been otherwise. Most importantly, we acknowledge the advice and support of John Langan, who first suggested to Townsend Press the need for a textbook such as this one and who brought the three of us together for the project. Without his help, this book would not exist.

David I. Daniels
Janet M. Goldstein
Christopher G. Hayes

How to Become a Better Reader and Writer

"Essay?" asked the red-headed student in the front row. "What do you mean—essay?"

The rest of the class laughed. The instructor had spent all week explaining what an essay is. But some of the other students laughed a little nervously. They had been asking themselves the same question the student in the front row dared to ask out loud. What *is* an essay, really?

An essay is a short piece of writing that expresses an author's idea or feeling about a particular topic. Many articles in books, magazines, and newspapers, as well as the papers you will be writing, follow the same basic pattern. An author makes a point of some kind and provides information that supports that point.

A Basic Reader for College Writers consists of this introductory chapter and 32 high-interest essays. This introduction will explain how understanding the concept of *point and support* can make you a better reader and writer. It will offer specific tips or strategies for reading more effectively. And while the book is not a composition text, some brief strategies will be suggested for more effective writing as well.

The rest of the book contains the 32 essays and a carefully-designed series of activities that accompanies each essay. As you read the essays and work closely with them, you will develop your own ideas for writing. At the end of each essay, you will be given specific paragraph and essay topics to write about.

Format of the 32 Reading Selections

This book assumes that we learn best through doing. You are asked, then, to answer brief questions as you read through the rest of this introduction.

Each of the 32 essays begins with a *Preview* that gives helpful background information and arouses your interest in the piece.

- What helpful information, for example, do you learn about the author of the first essay, "Bird Girl," by reading the preview?

_____

_____

Following the preview is a list of *Words to Watch*, which gives the definitions of difficult words taken from the reading.

- How many "Words to Watch" are provided for "Bird Girl" (page 2)?

_____

In parentheses next to each word is the number of the paragraph in which it appears. Also, each word is underlined in the reading itself.

Every essay is followed by a series of activities. The initial activity, *First Impressions*, asks you to write for ten minutes about the piece you have just finished reading.

- Turn to "First Impressions" on page 6 and note how many writing choices you are given: _____

Next there is a series of questions titled *Vocabulary Check*. Half of these questions will help you learn words in a research-proven way: by seeing how they are actually used in the selection. The other questions will help reinforce the meanings of selected words learned in "Words to Watch."

- Turn to the "Vocabulary Check" on page 6 and record how many vocabulary questions appear: _____

The vocabulary material is followed by a *Reading Check*. The questions here will help you to practice and develop several important reading skills.

- Turn to "Reading Check" (page 8) to note the number of comprehension questions that are asked: _____
- Complete the list below of the kinds of comprehension question provided:
  Central Point and Main Ideas

  _____

  _____

The Writer's Craft

You will next find an activity (page 11) in either *Outlining* or *Summarizing*: two processes that develop your ability to get to the heart of each piece and to think logically and clearly about what you have read.

- What kind of activity is given for "Bird Girl" (page 11)? _____

Next, there are *Discussion Questions* about the essay. These questions provide a final chance for you to deepen your understanding of a reading.

- Turn to page 12 and note how many discussion questions are provided for "Bird Girl" (and for every essay in the book): _____

Finally, two *Paragraph Assignments* and two *Essay Assignments* follow each essay. To get you started, the first paragraph assignment and the first essay assignment include sample main ideas and thesis statements. The second assignment in each pair offers specific hints for supporting your ideas. The selections are grouped into six units. Turn to the table of contents (page v) to complete the list below of the six units:

Personal Memories   Understanding Ourselves

_____   _____

Sports and Leisure   _____

Additional information you should know about includes a glossary of the "Words to Watch" that appear before each selection (pages 307-315) and also a reading performance chart on the last page of the book.

Point and Support

The most important principle in this book is that effective writing has two basic parts: (1) a *central point* and (2) *support* for that point. The central point states what the author thinks, and the support helps you, the reader, understand why the author holds this opinion. By keeping this principle in mind, you can become a better reader and writer. As you read, remember that an author's purpose is to make a point and support it with reasons, examples, and other details. When you write, remember that to communicate effectively, you should follow the same basic plan: make a point and support it.

Suppose you read an article in *Newsweek* about flexible working hours. By answering the question, "What is the point of this article?" you discover that the author thinks making working hours more flexible is a good idea. Next, you ask, "How does the author support the central point?" In fact, the article gives three supporting reasons. Flexible working hours would lead to fewer traffic jams, better use of building space, and more opportunities for parents to work. By asking and answering these two questions, you have found the meaning of the article. *This strategy can be applied to almost anything you read.*

You should follow the same principle when you write. Let us say you are writing a paper on the parking problem at your school. First, you need to decide what point to make about your topic. Suppose you decide to argue that the college should end its policy of reserving parking spaces for the faculty. Since your instructor, who will read (and grade) your paper, probably parks in a reserved space, you need some convincing reasons to support your central point. You might explain that the present policy makes poor use of space on an overcrowded campus since faculty parking spaces are often empty when the student section of the lot is full. You could also argue that students resent faculty parking privileges, making good relations between students and faculty more difficult. When you have thought of both your central point and enough support for that point, you are on your way to writing a solid, well-reasoned paper.

- What is an essay? _____

- The two basic parts of effective writing are to _____ a point and to _____ that point.

Reading Strategies

Most of your college reading is designed to help you learn about new subjects and new ideas. All too often, however, students have trouble understanding what they read. A familiar complaint is, "I read it, but I didn't understand it."

This section explains seven strategies that can make you a better reader. You will have many opportunities to apply them in this book. In fact, try to use them for *all* your reading. You'll then find yourself getting more from your other courses as well as from this one.

Strategy 1: Learn to Read Actively

One key to improved reading is getting actively involved in each stage of the reading process. Here are some ways to do so.

1. <u>Preview the selection</u>. In other words, look over what you will read—quickly but alertly—before you start to read it. Follow these steps:
    a. *Make the title into a question.* For example, before reading a short selection titled "TV Commercials and Children," you might ask the question "How do TV commercials affect children?" or "Why are TV commercials directed at children?" Searching for the answer to your question will give you a reason for reading.
    On the lines below, try out this tip by writing two questions based on "Learning to Give Up," the title of one of the selections in this book.

    _____

    _____

Are the questions you wrote on the lines above something like "Who learns to give up?" "Why do they learn to give up?" "What are the values or drawbacks of learning to give up?" If so, you've got the idea. Asking basic questions can make you a more active reader.
   b. *Read through the first several paragraphs and the last several.* They may give you a quick sense of the main idea of the article.
   c. *Look at the first sentence in each paragraph.* You won't get a complete picture of the selection by reading only these sentences, but you will get some idea of the selection's overall organization.
2. Read the selection straight through for pleasure. Don't get bogged down; instead, try to understand as much as you can this first time through.
3. Use any special features the book provides. In this book, a *Preview* introduces you to each selection. Also, *Words to Watch* defines the hard words in the selection in the order in which they appear. All these words are then underlined in the selection. Finally, the three *First Impressions* questions that follow each selection allow you to jot down some quick reactions to the selection and its relationship to your own life. Knowing that you'll be writing down your first impressions each time should focus your attention when you read the selections in this book. And once you get in the habit of writing about your first impressions, you'll be surprised by how many ideas you have.
4. Reread the selection, marking key information with a pen or pencil. Marking material will keep your mind alert and show you what to come back to later. Here are some suggestions on how and what to mark:
   a. Underline the ideas that seem important.
   b. Write *Ex* in the margin to set off important examples.
   c. Put question marks beside any material you don't understand.
   d. Number any important series of ideas.

This marking will help you answer the questions that follow each selection.

Following each selection in this book is a set of questions that help you practice basic reading skills. As you strengthen these skills enough to make them habits, your reading ability is sure to improve. Here are the skills:

Strategy 2: Understand Vocabulary in Context

Building your vocabulary is essential to becoming a better reader and writer. In fact, people who build strong vocabularies are more likely to be successful in school and in their careers. Yet few of us have the time or desire to open the dictionary every time we meet an unfamiliar word. Luckily, there is another way to learn new words: we can guess their meanings with the help of surrounding words (called *context*). For example, see if you can figure out the meaning of the word *prudent* from its context in this sentence:

> The appearance of AIDS has caused many people to be more prudent about romance.

Because you understand the rest of of this sentence, you can guess that *prudent* means "cautious" or "careful."

Following each selection in this book are eight vocabulary items. The first four have been chosen to help you learn how to guess what words mean from their contexts. The last four cover important words from "Words to Watch." Here's an example for you to try, taken from the paragraph on "TV Commercials and Children" that appears below. See if you can figure out the meaning of the word in italics just by reading the sentence in which it appears. Then circle the letter of the answer that best completes the item.

> The word *crave* in "such commercials often promote junk food. They encourage little children to crave sugary snacks and breakfast cereals" means
> a. be afraid of.   c. strongly desire.
> b. sell.   d. ignore.

What would TV ads for junk food make children do with "sugary snacks and breakfast cereals"? If you chose *c*, "strongly desire," you are correct.

Strategy 3: Look for a Basic Structure in What You Read

You should assume that a well-written selection, long or short, has two basic parts: (1) a central point and (2) support for the central point. As you read the selections in this book, you'll be answering two kinds of questions about the structure of each reading:

1. <u>Find the Central Point and Main Ideas</u>. If a selection is only one paragraph long, the central point is often (though not always) expressed in its first sentence. In fact, your instructor may ask you to start the paragraphs you write with *topic sentences*—that is, sentences that state the main idea in each paragraph. In an essay, which is made up of several paragraphs, the sentence that states the central point is known as the *thesis statement*.

   The sentence stating the central point of a selection is a one-sentence summary of the entire essay. It's the answer to the question "What is the point?" which you should ask about whatever you read. In addition to a central point, longer selections have main ideas that support the central point. Often these main ideas are stated in topic sentences that begin paragraphs, but sometimes they are found within or at the ends of paragraphs. And some of the time, both central points and main ideas are not stated directly. When this situation happens, you must draw your own conclusions about what they are.

2. <u>Locate Key Supporting Details</u>. The support for central points and main ideas may be in the form of reasons, examples, details, facts, statistics, quotations, or anecdotes (stories). Finding these details will help you recognize an author's point-and-support structure for an essay.

Look, for example, at the following paragraph:

TV Commercials and Children

Television commercials aimed at young children—the kind shown during Saturday morning cartoon shows, for example—should be banned. For one thing, such commercials often promote junk food. They encourage little children to crave sugary snacks and breakfast cereals made of tiny chocolate doughnuts or cookie nuggets. In addition, these commercials urge children to be greedy. At the same time parents are teaching their children to share what they have with others, TV commercials make them want more expensive toys and other products for themselves. The worst thing about these ads, however, is that they take advantage of children who have not yet learned what advertising is or how it works. If a beloved cartoon character tells a child a cereal or a toy is great, the child believes it. Children can't see how advertisers trick them into wanting a product or how ads make toys or games look better than they really are. Aiming ads at little children is unfair.

Can you find the central point and the three key supporting details in this paragraph? Answer the questions below, and then read the explanations that follow them.

1. Which sentence best expresses the central point of "TV Commercials and Children"?
   a. All television commercials should be banned.
   b. TV commercials aimed at young children should be banned.
   c. Commercials make young children want to eat junk food.
   d. Advertisers do not care what children eat.

In this selection, the central point is *b,* "TV commercials aimed at young children should be banned." Answer *a* is *too broad*—it refers to *all* television commercials, not just those aimed at youngsters. Answer *c* is *too narrow*—it is actually one of the supporting details for the central point. Answer *d* may or may not be true, but it is not what the whole paragraph is about. Only answer *b* states the central point of the paragraph.

2. On the lines below, write the three key supporting details for the central point. (Ask yourself, "What specific reasons does the author give for why TV ads are harmful to children?")

   a. _____

   b. _____

   c. _____

If you wrote answers similar to "They promote junk food," "They encourage greed," and "They take advantage of children," you are correct.

Strategy 4: Draw Inferences

Inferences are the reasonable guesses we make based on the facts presented. For example, if a crowd of people is smiling and talking after leaving a movie, we would probably assume that the movie is an enjoyable one. And if rolled-up newspapers accumulate on a neighbor's porch over a holiday weekend, we could conclude that the family is away on a brief vacation. Or if trucks that usually race along the highway are suddenly observing the speed limit, we could infer that a police radar trap is nearby. We make the same kinds of judgments when we draw conclusions about what we read. In this book, you'll be answering several inference questions each time you read a selection. Look again at the paragraph on "TV Commercials and Children" (page xxvi) and answer the following question. Then read the explanation that follows it.

_____ TRUE OR FALSE? We can infer from the paragraph that young children think that ads tell the truth.

You can find the answer to this question near the end of the paragraph, when the writer explains that young children haven't learned what advertising is. The paragraph goes on to state that if a cartoon character praises a cereal or toy, the child believes that character. Therefore, the author is suggesting that young children believe everything they see on TV—including ads. The inference is true.

Strategy 5: Appreciate the Writer's Craft

"Writer's craft" refers to techniques an author uses to communicate ideas. Being aware of these strategies will increase your understanding of what you read as well as improve your own writing. In this book questions on the writer's craft cover:

1. <u>Introductions and Conclusions.</u> What does an author do to interest you in reading what he or she has written? Sometimes a selection begins with an entertaining story (sometimes called an anecdote), a quotation,

a provocative question, or a definition. To provide an ending, authors may use one of these techniques or instead do something like summarize key points, plead for a change, or make a prediction.

2. <u>Type of Support.</u> How has the author supported his or her central point? Common methods of support in paragraphs and essays include facts, examples, statistics, quotations, material from surveys and studies, questions, one or more incidents, and the author's own reasons and personal experiences.

3. <u>Patterns of Organization.</u> How have the supporting details been arranged? Authors often choose time order (telling the parts of a story in the order that they happened) or order of importance (from least to most important). Or they may prefer space order (showing where something is located), comparison-contrast (showing how two things are alike or different), or cause and effect (showing why something happened).

4. <u>Tone.</u> Just as a speaker's tone of voice reveals how he or she feels, a writer's tone also communicates feelings. You should be able to tell whether a selection's tone is humorous or serious, angry or friendly, formal or informal, self-pitying or sarcastic, encouraging or discouraging, or simply objective (factual).

5. <u>Purpose.</u> Decide what type of writing you are reading. Is it intended to inform (give people information), to entertain (give people pleasure), or to persuade (change people's minds about an issue)?

6. <u>Audience.</u> Decide for what kind of reader the selection was probably written. Was it meant for the general reader (anyone)? Or was the author writing for a smaller audience, such as major league baseball players, a group of fellow researchers, or parents of high school students?

7. <u>Signal Words.</u> Just as traffic signals tell drivers what's coming next, signal words provide needed guidance for readers. Some of these signal words and phrases (also called <u>transitions</u>) are listed below:
   a. *Addition* words add a similar idea: and, also, in addition, finally.
   b. *Time* words show when something happened: first, next, then, last.
   c. *Location* words show where something is: above, between, in front of, next to.
   d. *Illustration* words show an example: for example, for instance.
   e. *Contrast* words show the next idea will be different: however, but, on the other hand.
   f. *Conclusion* words indicate that a conclusion or result will follow: thus, therefore, as a result.

8. <u>Intentional Repetition.</u> Some words and phrases appear again and again throughout a selection not because the author is careless, but because he or she wants to call attention to ideas he or she considers important.

9. <u>Titles</u>. Looking closely at titles gives you clues to authors' ideas and attitudes towards their subjects.

Here are some "Writer's Craft" questions for you to try. To answer them, you may have to look once again at "TV Commercials and Children" on page xxvi. After you have answered the questions, check your answers below.

1. The purpose of "TV Commercials and Children" is to
   a. entertain us with examples of clever ads.
   b. inform us that children's programs contain commercials.
   c. persuade us that children should watch less TV.
   d. persuade us that commercials can be harmful to children.
2. The words *for example* in "Television commercials aimed at young children—the kind shown during Saturday morning cartoon shows, for example" signal
   a. illustration.
   b. contrast.
   c. addition.
   d. time.

Did you choose *d* for question 1 and *a* for question 2? Then you are correct.

Strategy 6: Learn to Outline and Summarize

Outlining and summarizing are two time-honored ways of highlighting the point and support in a piece of writing. An *outline* is a diagram that shows the central point and major supporting details. (In this book, capital letters, rather than Roman numerals, will be used to indicate the largest support.) A *summary* is a much shorter version of the selection, written in paragraph form. Usually the first sentence in a summary expresses the point, and the sentences that follow express the support.

Everyone agrees that outlining and summarizing are central to thoughtful reading and writing at the college level. The outlining or summarizing activity that follows each selection in the book will help you become more comfortable with these essential skills.

Strategy 7: Discuss Your Ideas

In class, your instructor will probably ask you to respond to one or more of the four discussion questions that follow each essay. After reading the selection, writing about your first impressions, and completing the activities, you'll find that you have a lot to say about the topic of the selection. When you discuss your ideas in class, you'll then be more ready and able to express *informed* opinions, based on all the reading and writing you've already done.

- _____ and _____ are two activities that are central to college reading and writing.
- According to Strategy 7, three ways to get ideas for what to say about a reading selection in class discussion are to

   a. _____

   b. _____

   c. _____

Writing Strategies

While the focus of this reader is on the effective reading of the selections, some brief hints will be offered here on effective writing.

When you write a paper, your aim should be to communicate clearly and thoughtfully. To do so, remember that all effective writing has two basic parts: (1) it makes a point, and (2) it supports and develops that point. If you focus on these two goals in your writing, you will take the single most important step needed to write well.

Read the following example of effective writing. Then answer the questions that follow it.

Drunk Drivers

People caught driving while drunk—even first offenders—should be jailed. First of all, drunk driving is more dangerous than carrying a loaded gun. Drunk drivers are in charge of three-thousand-pound weapons at a time when they have little coordination or judgment. Instead of getting off with a license suspension, the drunk driver should be treated as seriously as someone who walks into a crowded building with a ticking time bomb. In addition, views on drunk driving have changed. We are no longer willing to make jokes about funny drunk drivers, to see drunk driving as a typical adolescent stunt, or to overlook repeat offenders who have been lucky enough not to hurt anybody—so far. Finally, a jail penalty might encourage solutions to the problem of drinking and driving. People who go out for a good time and intend to have several drinks would be more likely to select one person as the driver. That person would stay completely sober. Bars would probably start promoting tasty and trendy nonalcoholic drinks such as fruit daiquiris and "virgin" pina coladas. And perhaps beer and alcohol advertising would be regulated so that young people would not learn to associate alcohol consumption with adulthood. By taking drunk driving seriously enough to require a jail sentence, we would surely save lives.

- What is the writer's central point in this paragraph?

- What support does the writer give for this central point?

    1. _____

    2. _____

    3. _____

The student who wrote this paragraph, Eva Williams, has *made a clear point*—that drunk drivers should be jailed—and expressed it in the first sentence of her paragraph, where readers expect to find it. As a reader, you should have had the following response after seeing her point: "Okay, here's her main idea. Now can she defend it? Can she give some solid reasons why she feels the way she does? Then I can decide whether or not I agree with her." In fact, Eva *solidly supports the central point* by discussing three reasons why drivers should be jailed:

1. A car is more dangerous than a loaded gun.
2. We are no longer willing to accept drunk drivers.
3. Jail sentences would encourage people to find solutions to the drunk driving problem.

You may still not agree with her. You might feel, perhaps, that such a penalty is too rigid or severe. But you have to grant that you know just where she stands. She has presented her thinking in a clear and thoughtful manner, making a point and then backing up that point.

Very few people—including professional writers—sit down and decide "This is my point" and "This will be my support." Instead, writing involves a good deal of trial and error. Usually you will go through a series of stages as you create a paper that clearly makes and develops a point. Here are six strategies you might reasonably expect to follow to produce a good paragraph or essay:

Strategy 1: Get Some Ideas Down on Paper

An excellent way to get started on a paper is to use a *prewriting activity* such as freewriting, brainstorming, or questioning. These strategies are called prewriting activities because they take place before the actual writing of the first draft. Using these approaches will help you discover and start to shape your feelings and ideas.

Freewriting is writing freely about whatever comes to mind about your subject. When freewriting, put down words as they occur to you without worrying at all about punctuation, grammar, spelling, or organization. (Remember, your instructor will not be seeing this paper.) Try to write without stopping. Here is part of the freewriting prepared by Eva, the writer of the drunken driving paragraph. (Mistakes have been corrected for the sake of easy reading.)

Drunk drivers have been around for a long time. We talk about them and how bad they are and then what happens? Very often nothing happens in my opinion. They just get off with a light fine or a short time in jail and so what if they have injured someone or maybe even killed people in some cases. Their cars are like loaded guns and they are crazy people with them. They should be made to pay, and they should go to jail and there should be no two ways about it. . . .

Brainstorming is listing ideas rather than writing them in sentences. When you brainstorm, the goal is to accumulate as many ideas and details as you can without worrying at this stage about putting them in order. Here is the list that Eva prepared while brainstorming her topic:

- Jail sentence needed
- Newspaper stories all the time
- Penalties to date are not working
- Beer ads glorify drinking
- Many young people are victims
- Bars should be responsible
- Bars should promote nonalcoholic drinks
- More warnings needed on TV
- Cars are loaded guns
- Danger must be regulated
- Sick of jokes about drunken drivers

A third helpful prewriting activiting is *questioning*. This means asking and answering a number of questions about your topic. These questions will help you think of better main points and supporting details to put in your paragraphs and essays. Here are some of the questions Eva asked and answered about her topic:

<u>What</u> is my topic?	Drunk drivers
<u>What</u> is my point?	Drunk drivers should be put in jail
<u>Why</u> put them in jail?	Only way to make people take the issue as seriously they should. They must realize their cars are like loaded guns.
<u>How</u> will this help?	People will start taking steps to deal with the problem.

By practicing these prewriting techniques, you'll be able to think more deeply about your subject and come up with better details to support your main ideas.

- Three prewriting techniques explained in Strategy I are _____,
  _____, and _____.
- Which of these prewriting techniques do you think will be most useful to you the next time you write a paper? _____.

Strategy 2: Express Your Central Point in One Sentence

Prewriting activities provide a foundation to build on as you move to the next stage of the writing process, stating the point of your paper in a single sentence. Eva's point was:

People caught driving while drunk should be jailed.

Be sure you write a sentence that really does express your point. Some statements that seem at first glance to express central points actually do not. Look over the following statements to see if you can tell what is wrong with each of them:

Drunk driving is the subject of this paper.
Our entire nation must fight the problem of drunk driving.
Few drunk drivers are put in jail.

The first statement is just an announcement of the topic; it does not make a point about the topic. The second sentence covers too much to be treated in a short essay. In fact, it is so broad that supporting it might require an entire book. The third statement is simply a fact—not an idea that needs any support. Statements of facts are "dead-end sentences" because there is nowhere to go with them; they are too narrow. Instead, you should write a topic sentence or thesis statement that advances an idea broad enough to expand into a paragraph or an essay.

- Which of the following would be the best thesis statement for a paper on how to get more students to use the campus library?
   a. Our college library is the topic of this essay.
   b. Last Friday, only two students were using our library's main reading room.
   c. A few changes would make our college library a much more popular place for students.
   d. Students at this school do not appreciate all the services that are provided for their use.

Strategy 3: Support Your Central Point with Specific Details

Now that you have a central point, the next step is finding evidence to develop and support this point. Ask yourself, "What kind of support is needed?" Do you need a few convincing *examples*? One or more dramatic *incidents*? Several strong *reasons* to explain why something is the way it is or how you feel about it? A few *facts* or *statistics* so that no one can argue with you? Will your own personal observations and experiences be enough, or would it be a good idea to do a little library research? Whatever you decide, your brainstorming, freewriting, or questions should give you a good start. In fact, they might contain everything you need to prove your point.

At this stage, it's a good idea to prepare a *scratch outline* for your paper. This is an informal outline that shows, in a nutshell, the point you plan to make in your paper and the ideas and examples you will use to support that point. In order to make this outline, you'll need to decide on a way of organizing your supporting details.

Strategy 4: Organize Your Support

The two most common ways to put ideas in order are *time order* and *order of importance*. Using time order means giving the details in the order in which they happened. The second type of organization, order of importance, is most effective when details are put in order from least important to most important. This works well because it means saving the most important detail until last, and people are likely to remember the last thing they read. Notice that Eva put her ideas in order of importance. She felt the most significant reason for the jail sentence was that it would promote solutions to the drunk driving problem.

Other ways to put ideas in order are by location (space order), cause and effect, and comparison-contrast. Further details about patterns of organization may be found in the "Reading Strategies" section of this introduction on page xxviii.

- What is the purpose of a scratch outline? _____

- The two most common ways of organizing a paper are _____ order and order of _____.

Strategy 5: Polish the Paper

As you know, a paper does not happen all at once but is the result of a series of strategies and drafts. Eva wrote three versions of her paper, each an improvement over the one before it. Given below are the opening points of these three drafts:

First   People who drive while drunk should be jailed.
draft   Drunken driving is as dangerous as a gun that is loaded. . . .

Second draft	People caught driving while drunk should be jailed. One reason is that drunken driving is as dangerous as a loaded gun. . . .
Third draft	People caught driving while drunk—even first offenders—should be jailed. First of all, drunk driving is more dangerous than carrying a loaded gun. . . .

- What is the advantage of writing more than one draft of a paper? _____

_____ .

Strategy 6: Get Feedback on What You Have Written

The main idea of writing is to communicate ideas. To find out whether you have communicated effectively, you need readers—yourself, first of all, and then other people. First, try seeing your own paper as if a stranger had written it. After you finish writing, put the paper away for a while. (24 hours is ideal.) Then read your paper again as if it were someone else's. Another good technique is to get a friend or family member to read the paper aloud to you. (Reading your own paper into a tape recorder and playing it back can work just as well.) If anything seems awkward or unclear to you as you read or hear your paper, fix it. If you don't, it will seem just as awkward or unclear to other people.

Try showing your paper to other people as well. Your instructor may suggest that you discuss your paper with small groups of your classmates. Your fellow students can ask you questions and make comments about what you have written that will help you improve your paper.

Although this is only a brief overview of the key strategies in effective writing, it should give you a good idea of how to do the writing assignments for each of the selections in this book. Two paragraph assignments and two essay assignments are given for each selection. (Turn to page 12 for the first set of these assignments.) For each one, notice that you are asked to make and support a point. (A sample topic sentence and thesis statement are always given for the first paragraph and essay assignment as a way of helping you get started.) Thus, in writing as well as in reading, you will have a chance to practice and perfect the point-and-support philosophy of this book.

- What are two ways to get feedback on what you have written?

    a. _____

    b. _____

- What help does this book give you in getting started on the first paragraph or essay assignment for each selection?

_____

A Final Word

You are now ready to move on to the 32 selections in the book. As you study each selection, read it first to enjoy whatever it may have to say about human nature and life today. Then reread the selection and work on the activities with the intention of learning as much as you can.

To help you learn, we have provided an answer key at the back of the book for the first selection in each of the last five units of the book. (Answers to the questions on "Bird Girl" appear immediately following the questions themselves.) Use the answer key to check your answers *after* you have worked through the activities. Be sure you understand why any items you missed are wrong. This information will help prepare you to do well on the remaining selections in each unit, for which answers are not given.

Finally, remember throughout that learning is, in the end, up to you. If you have the intention of gaining as much as you can from this book, then *A Basic Reader for College Writers* will offer you a great deal. As you discover how to apply the questions "What is the point?" and "What is the support for that point?" you will acquire a powerful learning and reasoning tool—a tool that can make you a skilled and independent learner for the rest of your life.

Personal Memories

Bird Girl

Clark DeLeon

Preview

We all remember how cruel children can be to each other. We may recall "ganging up" on a helpless classmate at recess when we were in junior high. Or maybe *we* were the victims. The scars from these childhood incidents can last a lifetime—or even shorten a life. In the following selection, a series of three columns from *The Philadelphia Inquirer*, Clark DeLeon writes about such childhood cruelty, and his readers respond.

Words to Watch

sallow (1): sickly pale yellow
tacitly (1): silently
lest (2): for fear that
greasers (3): tough, bullying teenagers
defiant (5): bold
unrelenting (7): not stopping
touched a chord in (7): sounded familiar to
contend (8): struggle
malicious (8): mean
taunts (8): insults
gross (8): very obvious
encounter (9): meeting
eluded (10): escaped
mobile (11): movable
instigators (11): leaders

Targets: A Lesson in Life

There was a weird girl in my high school whom we all called the Bird. We called her that because of her nervous, birdlike movements and the way she would hunch her shoulders toward her ears as if she was hoping her head would disappear into her body. She had sallow skin that looked as if it had never felt the sun, and there was usually a blotchy red rash in the middle of her forehead. She had fine black hair on her arms long enough to comb, and she wore clothes that had been out of fashion since Shirley Temple was singing "The Good Ship Lollipop." She was also the object of such contempt and scorn, such cruel ridicule, that it shames me to this day to think I was part of it, even tacitly.

Oh, I was never one to say anything to her face. I wasn't that brave. I'd wait until she hurried by with her books held tightly to her chest and join in the chorus of birdcalls with the other guys. She was always good for a laugh. And it's important when you're a teenager to join the laughter, lest the laughter turn on you.

I remember one day when the Bird was surrounded by three or four suburban-variety greasers who had stopped her in the corridor between classes. They were flapping their arms and screeching in her ear. She was terrified. Her eyes darted in panic. A couple of her books fell to the floor. When she stopped to pick them up, they bent over her in a circle, closing in, screeching, screeching.

Then this girl came out of nowhere. I'd never seen such anger in a girl before. She went up to the leader of the tormentors and ripped into him with a hot fury. "Stop it!" she shouted. "Can't you see what you're doing?" The guys backed off, stunned. Then the girl went over to the Bird and put her arm around her shoulder and walked her to class.

I thought about the Bird when I read about Nathan Faris, the little boy who shot a classmate and killed himself after being the target of teasing by the kids in his school. I thought of how I had been a part of her misery, how more than 20 years later it still bothers me. But I also think of what I learned that day about decency and bravery, about being a human being, from a girl whose name I don't even know. And I wonder if that one act of defiant kindness may have saved another girl's life.

Targets: Why Are Kids So Cruel?

"I just had to write to you in regard to your item 'Targets' that appeared in today's (March 8) *Inquirer*," wrote Ray Windsor of Lansdowne.

I received several letters about that piece, a girl I knew in high school who was the victim of cruel and unrelenting ridicule because she was unattractive, uncool and unable to defend herself. That piece touched a chord in people, and I think Ray's story will, too. Here it is:

"Back in high school (Monsignor Bonner) I had to contend with many of the malicious deeds and taunts from my 'fellow students,' similar but different. With me, however, I was a victim of gross physical immaturity. . . . I actually didn't start shaving regularly until I was 25 or so.

"This problem was very hard for me to deal with, even though it was out of my control. The class 'bullies' and insensitive and uncaring types never hesitated for one moment to knock me around, having read my problems like a book. Gym class, especially, was my psychological encounter with hell —twice weekly. Because of my outward appearance, I always skipped showering with the rest of the class. Eventually, they caught on to this and many of the guys would either throw me in the showers, or if they didn't do this, they would spit in my underwear or socks or shoes and then (usually) chuck them out of the window to the ground two stories below.

"Is it no wonder I was sick as often as I could be on Gym Day? Oh, all the wonderful FUN they had at my emotional expense. I once mustered the courage to talk to my 'guidance counselor' about the problems I was contending with, and all he was able to tell me was that this was the type of thing that students like myself go through to become a man. How I was to become a man through all this eluded me, primarily because I was being treated as less-than-human by these jerks.

"Once this pattern was set up, I easily became a target for much the same outside of gym. Often I was pushed and shoved in the hallway. On occasion, I was tripped or punched, and on special occasions, I would even be tossed into the mobile trash cans and rolled into classrooms that weren't even mine. I may have been bigger than some of these instigators, but I could never seem to get the courage to bring a fist up to their ugly faces. It was always THEM against ME. How often I broke down and cried out of sheer frustration is uncountable. What really gets me is that I let this happen. Is it any wonder that I turned to alcohol and had two major ulcer operations before I was 25?

"As I suspect you know by now, I have picked up the shattered pieces of my adolescence and have gotten my life back together again. The HATE and RAGE I once felt for these ne'er-do-wells has since turned to pity. In fact, they are no doubt half-decent guys now. But if they only knew how much harm they'd caused me, they'd become a little upset with themselves. At least I hope so, anyway. I only wish that someone had yelled, 'Stop it! Can't you see what you're doing?' back at school. It may have saved me from much of the misery I was forced to endure until I graduated from that hell hole."

That's Ray's story. I've got my own, and you probably have yours.

How did we survive those years? How did we endure the anger, the shame, the emotional brutality? And we're talking middle-class suburban kids, here. We're talking the seeds of the promised land. If parents only knew what their kids were going through, what their kids are going through.

I don't know if there's an answer. How can we make teenagers treat each other like human beings? How can we penetrate that closed society of adolescence? How can we let the victims know that life gets better? How can we shame the bullies with what they will feel about their actions, if they ever grow up?

Kids: Lessons Learned Early

I want to share something with you, something nice.

It's what some kids have had to say in letters to me about the column about the Bird, the girl I knew in high school who was teased and tormented by everyone, until one day another girl stood up to a group of guys who were picking on the Bird. You wonder when you write something like this about growing up, how kids will receive your message. Here are some of their reactions:

"I read your article about the weird girl called the Bird," wrote Stephanie K. "I am in the sixth grade, and one of my classmates is weird like in your article, and we too make fun of him. We don't make fun of him as much anymore. We used to make fun of him all day long. . . . I really thought about what you've said and I want to thank you for taking time to write something that will prevent other people from feeling bad."

"I have read your story about the girl that was called the Bird because she had pale skin and acted weird. In the story, you said that you were one of the ones who teased the Bird," wrote Cuong N. "You also spoke highly of the girl who came up to you and your friends and told you guys to stop teasing the Bird. If you spoke highly of that girl, why didn't you do the same thing, or were you scared of being teased too? If I was in your place, I would have done the same thing you did and prevented myself from being teased. Please write back to me if you can."

"I would probably have done the same thing as you did," wrote Katie M. "Now that I read the story and understand the problem going on, I wonder why more people aren't like the kid who came and helped the Bird."

"I think the girl who stood up for the Bird was very brave," wrote Nicole G. "She could have been beaten up or teased, but she did it anyway. I really look up to and respect people like that."

"I think that you shouldn't have held back what you thought about the other kids teasing the Bird, because that makes you in a way worse than the others," wrote Michael C. "If you felt that the girl reacted bravely for sticking up for the Bird and that she was a good person for doing what she did, why didn't you at least find out who she was?"

I wish I had found out her name, Michael. And I respect people like that too, Nicole. And I too wonder why more people aren't like the girl who helped the Bird, Katie. And the reason I spoke highly of the girl is that I was afraid to do what she did, and her bravery inspired me, Cuong. And I'm especially glad that you've stopped teasing your sixth-grade classmate, Stephanie. Thank you all for thinking about the story the way you did.

First Impressions

To the Student: The three "First Impressions" questions that follow each selection allow you to write freely about your first reactions to what you have read. Normally, you won't be handing in this writing to your instructor. It is personal writing that focuses your ideas about the selection and its relationship to your own life. Don't worry about making mistakes. Just get your reactions down on paper.

Freewrite for ten minutes on one of the following.

1. Did you enjoy reading this selection? Why or why not?
2. Were you ever teased as a child? Or did you take part in teasing someone else? If so, describe what happened.
3. What is the best or worst thing you remember about your high school years?

Vocabulary Check

The explanations below are provided to help you understand how to answer the questions and complete the other items in this book. Try to figure out each answer yourself first. Then check your answer. Study the explanation, especially if your response wasn't correct. As you work on the exercises, cover the explanations below the items with a card or piece of paper so you're not tempted to look at them until <u>after</u> you've tried the items yourself.

The vocabulary words covered in the first four items are not defined in "Words to Watch" or in the glossary at the back of the book, so it's up to you to figure out what they mean. But that doesn't mean you have to guess the answers blindly. First, read each item to see if you already know the answer. If you don't, start by crossing off one or more of the words that you're sure are wrong. Then try replacing the word in the item with each answer that's left. The word that fits best is right.

Circle the letter of the word or phrase that best completes each of the following four sentences.

1. The word *contempt* in "She was also the object of such contempt and scorn, such cruel ridicule, that it shames me to this day" (paragraph 1) means
   a. praise.   c. envy.
   b. disgust. d. love.

The sentence suggests that *contempt* has a meaning similar to that of "scorn" and "cruel ridicule." Knowing this should help you rule out "praise" and "love." Then you can try "disgust" and "envy" in place of *contempt* in the sentence. "Envy" doesn't make sense, so your answer is "disgust" *(b)*.

2. The word *insensitive* in "The class 'bullies' and insensitive and uncaring types never hesitated for one moment to knock me around, having read my problems like a book" (paragraph 9) means
   a. intelligent. c. unfeeling.
   b. friendly.   d. far away.

To answer this item, ask yourself how bullies would feel about someone else's problems. The sentence says they are "uncaring," a clue that the answer is *c*, "unfeeling."

3. The word *mustered* in "I once mustered the courage to talk to my 'guidance counselor' about the problems" (paragraph 10) means
   a. fought.   c. refused.
   b. gathered. d. seasoned.

Here, the question to ask yourself is what Ray would do to his courage before talking to someone about his problems. Discussing personal problems would take courage for anyone and would probably have been especially difficult for Ray. He wouldn't want to fight or refuse or season his courage, would he? So the right answer is *b*, "gathered."

4. The word *endure* in "It may have saved me from much of the misery I was forced to endure until I graduated from that hell hole" (paragraph 12) means
   a. commit. c. borrow.
   b. enjoy.   d. put up with.

What would the writer be forced to do with misery he couldn't avoid? He would have to "put up with" it, so the correct answer to this one is *d*.

Circle the letter of the answer that best completes each of the following four items. Each sentence uses a word (or form of a word) from "Words to Watch."

The second set of vocabulary items checks your understanding of terms from "Words to Watch." Different kinds of items are used elsewhere in the book, but this time each one requires you to choose the word from "Words to Watch" that best fits into the sentence. If you need to, look back at the definitions that appear before the essay on page 2. Then try each possible definition to see how well it fits. Cover the answers at the end of this exercise while you do the items. Then check to see how well you did.

PERSONAL MEMORIES

5. The police were unable to round up the entire gang because several of its members _____ every attempt to capture them.
   a. eluded
   b. instigated
   c. encountered
   d. taunted

6. The pressure on our team was _____; it seemed as if it would never end.
   a. contending
   b. sallow
   c. tacit
   d. unrelenting

7. The audience threw tomatoes onto the stage and shouted _____ at the cast.
   a. tacitly
   b. encounters
   c. instigators
   d. taunts

8. First the campers _____ with sandstorms and then with extreme cold.
   a. contended
   b. taunted
   c. eluded
   d. instigated

Check your answers: 5. *a*   6. *d*   7. *d*   8. *a*

Reading Check

Central Point and Main Ideas

1. Which sentence best expresses the central point of the selection?
   a. Gym class is the worst place for teenagers who are victims of teasing.
   b. Childhood and adolescence are difficult times for many people.
   c. A classmate's courageous action may have saved a girl's life.
   d. Teenagers should learn to stop being cruel to people who are different.

Sometimes all of the possible answers for an item like this one are true, but some are too narrow, which means they give only details, not main ideas. Others are too broad, giving ideas that are more like the subjects of whole books than the central points of essays. If you can't find the correct answer right away, cross out the sentences that give details instead of general ideas. Here, sentences *a* and *c* give supporting details, so they're definitely wrong. That leaves sentences *b* and *d*. Can you tell which of these two sentences is too broad? It's sentence *b*, which contains a bigger subject than the selection does, a subject that could have a whole book devoted to it instead of just three newspaper columns. So, by eliminating the wrong answers, you've found the right one, sentence *d*.

2. Which sentence best expresses the main idea of paragraph 11?
   a. Ray was teased a great deal while in school.
   b. Once the teasing started, it took over Ray's life.

c. Ray eventually began drinking and had two major ulcer operations.
d. Ray didn't have the courage to fight back.

To answer an item like this one, look back at the paragraph it covers (11) to remind yourself of what it's about. Then, try to choose the correct answer. If you can't, go back to read the paragraph again. Sometimes the paragraphs you'll look back at will have topic sentences, but this one doesn't. Therefore, you'll have to decide for yourself what it means. A good way to start is by crossing out the sentences that are too narrow, *c* and *d*. These sentences both give details. This leaves two general sentences, *a* and *b*. Sentence *b* is the better of the two because it includes the idea that the teasing affected Ray's life.

3. Which sentence best expresses the main idea of paragraph 19?
    a. Cuong had read the story of the Bird.
    b. Cuong thought the author should not have admitted being scared.
    c. Cuong wanted the author to write to him.
    d. Cuong would not have stopped the teasing but wondered why the author had not tried to stop it either.

Again, look back at the paragraph (19). Then cross out the sentences that state details rather than main ideas—*a* and *c*. (Notice that although sentence *a* refers to the first sentence of the paragraph, which is often the topic sentence, this time that sentence is not broad enough to be a topic sentence.) To choose between the remaining sentences, *b* and *d*, look for the one that does a better job of stating the overall idea of the paragraph. The sentence that does the best job of stating the main idea is sentence *d*.

Key Supporting Details

Questions about key details give you a chance to check your understanding of the support the author provides for the central point and main ideas. To answer this type of question, you may need to look back at the selection to check on details you've forgotten.

4. The girl in the article had gotten the nickname of the Bird because of
    a. her movements and posture.
    b. the hair on her arms.
    c. the whistling sounds she made.
    d. her high voice.

Did you look back at the description of the Bird in paragraph 1? It says that the Bird's nickname was based on "her nervous, birdlike movements and the way she would hunch her shoulders," so the answer is *a*.

5. _____ TRUE OR FALSE? Ray Windsor tried not to take showers with the other boys in his gym class.

This question is answered in paragraph 9, where Ray explains that he skipped showering until the other boys in the class caught on. Ray tried to avoid taking showers, so the answer is TRUE.

Inferences

For this group of questions you will be drawing conclusions about what the author means but does not state directly.

6. The author suggests that Nathan Faris
   a. might have been helped like the Bird if someone had only defended him.
   b. was probably very different from the Bird.
   c. was justified in shooting one of his classmates.
   d. was too weak to defend himself.

You can find the answer to this question by skimming rapidly to find Nathan Faris's name. It's mentioned in paragraph 5. Reading the whole paragraph will give you some clues to the answer, but the best clue is in the last sentence: "And I wonder if that one act of defiant kindness may have saved another girl's life." This means that DeLeon thinks the girl who spoke up to protect the Bird may have prevented her suicide. If that's the case, just one person speaking up might have kept Nathan Faris from shooting another person and killing himself, so the answer to this question is *a*.

7. _____ TRUE OR FALSE? The author implies that the problem of teasing in adolescence is not very important.

You have to think about the whole selection to answer this item. Think back to the examples of the Bird, Ray Windsor, and Nathan Faris. Would you call the teasing and problems they had to put up with "not very important"? No, especially when you consider the effects the teasing had on their lives. So the answer is FALSE.

The Writer's Craft

This group of items asks about the way the selection was written. It includes questions about topics such as how the author organized the selection and supported general ideas.

8. The tone of Ray Windsor's letter can be described as
   a. humorous.
   b. angry.
   c. objective.
   d. formal.

What tone of voice do you think Ray would use if he read his letter out loud? Other people might have thought Ray's situation was funny, but Ray certainly didn't. That means you can cross out choice *a*. Ray isn't trying to present both sides of his story in a factual way, so "objective" *(c)* is also wrong. His general approach is more informal (casual) than formal, so the right answer is *b*, "angry."

BIRD GIRL   11

9. As the signal words *when* and *then* indicate, paragraphs 3 and 4 present
   a. items in no particular order.
   b. events in time order.
   c. comparisons and contrasts.
   d. examples.

Think about the words *when* and *then* in each of the types of situations mentioned in the answers. *When* and *then* wouldn't be needed if details were given in no special order *(a)*, nor do they point out similarities and differences *(c)* or examples *(d)*, so you've found the right answer: *b*.

10. The author's purpose in writing this article is
    a. to entertain readers with stories of schoolchildren.
    b. to inform readers of ways to combat teasing.
    c. to persuade readers that childhood is an important time in life.
    d. to persuade readers that young people's cruelty to each other must be stopped.

Was this selection meant just as entertainment? If you look back, you'll see that the ideas in it are rather serious, so you can eliminate *a*. Among the answers that are left, *b* can be dropped because DeLeon is more emotional about his subject than someone who was just giving information would be. Between *c* and *d*, *d* is the better choice because it is about the central point of the piece, young people's cruelty toward each other.

Summarizing Activity

Complete the following summary of "Bird Girl" by filling in each blank with one or more words.

A summary of an essay is a brief statement of its main ideas. The details in a summary follow the order of the original selection. That means the first answer can be found toward the beginning of the selection, and the later answers will be found further along in it. Fill in the answers after looking back at the essay to find any you're not sure of. Then check your answers below.

   Many students in the author's high school teased a girl called the Bird because of her strange, birdlike gestures and appearance. One day, several boys surrounded the Bird and began to flap their arms and (1) _____.
   When she bent down to pick up some books that had fallen, they closed in on her. Suddenly, another girl stopped them by shouting at them. She then put her arm around the Bird and walked her to class. A reader wrote in with a similar story. He too was (2) _____ in high school because of his appearance. (3) _____ class was the worst experience for

him, but the halls were dangerous, too. The teasing was so bad that he took up drinking and needed two (4) _____ operations before age 25. Even today, he still remembers the agony he lived through. The author wonders how teenagers can be taught to be less cruel. However, he was glad to receive (5) _____.

Check your answers: (1) screech, (2) teased, (3) gym, (4) ulcer, (5) letters from young people who shared his concerns. (Sometimes your answers won't be in exactly the same words as those in the Answer Key, especially for the last long blank. The important thing is to get as close as you can to the right idea.)

Discussion Questions

1. What did the author learn from the girl who defended the Bird?
2. In paragraph 2, DeLeon says that "it's important when you're a teenager to join the laughter, lest the laughter turn on you." What does he mean? Is he correct?
3. Why do you think so many readers wrote to DeLeon about the story of the Bird?
4. DeLeon asks, "How can we make teenagers treat each other like human beings?" How would you answer this question?

Paragraph Assignments

1. Add another example to DeLeon's selection by writing your own paragraph about a person who was teased or bullied in your school or neighborhood. Describe the person and then explain how others treated him or her. Make your description detailed enough so that your readers can picture the person clearly and understand what happened. Use a topic sentence such as "Carolyn always got picked on because she was different from the other girls in my eighth grade class."
2. Considering the social pressures on teenagers, the girl who helped "the Bird" was especially brave. Even with seemingly fewer social pressures, college students and other adults do not always go out of their way to help others through an act of kindness. Write an essay about a time someone you know did help someone else. You could describe a situation similar to one of the following:

   - lending money
   - taking children on outings
   - visiting someone who's sick
   - helping old people
   - taking in a foster child
   - doing volunteer work in a hospital
   - coaching

   Include vivid details so your readers can clearly picture what happened.

Essay Assignments

1. DeLeon admits that he regrets two things: taking part in teasing the Bird and not finding out who the girl was who stepped in to stop the teasing. Write an essay about something you regret—perhaps something you did or something you didn't do when you were younger. Explain what happened, and tell why you wish things had turned out differently. Try to support your general ideas with details as interesting as those DeLeon uses. Your thesis statement might be similar to one of the following:

   I regret working two jobs in high school instead of taking part in school activities.
   I wish I had gotten to know my father better before he died.
   Moving in with my brother was not my wisest decision.

2. What would you do if you were the principal of a high school who had been asked to develop specific programs to help students treat each other better? What would you advise teachers to tell their students that they don't usually tell them? What could students do to prevent teasing? Write an essay in which you explain your suggestions for what teachers and students could do to make your school a friendlier place. You might want to include such ideas as buddy systems, in which seniors act as personal counselors to younger students; discussion groups of students and teachers; or an anti-teasing poster campaign.

Being a Boy
Julius Lester

Preview

Most young boys find fighting and rough games very natural, but for Julius Lester, growing up was a struggle. Even as a five-year old, he was an outsider, and as a teenager he continued to have problems—this time, with girls. In an article originally written for *MS.* magazine, Lester jokes about his poor showing as a boy, but his comments show a serious concern with the question of what being male or female really means.

Words to Watch

pummeling (1): hitting
adept (1): skillful
assertion (3): statement
decathlon (4): contest made up of ten athletic events
asset (6): useful quality
initiative (6): lead
prospect (7): something expected
substantial (7): solid
syphilis (8): a disease spread by sexual contact
covertly (8): secretly
procedure (9): process
cubicles (11): small rooms or spaces

As boys go, I wasn't much. I mean, I tried to be a boy and spent many childhood hours <u>pummeling</u> my hardly formed ego with failure at cowboys and Indians, baseball, football, lying, and sneaking out of the house. When our neighborhood gang raided a neighbor's pear tree, I was the only one who got sick from the stolen fruit. I also failed at setting fire to our garage, an art at which any five-year-old boy should be <u>adept</u>.

I was, however, the neighborhood champion at getting beat up. "That Julius can take it, man," the boys used to say, almost in admiration, after I emerged from another battle, tears brimming in my eyes but refusing to fall.

My efforts at being a boy earned me a pair of scarred knees that are a record of a childhood spent falling from bicycles, trees, the tops of fences, and porch steps; of tripping as I ran (generally from a fight), walked, or simply tried to remain upright on windy days.

I tried to believe my parents when they told me I was a boy, but I could find no objective proof for such an <u>assertion</u>. Each morning during the summer as I cuddled up in the quiet corner with a book, my mother would push me out the back door and into the yard. And throughout the day as my blood was let as if I were a patient of 17th century medicine, I thought of the girls sitting in the shade of porches, playing with their dolls, toy refrigerators and stoves.

There was the life, I thought! No constant pressure to prove oneself. No necessity always to be competing. While I humiliated myself on football and baseball fields, the girls stood on the sidelines laughing at me, because they didn't have to do anything except be girls. The rising of each sun brought me to the starting line of yet another day's Olympic <u>decathlon</u>, with no hope of ever winning even a bronze medal.

Through no fault of my own I reached adolescence. While the pressure to prove myself on the athletic field lessened, the overall situation got worse—because now I had to prove myself with girls. Just how I was supposed to go about doing this was beyond me, especially because, at the age of 14, I was four foot nine and weighed 78 pounds. (I think there may have been one 10-year-old girl in the neighborhood smaller than I.) Nonetheless, duty called, and off I went.

To get a girlfriend, though, a boy had to have some <u>asset</u> beyond the fact that he was alive. I wasn't handsome like Bill McCord, who had girls after him like a cop-killer has policemen. I wasn't ugly like Romeo Jones, but at least the girls noticed him: "That ol' ugly boy better stay 'way from me!" I was just there, like a vase your grandmother gives you at Christmas that you don't like or dislike, can't get rid of, and don't know what to do with. More than ever I wished I were a girl. Boys were the ones who had to take the <u>initiative</u> and all the responsibility. (I hate responsibility so much that if my heart didn't beat of itself, I would now be a dim memory.)

It was the boy who had to ask the girl for a date, a frightening enough <u>prospect</u> until it occurred to me that she might say no! That meant risking my ego, which was about as <u>substantial</u> as a toilet-paper raincoat in the African rainy season. But I had to thrust that ego forward to be judged, accepted, or rejected by some girl. It wasn't fair! Who was she to sit back like a queen with the power to create joy by her consent or destruction by her denial? It wasn't fair—but that's the way it was.

But if (God forbid!) she should say Yes, then my problem would begin in earnest, because I was the one who said where we would go (and waited in terror for her approval of my choice). I was the one who picked her up at her house where I was inspected by her parents as if I were a possible carrier of <u>syphilis</u>. Once we were on our way, it was I who had to pay the bus fare, the price of the movie tickets, and whatever she decided to stuff her stomach with afterward. (And the smallest girls are all stomach.) Finally, the girl was taken home where once again I was inspected (the father looking <u>covertly</u> at my fly and the mother examining the girl's hair). The evening was over and the girl had done nothing except honor me with her presence. All the work had been mine. 8

Imagining this <u>procedure</u> over and over was more than enough: I was a sophomore in college before I had my first date. 9

Now, of course, I know that it was as difficult being a girl as it was a boy, if not more so. While I stood paralyzed at one end of a dance floor trying to find the courage to ask a girl for a dance, most of the girls waited in terror at the other, afraid that no one, not even I, would ask them. And while I resented having to ask a girl for a date, wasn't it also horrible to be the one who waited for the phone to ring? And how many of those girls who laughed at me making a fool of myself on the baseball diamond would have gladly given up their places on the sidelines for mine on the field? 10

No, it wasn't easy for any of us, girls and boys, as we forced our beautiful free-flowing child-selves into those narrow, constricting <u>cubicles</u> labeled *female* and *male*. I tried, but I wasn't good at being a boy. 11

First Impressions

Freewrite for ten minutes on one of the following.

1. Did you enjoy reading this selection? Why or why not?
2. Which years of your life would you most want to live through again? Which years would you not want to repeat? Why?
3. Lester says in paragraph 10 that being a girl is as difficult as being a boy. Do you agree?

Vocabulary Check

Circle the letter of the word or phrase that best completes each of the following four sentences.

1. The word *brimming* in "tears brimming in my eyes but refusing to fall" (paragraph 1) means
   a. filling up.
   b. closing.
   c. smiling.
   d. clearing.
2. The word *upright* in "tripping as I ran (generally from a fight), walked, or simply tried to remain upright on windy days" (paragraph 2) means
   a. cold.
   b. correct.
   c. standing up.
   d. alone.
3. The word *objective* in "I tried to believe my parents when they told me I was a boy, but I could find no objective proof" (paragraph 3) means
   a. factual.
   b. weak.
   c. emotional.
   d. stupid.
4. The word *constricting* in "those narrow, constricting cubicles labeled *female* and *male*" (paragraph 11) means
   a. exciting.
   b. freeing.
   c. encouraging.
   d. limiting.

Circle the letter of the word (or form of the word) from "Words to Watch" that best completes each of the following four sentences.

5. That cabin does not look very _____; it's in such bad shape that a heavy wind might blow it down.
   a. adept
   b. initiating
   c. substantial
   d. covert
6. The teachers' offices were a series of _____, each one so small that a desk and chair took up almost all the space inside.
   a. assertions
   b. cubicles
   c. prospects
   d. procedures
7. When we have a practical problem, Michael usually takes the _____ and suggests a good solution.
   a. initiative
   b. decathlon
   c. cubicle
   d. pummeling
8. One of my boyfriend's _____ is his sense of humor.
   a. assertions.
   b. initiatives.
   c. assets.
   d. cubicles.

Reading Check

Central Point and Main Ideas

1. Which sentence best expresses the central point of the selection?
   a. Growing up is very difficult.
   b. Strict definitions of "male" and "female" behavior can cause problems for young people.

c. Dating was extremely difficult for the author because he was unattractive and no good at sports.
d. The author's childhood was unhappy.
2. Which sentence best expresses the main idea of paragraph 3?
   a. Lester's mother wouldn't let him read.
   b. Girls prefer sitting in the shade to playing in the sun.
   c. Lester did not enjoy the activities boys were supposed to enjoy.
   d. Lester frequently got beaten up when he was young.
3. Which sentence best expresses the main idea of paragraph 8?
   a. Lester disliked dating because it was so expensive.
   b. Lester felt uncomfortable meeting his dates' parents.
   c. Lester thought that on a date the boy had to do all the work.
   d. Lester had to take his dates to the movies and out to eat.

Key Supporting Details

4. Lester thought it was unfair that
   a. girls were smarter than boys.
   b. people had to wear raincoats in Africa.
   c. he had to grow up.
   d. girls could refuse to go out with him.

5. _____ TRUE OR FALSE? As Lester became an adolescent, he gained more self-confidence.

Inferences

6. The author implies that as a boy he was
   a. handsome.
   b. awkward.
   c. ugly.
   d. aggressive.
7. From the article, we can assume the author thinks that
   a. boys should be encouraged to be athletic.
   b. boys should be discouraged from participating in sports.
   c. it's better to be a girl than a boy.
   d. it's all right for girls to participate in sports.

The Writer's Craft

8. The tone of this essay is often
   a. humorous.
   b. matter-of-fact.
   c. formal.
   d. joyous.
9. The main type of support used in the article is
   a. the author's own experiences.
   b. statistics.
   c. surveys.
   d. quotations from experts.

10. In paragraph 8, the author organizes the details of a date
    a. from most important to least important.
    b. from least important to most important.
    c. in time order.
    d. in no special order.

Summarizing Activity

Complete the following summary of "Being a Boy" by filling in each blank with one or more words.

Julius Lester felt he was (1) _____ at being a boy. He wasn't very good at boys' games, and he also got (2) _____ often by the other boys in the neighborhood. When he reached adolescence, he had a new problem: proving himself with (3) _____. Lester didn't think he could get a girlfriend because he was both small and plain looking.

Also, he was afraid to ask a girl out because she might (4) _____.

If she did go out with him, he would have to make all the plans and pay for everything. He thought girls had much easier lives than boys did. When he was older, he realized that girls (5) _____.

Discussion Questions

1. According to Lester, what does "being a boy" consist of? Why wasn't he very good at it?
2. Are there times when you think the opposite sex has life easier than you do? Why or why not?
3. Throughout his essay, Lester uses humor and exaggeration, as when he refers to each new day as an "Olympic decathlon" (paragraph 4). Find other examples. Why do you think he is making fun of such a serious subject?
4. Why does Lester refer to "female" and "male" as "narrow, constricting cubicles"? Do you think he would still refer to them in this way today, or have the expectations for boys and girls changed? If so, how?

Paragraph Assignments

1. Julius Lester believes that the expectations for boys that existed while he was growing up were too demanding. Write a paragraph about something that seemed unfair to you when you were a child or young teenager. For example, you might choose to write about having your TV time limited, having to do household chores, or having to visit elderly relatives. Your topic sentence could be similar to the following:

When I was a child, I didn't like being forced to go to bed just when I was beginning to have fun.

As I was growing up, I resented my parents not allowing me to choose my own clothes.

Having to take my little brother Billy to the movies every Saturday afternoon for years was unfair.

2. Lester feels he was a failure at being a boy. Write about something you were forced to do or be which you did not do very well. For instance, you could write about being the "world's worst" bridesmaid, altar boy, babysitter, camper, or card player. You could write humorously, as Lester does, or seriously, warning about the dangers of forcing people to do something they won't enjoy or won't do well.

Essay Assignments

1. Lester found dating so frightening that he avoided it until college. Were you ever as frightened of dating as he was? Write an essay about your first real date or about your first important date (such as going to a rock concert or a prom). Explain what worries you had beforehand; then describe how the date actually went. Conclude the essay by revealing how you felt afterwards about the date and how future dates, with the same person or with others, were either similar or different. Your thesis statement could be something like this: "Although I dreaded going to the homecoming dance with Loretta, I ended up having a good time." As an alternative, write about the reasons that you, like Lester, didn't date in high school.
2. Write your own "Being a Boy" (or "Being a Girl") essay. Like Lester, arrange your article in time order, discussing what was expected of you at different stages in your life. At each age level, were you able to be the boy or girl that other people wanted you to be? Or did you have problems—perhaps because your abilities or goals were different? How do the different expectations for men and women affect you now?

The Back of the Bus
Mary E. Mebane

Preview

To most of us, segregation in the American South is just something we read about in history books. It was very real, however, to Mary E. Mebane, who experienced segregation firsthand as a child before going on to earn M.A. and Ph.D. degrees at the University of North Carolina. In her childhood "world without options," Mebane had to endure fear, anger, and hatred. In this selection from her autobiography *Mary*, she narrates an incident that vividly shows how difficult daily life was for black people at that time.

Words to Watch

restrictive (1): limiting
unwary (4): not alert
industriously (5): busily
complacently (7): contentedly
disputed (13): argued over
exodus (19): departure
apprehensive (20): worried
insouciance (21): lack of concern
nondescript (21): ordinary
devastated (22): completely destroyed
frieze (26): picture
articulate (26): clear and expressive
antagonist (39): opponent
devised (41): designed

Historically, my lifetime is important because I was part of the last generation born into a world of total legal segregation in the Southern United States. When the Supreme Court outlawed segregation in the public schools in 1954, I was twenty-one. When Congress passed the Civil Rights Act of 1964, permitting blacks free access to public places, I was thirty-one. The world I was born into had been segregated for a long time—so long, in fact, that I never met anyone who had lived during the time when <u>restrictive</u> laws were not in existence, although some people spoke of parents and others who had lived during the "free" time. As far as anyone knew, the laws as they then existed would stand forever. They were meant to—and did—create a world that fixed black people at the bottom of society in all aspects of human life. It was a world without options.

Most Americans have never had to live with terror. I had had to live with it all my life—the psychological terror of segregation, in which there was a special set of laws governing your movements. You violated them at your peril, for you knew that if you broke one of them, knowingly or not, physical terror was just around the corner, in the form of policemen and jails, and in some cases and places white vigilante mobs formed for the exclusive purpose of keeping blacks in line.

It was Saturday morning, like any Saturday morning in dozens of Southern towns.

The town had a washed look. The street sweepers had been busy since six o'clock. Now, at eight, they were still slowly moving down the streets, white trucks with clouds of water coming from underneath the swelled tubular sides. <u>Unwary</u> motorists sometimes got a windowful of water as a truck passed by. As it moved on, it left in its wake a clear stream running in the gutters or splashed on the wheels of parked cars.

Homeowners, bent over <u>industriously</u> in the morning sun, were out pushing lawn mowers. The sun was bright, but it wasn't too hot. It was morning and it was May. Most of the mowers were glad that it was finally getting warm enough to go outside.

Traffic was brisk. Country people were coming into town early with their produce; clerks and service workers were getting to the job before the stores opened at ten o'clock. Though the big stores would not be open for another hour or so, the grocery stores, banks, open-air markets, dinettes, were already open and filling with staff and customers.

Everybody was moving toward the heart of Durham's downtown, which waited to receive them rather <u>complacently</u>, little knowing that in a decade the shopping centers far from the center of downtown Durham would create a ghost town in the midst of the busiest blocks on Main Street.

Some moved by car, and some moved by bus. The more affluent used cars, leaving the buses mainly to the poor, black and white, though there were some businesspeople who avoided the trouble of trying to find a parking place downtown by riding the bus.

I didn't mind taking the bus on Saturday. It wasn't so crowded. At night or on Saturday or Sunday was the best time. If there were plenty of seats, the blacks didn't have to worry about being asked to move so that a white person could sit down. And the knot of hatred and fear didn't come into my stomach.

I knew the stop that was the safety point, both going and coming. Leaving town, it was the Little Five Points, about five or six blocks north of the main downtown section. That was the last stop at which four or five people might get on. After the stop, the driver could sometimes pass two or three stops without taking on or letting off a passenger. So the number of seats on the bus usually remained constant on the trip from town to Braggtown. The nearer the bus got to the end of the line, the more I relaxed. For if a white passenger got on near the end of the line, often to catch the return trip back and avoid having to stand in the sun at the bus stop until the bus turned around, he or she would usually stand if there were not seats in the white section, and the driver would say nothing, knowing that the end of the line was near and that the standee would get a seat in a few minutes.

On the trip to town, the Mangum Street A&P was the last point at which the driver picked up more passengers than he let off. These people, though they were just a few blocks from the downtown section, preferred to ride the bus downtown. Those getting on at the A&P were usually on their way to work at the Duke University Hospital—past the downtown section, through a residential neighborhood, and then past the university, before they got to Duke Hospital.

So whether the driver discharged more passengers than he took on near the A&P on Mangum was of great importance. For if he took on more passengers than got off, it meant that some of the newcomers would have to stand. And if they were white, the driver was going to have to ask a black passenger to move so that a white passenger could sit down. Most of the drivers had a rule of thumb, though. By custom the seats behind the exit door had become "colored" seats, and no matter how many whites stood up, anyone sitting behind the exit door knew that he or she wouldn't have to move.

The <u>disputed</u> seat, though, was the one directly opposite the exit door. It was "no-man's-land." White people sat there, and black people sat there. It all depended on whose section was fuller. If the back section was full, the next black passenger who got on sat in the no-man's-land seat; but if the white section filled up, a white person would take the seat. Another thing about the white people: they could sit anywhere they chose, even in the "colored" section. Only the black passengers had to obey segregation laws.

On this Saturday morning Esther and I set out for town for our music lesson. We were going on our weekly big adventure, all the way across town, through the white downtown, then across the railroad tracks, then through the "colored" downtown, a section of run-down dingy shops, through some fading high-class black neighborhoods, past North Carolina College, to Mrs. Shearin's house.

We walked the two miles from Wildwood to the bus line. Though it was a warm day, in the early morning there was dew on the grass and the air still had the night's softness. So we walked along and talked and looked back constantly, hoping someone we knew would stop and pick us up.

I looked back furtively, for in one of the few instances that I remembered my father criticizing me severely, it was for looking back. One day when I was walking from town he had passed in his old truck. I had been looking back and had seen him. "Don't look back," he had said. "People will think that you want them to pick you up." Though he said "people," I knew he meant men—not the men he knew, who lived in the black community, but the black men who were not part of the community, and all of the white men. To be picked up meant that something bad would happen to me. Still, two miles is a long walk and I occasionally joined Esther in looking back to see if anyone we knew was coming.

Esther and I got to the bus and sat on one of the long seats at the back that faced each other. There were three such long seats—one on each side of the bus and a third long seat at the very back that faced the front. I liked to sit on a long seat facing the side because then I didn't have to look at the expressions on the faces of the whites when they put their tokens in and looked at the blacks sitting in the back of the bus. Often I studied my music, looking down and practicing the fingering. I looked up at each stop to see who was getting on and to check on the seating pattern. The seating pattern didn't really bother me that day until the bus started to get unusually full for a Saturday morning. I wondered what was happening, where all these people were coming from. They got on and got on until the white section was almost full and the black section was full.

There was a black man in a blue windbreaker and a gray pork-pie hat sitting in no-man's-land, and my stomach tightened. I wondered what would happen. I had never been on a bus on which a black person was asked to give a seat to a white person when there was no other seat empty. Usually, though, I had seen a black person automatically get up and move to an empty seat farther back. But this morning the only empty seat was beside a black person sitting in no-man's-land.

The bus stopped at Little Five Points and one black got off. A young white man was getting on. I tensed. What would happen now? Would the driver ask the black man to get up and move to the empty seat farther back? The white man had a businessman's air about him: suit, shirt, tie, polished brown shoes. He saw the empty seat in the "colored" section and after just a little hesitation went to it, put his briefcase down, and sat with his feet crossed. I relaxed a little when the bus pulled off without the driver saying anything. Evidently he hadn't seen what had happened, or since he was just a few stops from Main Street, he figured the mass exodus there would solve all the problems. Still, I was afraid of a scene.

The next stop was an open-air fruit stand just after Little Five Points, and here another white man got on. Where would he sit? The only available seat was beside the black man. Would he stand the few stops to Main Street or would the driver make the black man move? The whole colored section tensed, but nobody said anything. I looked at Esther, who looked apprehensive. I looked at the other men and women, who studiously avoided my eyes and everybody else's as well, as they maintained a steady gaze at a far-distant land.

Just one woman caught my eye; I had noticed her before, and I had been ashamed of her. She was a stingy little black woman. She could have been forty; she could have been fifty. She looked as if she were a hard drinker. Flat black face with tight features. She was dressed with great insouciance in a tight boy's sweater with horizontal lines running across her flat chest. It pulled down over a nondescript skirt. Laced-up shoes, socks, and a head rag completed her outfit. She looked tense.

The white man who had just gotten on the bus walked to the seat in no-man's-land and stood there. He wouldn't sit down, just stood there. Two adult males, living in the most highly industrialized, most technologically advanced nation in the world, a nation that had devastated two other industrial giants in World War II and had flirted with taking on China in Korea. Both these men, either of whom could have fought for the United States in Germany or Korea, faced each other in mutual rage and hostility. The white one wanted to sit down, but he was going to exert his authority and force the black one to get up first. I watched the driver in the rearview mirror. He was about the same age as the antagonists. The driver wasn't looking for trouble, either.

"Say there, buddy, how about moving back," the driver said, meanwhile driving his bus just as fast as he could. The whole bus froze—whites at the front, blacks at the rear. They didn't want to believe what was happening was really happening.

The seated black man said nothing. The standing white man said nothing.

"Say, buddy, did you hear me? What about moving on back." The driver was scared to death. I could tell that.

"These is the niggers' seats!" the little lady in the strange outfit started screaming. I jumped. I had to shift my attention from the driver to the <u>frieze</u> of the black man seated and white man standing to the <u>articulate</u> little woman who had joined in the fray.

"The government gave us these seats! These is the niggers' seats." I was startled at her statement and her tone. "The president said that these are the niggers' seats!" I expected her to start fighting at any moment.

Evidently the bus driver did, too, because he was driving faster and faster. I believe that he forgot he was driving a bus and wanted desperately to pull to the side of the street and get out and run.

"I'm going to take you down to the station, buddy," the driver said.

The white man with the briefcase and the polished brown shoes who had taken a seat in the "colored" section looked as though he might die of embarrassment at any moment.

As scared and upset as I was, I didn't miss a thing.

By that time we had come to the stop before Main Street, and the black passenger rose to get off.

"You're not getting off, buddy. I'm going to take you downtown." The driver kept driving as he talked and seemed to be trying to get downtown as fast as he could.

"These are the niggers' seats! The government plainly said these are the niggers' seats!" screamed the little woman in rage.

I was embarrassed at the use of the word "nigger" but I was proud of the lady. I was also proud of the man who wouldn't get up.

The bus driver was afraid, trying to hold on to his job but plainly not willing to get into a row with the blacks.

The bus seemed to be going a hundred miles an hour and everybody was anxious to get off, though only the lady and the driver were saying anything.

The black man stood at the exit door; the driver drove right past the A&P stop. I was terrified. I was sure that the bus was going to the police station to put the black man in jail. The little woman had her hands on her hips and she never stopped yelling. The bus driver kept driving as fast as he could.

Then, somewhere in the back of his mind, he decided to forget the whole thing. The next stop was Main Street, and when he got there, in what seemed to be a flash of lightning, he flung both doors open wide. He and his black <u>antagonist</u> looked at each other in the rearview mirror; in a second the windbreaker and porkpie hat were gone. The little woman was standing, preaching to the whole bus about the government's gift of these seats to the blacks; the man with the brown shoes practically fell out of the door in his hurry; and Esther and I followed the hurrying footsteps.

We walked about three doors down the block, then caught a bus to the black neighborhood. Here we sat on one of the two long seats facing each other, directly behind the driver. It was the custom. Since this bus had a route from a black neighborhood to the downtown section and back, passing through no white residential areas, blacks could sit where they chose. One minute we had been on a bus in which violence was threatened over a seat near the exit door; the next minute we were sitting in the very front behind the driver.

The people who <u>devised</u> this system thought that it was going to last forever.

First Impressions

Freewrite for ten minutes on one of the following.

1. Did you enjoy reading this selection? Why or why not?
2. Imagine that you had been on the bus. How would you have felt? What would you have done?
3. Have you ever seen someone act courageously in a difficult situation? If so, describe what happened and how you felt about it.

Vocabulary Check

Circle the letter of the word or phrase that best completes each of the following four sentences.

1. The word *peril* in "You violated them at your peril, for you knew that if you broke one of them, . . . physical terror was just around the corner" (paragraph 2) means
   a. desire for profit.   c. own place.
   b. own age.   d. risk of danger.
2. The word *affluent* in "The more affluent used cars, leaving the buses mainly to the poor" (paragraph 8) means
   a. wealthy.   c. elderly.
   b. alcoholic.   d. sinful.
3. The word *discharged* in "whether the driver discharged more passengers than he took on near the A&P on Mangum was of great importance" (paragraph 12) means
   a. recognized.   c. stopped for.
   b. wanted.   d. let off.

4. The word *furtively* in "I looked back furtively, for in one of the few instances that I remembered my father criticizing me severely, it was for looking back"(paragraph 16) means
   a. openly.
   b. pleasantly.
   c. slowly.
   d. secretly.

Circle the letter of the word (or form of the word) from "Words to Watch" that best completes each of the following four sentences.

5. Julia is a (an) _____ speaker; she is never at a loss for words.
   a. disputed
   b. apprehensive
   c. nondescript
   d. articulate

6. Our committee worked _____ on the project because we all wanted it to be a success.
   a. industriously
   b. unwarily
   c. insouciantly
   d. antagonistically

7. The bank robbers thought they had _____ the perfect scheme, but they were arrested the minute they demanded the money.
   a. restricted
   b. devised
   c. disputed
   d. devastated

8. Harry felt _____ because the road was already bad and the storm was getting worse.
   a. complacent
   b. apprehensive
   c. insouciant
   d. articulate

Reading Check

Central Point and Main Ideas

1. Which sentence best expresses the central point of the selection?
   a. Before the Civil Rights Act, blacks should not have used buses.
   b. Durham, Mary's home town, was one of the worst places for blacks before 1964.
   c. Mary's bus ride shows how segregation laws terrorized black people.
   d. The Civil Rights Act ended public segregation in the South.

2. Which sentence best expresses the main idea of paragraph 16?
   a. Mary led a dangerous life.
   b. Although her father told her not to, Mary occasionally looked back.
   c. Mary was afraid of black men who were not part of her community.
   d. Mary thought that two miles was too far to walk.

3. Which sentence best expresses the main idea of paragraph 40?
   a. Mary and Esther didn't have to walk far to catch the next bus.
   b. Mary and Esther sat directly behind the bus driver because the bus was almost empty.
   c. The bus did not pass through any white areas.

d. When Mary and Esther left the white neighborhood, they didn't have to obey its laws.

Key Supporting Details

4. At the time Mary was growing up, the people in Durham believed that segregation
   a. was illegal.
   b. would never end.
   c. would end in 1964.
   d. would end by the next generation.
5. Crowded buses frightened Mary because
   a. she disliked crowds.
   b. too many poor blacks and whites rode them.
   c. a dangerous argument over seating could occur.
   d. she couldn't study her music with so many people around.

Inferences

6. _____ TRUE OR FALSE? Before 1964, part of a Southern bus driver's job was to control segregated seating.
7. From the selection, we can conclude that the author is probably writing about a time when she was
   a. twenty-one.
   b. over thirty-one.
   c. in college.
   d. younger than eighteen.

The Writer's Craft

8. The author begins this selection with
   a. the first scene of her story.
   b. statistics.
   c. quotations.
   d. historical background.
9. In paragraphs 9 through 13, the author
   a. continues her story.
   b. makes a comparison.
   c. gives some background.
   d. makes a recommendation.
10. The story of the dramatic event on the bus ends in paragraph 39. The next paragraph provides
    a. a summary.
    b. a contrast.
    c. examples.
    d. a conversation.

Outlining Activity

Complete the following outline of "The Back of the Bus" by writing the letters of the missing items where they belong.

Items Missing from the Outline
a. The bus driver reacted to the mounting tension by driving very fast.
b. The black man would not leave "no-man's land" when the bus driver told him to.

Central point: Legal segregation in America's South caused black people to live in terror of conflict and violence.

   A. Mary worried when a white man sat in the black section.
   B. Mary's tension increased when a white man refused to sit beside a black man in "no-man's land."
   C. _____
   D. A strangely dressed little black woman added to the tension by screaming, "The government gave us these seats!"
   E. The bus driver threatened to take the black man to the police station.
   F. _____
   G. Finally, the bus driver decided to end the incident by letting everyone out on Main Street.

Discussion Questions

1. Have you experienced (or seen someone else experience) prejudice or other unfair treatment? If so, what happened, and how did you feel about it?
2. Which of the characters in Mebane's narrative do you admire the most? Do you think any of them act unwisely? If so, who and why?
3. We can easily understand why the segregation laws made blacks angry. How do the various white people in Mebane's narrative seem to feel about these laws? Why do you think they feel the way they do?
4. Why do you think Mebane ends her narrative with the sentence, "The people who devised this system thought that it was going to last forever"? Are there any laws or customs existing today that you think will disappear in the future?

Paragraph Assignments

1. Write a paragraph about a time of terror in your own life or a tense situation you experienced. The incident could be a fire, a robbery, a medical emergency, a death, a threat, or an intense confrontation. Explain in detail what led to the event (if you know), what actually happened, what you feared, how it all ended, and why you still remember the inci-

dent. A possible topic sentence might be, "One of the most frightening experiences of my life was the time _____."

2. Segregation was the law thorughout the South before 1964. What do you think people should do when they feel a law or custom is unjust or immoral? In a paragraph, give an example of a law many people disagree with, and tell what you think they could do to change it. Some of the issues you might want to write about could include the following:

- raising the 55-mile-an-hour speed limit
- allowing women to have abortions
- forcing people to retire at age 65
- legalizing marijuana
- experimenting on animals
- raising or lowering the drinking age

Be sure to say whether or not people who disagree with a law are justified in breaking it in order to call attention to their beliefs.

Essay Assignments

1. Public places often provide excellent opportunities to observe human behavior. Some of these places include buses, trains, planes, parks, fast-food restaurants, sports arenas, or college campuses. Write an essay about what can happen, or has happened, in one of these places. You might tell about one particular incident or several different incidents you have observed. Your central point could be similar to one of the following:

   A recent train ride revealed some interesting truths about human behavior.
   I enjoy going to baseball games these days, not to watch the game on the field but to watch what's going on in the stands.
   At a rock concert I learned more about abnormal behavior than I learned in my psychology class.

2. Mary Mebane didn't realize the true meaning of the experience she describes in this essay until she was an adult. Write an essay about an experience that taught you a lesson you didn't completely understand until later. You could write about finding out that someone was untrustworthy, understanding that parents have problems too, or finding out something important about yourself that you didn't realize before. Put your details in the essay in the order in which they happened.

To Get a Story, I Flimflammed a Dead Man's Mother

Bob Teague

Preview

Everyone has seen television news shows that feature the sobbing relatives of crime and accident victims and expose the personal lives of politicans. This invasion of privacy, admits Bob Teague, one of the first blacks to become a television reporter, is often the basis of news coverage. But how far should reporters go to get a story? In this chapter from his book *Live and Off-Color: News Biz*, Teague, who has over twenty years' experience with New York City's WNBC-TV, reveals his views on that question.

Words to Watch

goad (1): urge
pathos (2): ability to arouse pity
enterprising (6): clever and hard-working
magnitude (11): great importance
zeal (16): enthusiasm
speculating (21): guessing
anguished (22): with great suffering
vested interests (25): people with something to gain
protocols (25): customs and rules
circumvent (25): get around
perpetrated (26): committed
gaucheries (28): actions in bad taste
quid pro quo (37): something given in exchange for something else
mitigated (37): reduced
indiscretions (37): small sins

Working the street as a local TV reporter often makes it necessary to grow a callus on your heart. When covering a murder, for example, you have to delve into the gruesome details of the bloodletting. If at all possible, you must also show the victim's friends or family, preferably in a rage or in tears. If you are covering a political campaign, you must goad the candidates into spitting obscenities at each other. Like: "He said you're incompetent and unqualified. What's your reaction to that?"

Even when you feel that you are doing something disgusting, or merely in bad taste—displaying insensitivity to the point of being inhuman—you have to hang tough and follow through, like sticking a mike under the nose of a weeping old woman whose grandson has been stabbed to death in a New York gang rumble. I did all that and worse. It came with the territory. If I failed to do it for dear old Ch. 4, some other streetwalker made of sterner stuff would certainly do it for dear old Ch. 2, Ch. 5 or Ch. 7. And if my masters saw that kind of pathos on a competing station—they all had a shelf full of TV monitors in their offices—they would ask me, "Where were you when Channel Blank was getting the good stuff?" No one has yet devised a satisfactory answer to that one.

My friend Gloria Rojas of Ch. 7 says that's exactly what happened to her in covering the aftermath of a plane crash. While other members of the Eyewitness News team blanketed the crash site, Gloria was sent to the nearest hospital. "What a scene," she told me. "Chaos all over the place. I just walked into the emergency section with my crew, and nobody tried to stop us. We took pictures of the injured, some of them barely conscious, struggling to live. I didn't want to bother any of them. Just being there meant that we were increasing their chances of infection. So we just took pictures, talked with one of the surgeons, then packed up to leave. That's when a reporter from Channel 11 showed up with his crew and started interviewing some of the victims, including a guy who was obviously dying. I said to myself: This is an abomination. I am not going to stoop to anything so gross. I'm going to leave.

"Back at the station," Gloria went on, "our executive producer saw Channel 11's exclusive on the 10 o'clock news. He wanted to know whether I'd interviewed the same guy or even somebody else in critical condition. When I said I had decided not to do it as a matter of decency, he damn near had a fit. He said I should have done it, too. So what finally happened was, our station called Channel 11 and begged a copy of their tape. We ran the interview on our program at 11 with a credit line that said, 'Courtesy of WPIX.' I was so mad I couldn't even cry."

The fact is, you never know which of the many damned-if-you-do, damned-if-you-don't choices you will have to make on a given day.

Once upon a time in the Bronx, police discovered several tons of toxic chemicals illegally dumped on scattered vacant lots—a menace to neighborhood youngsters. An enterprising Ch. 2 reporter, poking through an isolated pile of glass and cardboard containers being collected by sanitation trucks, found a ledger. It gave away the manufacturer's name and address, with a catalogue of the lethal compounds in that load.

"After doing my stand-upper with the ledger," the WCBS man said later, "I planned to turn it over to the cops. Then a Channel 7 reporter showed up with his crew. I decided to share the ledger with him. You know, like some day I'll be the guy playing catch-up and maybe he will give me a clue.

"You won't believe this, but he put the ledger back in the pile, hiding it under some boxes. Then, with his camera rolling, he starts prowling through the stuff. All of a sudden he picks it up, turns to the camera and says, 'Look what I've found.'

"I was so mad I could have killed him. No point in trying to talk him out of it. I knew that. So after giving the ledger to the cops, I called his boss [then news director Ron Tindiglia] at Channel 7. Tindiglia thanked me. 'I'll take care of it,' he said. Tindiglia is a gentleman. That crummy bit with the ledger never got on the air."

The line between creative coverage and faking the news is a thin one indeed. The WABC reporter, however, had clearly gone too far.

Conflicts between local newspeople rarely involve questions of that magnitude. A typical hassle developed between Heather Bernard of Ch. 4 and Arnold Diaz of Ch. 2 on the hottest story in New Jersey at that time. The family of Karen Anne Quinlan was in a legal battle with the state for the right to disconnect the life-support apparatus that prevented their comatose daughter from "dying with dignity." When Heather reached the home of the Quinlan family, several competing camera teams were standing in line at the front door awaiting their turns to shoot.

"Arnold Diaz was next in line ahead of me," Heather recalled with rancor. "The other crews ahead of us took only 15 to 20 minutes each. Arnold was in there for over an hour. I was furious. Finally, I went inside to see what the heck was taking so long. I couldn't believe it. His crew was all packed up. He was sitting at the table with the Quinlans, having lunch.

"OK. The family had to eat anyway. No harm done. Then as they finished lunch—Arnold and his crew were starting to leave—I noticed a stack of letters on a table in the corner. I made the mistake of asking Mrs. Quinlan about all that mail. She said it was the letters and cards they had received in recent weeks expressing sympathy for their daughter and the family. Arnold had missed that angle completely. Now he tells his crew to unpack their gear. He wants to do another sound bite and shoot the letters. I grab him by the arm and say, 'Arnold, come on. Enough is enough.'

"We had such a big argument about it that Mrs. Quinlan butted in. 'Now, children. No fighting in this house.' Arnold backed off and I did my piece first.

"The next day he called NBC and told [then news director] Earl Ubell that Heather Bernard had been bitchy and obnoxious, very unprofessional on the Quinlan story. When I saw Arnold again a day later, I thanked him. I said: 'NBC had been threatening to fire me because they said I'm not aggressive enough in the field. You've saved my job.'"

If your zeal propels you into conflict with another reporter, you can huff and puff with reckless abandon. You know the other guy does not want to risk damage to his money-in-the-bank profile or risk a multimillion-dollar lawsuit for damaging yours.

From Square One of my career in the news biz, I had bent my personal rules of good conduct, decency and integrity again and again to get news stories on the tube. Sure, I worried about it some, but I kept on doing it. One particular incident in the field, though, left me with a churning knot of self-loathing. In Coney Island, covering the suicide leap of a 23-year-old man from the roof of a 21-story apartment building, I flimflammed the dead man's mother into giving me the exclusive sound bite I needed to flesh out my scenario. My excuse was: Who knows what Ch. 2 or Ch. 7 might have filmed before I reached the scene some three hours later?

After picking the brains of neighbors who had known the victim, I still had no idea why he did it. There was no suicide note. My cameraman suggested that somebody in the family might be able to fill in the blank, and added that they also might have a picture of the guy that we could put on film.

I didn't hesitate. Nothing seemed more important than getting those elements.

The man's mother, a middle-aged, red-eyed widow in a blue-and-white flower-print kimono, cracked the door only an inch or so when I rang her bell. She did not want to go on television. "Go away," she sobbed. "I'm in mourning."

In my best phony sympathetic manner I advised her that neighbors were saying that her son had killed himself because he was heavily into hard drugs. "They're claiming he started selling it, then got hooked on scag himself. I'd hate to put that on the air if it's not true. I'm sure your son was a decent guy. Unless I get the real story from you, I'll have no choice." The truth is, only one person, speculating off-camera, had suggested any such thing. Nevertheless, it worked.

While the camera rolled, the woman launched into an anguished tirade against people who will say anything to get on TV. Then she told me that her son had been depressed for several days. His 19-year-old girl friend had been devastated by his confession that he also liked to have sex with men occasionally; she had broadcast his shame to their friends.

That interview—plus an exclusive snapshot of the dead man—boosted my stock in the trade but not with my girl friend at that time. As the two of us watched that story on the TV set in my pad, she accused me with her eyes and with the question: "Wouldn't it have been better to let the reason for his suicide remain a mystery, to spare his mother that kind of useless humiliation?"

I didn't know the answer at that point. I was trying to come to grips with the problem.

A willingness to defy authorities is one of several personality traits you have to develop to be effective as a streetwalker. In many instances, the story you're out to cover is not just lying there for the taking. It is hidden by vested interests and protected by protocols. To circumvent them and get the story, you may, for example, imply to a stubborn, tight-lipped district attorney that you already know more than he has told you—to draw him out at least far enough to confirm your hunches. You may ignore "No Trespassing" signs and sneak into a mental hospital where you have reason to believe that the patients are being mistreated. You may walk into someone's home or office with a concealed microphone and a camera that appears to be inactive, to catch the person off guard.

Deceitful? Yes, but morally correct in my judgment. Long before my time, society gave journalists the right to play by a slightly different set of rules. We are not, of course, above the law. On the other hand, some white lies and deceits can be justified if perpetrated solely for the purpose of digging up the truth and airing it, but not for the purpose of sensation-mongering as I did with the poor woman whose son committed suicide. Realizing that, belatedly, I never again went that far.

Witnesses on Bleecker Street in Greenwich Village reported that one building superintendent shot his next-door counterpart to death—the bloody climax of a long-running feud over who had been putting garbage in front of whose building on the sly. The dead man left a wife and two preteen-age children.

On this story, I vowed in advance, I was not going to be insensitive for a change. Instead, I would show compassion by leaving the bereaved survivors alone. I would use only sound bites of neighbors and homicide detectives on the case. Which was exactly how I did it at first. I could afford to on this particular outing; no other newsreel was present to coerce me into typical gaucheries.

My crew were packing their gear in the trunk, ready to leave Bleecker

Street, when two urchins with dirty faces tugged my elbow. "Put us on TV, mister. We saw the whole thing."

I explained that I already had interviewed witnesses. I didn't need them.

"But it was our father who got killed," one of the boys pleaded.

My professional instincts got the better of me. Since they had volunteered, I could put them on-camera with a relatively clear conscience. And great God in the foothills, what terrific sound bites they gave me! In simple, dramatic sentences, they took turns telling what they heard, what they saw. They could have been talking about the death of an alien from Mars. "And pow. He shot my father in the eye."

Again, my crew and I started to leave. An old guy wearing shabby and shapeless clothes tugged my elbow. "She's waiting for you," he announced. He pointed toward a frail young Puerto Rican woman in tears. She was wearing what had to be the prettiest dress she owned.

"The victim's wife?" I inquired.

The old man in the baggy suit nodded. "Yes, my granddaughter. She's waiting for you."

Reluctantly, I shoved the microphone under her quivering, freshly painted lips. She wailed about the loss of her husband, wept without embarrassment. Great TV. Some of her tears fell on my hand. That's when I got the message: she, as well as her kids, wanted the whole damn world to share their grief.

Experiences in that vein allowed me to feel more comfortable in my television role. There was a quid pro quo that mitigated my indiscretions to some degree. Just as I used people to suit my purposes, they used me. Why not? Television belonged to everybody.

First Impressions

Freewrite for ten minutes on one of the following.

1. Did you enjoy reading this selection? Why or why not?
2. Do you watch television news? Why or why not?
3. Have you ever been in a situation in which you chose to be dishonest or inconsiderate in order to gain what you wanted? If so, what happened? How did you feel afterward?

Vocabulary Check

Circle the letter of the word or phrase that best completes each of the following four sentences.

1. The word *abomination* in "a reporter ... started interviewing some of the victims, including a guy who was obviously dying. I said to myself: This is

an abomination. I am not going to stoop to anything so gross" (paragraph 3) means
   a. something admirable.   c. something slow.
   b. something courageous.   d. something dreadful.

2. The word *rancor* in "A typical hassle developed between Heather Bernard . . . and Arnold Diaz. . . . 'Arnold Diaz was next in line ahead of me,' Heather recalled with rancor. . . . 'I was furious'" (paragraphs 11 and 12) means
   a. affection.   c. resentment.
   b. joy.   d. no feeling.

3. The word *flimflammed* in "I flimflammed the dead man's mother into giving me the exclusive sound bite I needed. . . . In my best phony sympathetic manner I advised her that neighbors were saying that her son had killed himself because he was heavily into hard drugs" (paragraphs 17 and 21) means
   a. tricked.   c. reminded.
   b. discouraged.   d. followed.

4. The word *tirade* in "While the camera rolled, the woman launched into an anguished tirade against people who will say anything to get on TV" (paragraph 22) means
   a. long, forceful speech.   c. compliment.
   b. prediction.   d. amusing joke.

Circle the letter of the answer that best completes each of the following four items. Each sentence uses a word (or form of a word) from "Words to Watch."

5. George is always trying to _____ the library rules. Last week, he deliberately did not return three books that were on overnight reserve.
   a. mitigate   c. circumvent
   b. speculate   d. perpetrate

6. We have to admire the fans' _____. They are still cheering for the team even though it has lost seven games in a row.
   a. zeal   c. gaucheries
   b. protocols   d. indiscretions

7. _____ salespeople often use imaginative methods to close a sale.
   a. Anguished   c. Enterprising
   b. Pathetic   d. Gauche

8. Getting my driver's license was an event of great _____ in my life.
   a. magnitude   c. indiscretion
   b. pathos   d. protocol

Reading Check

Central Point and Main Ideas

1. Which sentence best expresses the central point of the selection?
    a. Being a television reporter is risky.
    b. Television reporters have the right to do anything to get their story, even lie and break the law.
    c. Television reporters must often be tough and even untruthful, but they should have limits.
    d. Most people would do almost anything to get on television.
2. Which sentence best expresses the main idea of paragraph 21?
    a. Teague got his interview by lying to the victim's mother.
    b. Teague had met the dead man's mother years before.
    c. Teague believed that the son was on drugs.
    d. Teague would have used the untrue story if the victim's mother had not explained what really happened.
3. Which sentence best expresses the main idea of paragraph 36?
    a. The building superintendent died a tragic death.
    b. Some of the woman's tears fell on Teague's hand.
    c. Teague gave the victim's wife the microphone.
    d. The victim's wife wanted to express her grief on television.

Key Supporting Details

4. By Bob Teague's standards, a good television reporter
    a. never lies.
    b. does anything to get an exclusive story.
    c. is tough and follows through.
    d. may fake the news if it will help the reporter's career.
5. The Channel 7 reporter who claimed that he had found a ledger at a dump site
    a. was the first person to find it.
    b. was not allowed to tell the story on the air.
    c. kept the ledger for himself.
    d. got promoted as a result of his story.

Inferences

6. Teague implies that
    a. news directors want their reporters to be aggressive.
    b. it's not necessary for TV reporters to be aggressive.
    c. TV reporters are less aggressive than newspaper reporters.
    d. reporters never help each other.
7. The author implies that competition between stations
    a. is always beneficial.
    b. does not exist in New York City.

c. does not cause conflicts among reporters.
d. encourages sensationalism.

8. _____ TRUE OR FALSE? Teague regrets the way he treated the suicide victim's mother.

The Writer's Craft

9. The word *however* in "The line between creative coverage and faking the news is a thin one indeed. The WABC reporter, however, had clearly gone too far" signals
   a. an illustration.
   b. a contrast.
   c. a conclusion.
   d. an example.
10. To support his points, the author uses
    a. statistics.
    b. viewers' opinions.
    c. anecdotes.
    d. definitions.

Summarizing Activity

Complete the following summary of "To Get a Story, I Flimflammed a Dead Man's Mother" by filling in each blank with one or more words.

Street reporters for television must be (1)_____. If they are not, they risk another reporter getting a better or at least a more sensational story. Reporters soon learn that news directors want sensationalism.

The (2)_____ between stations can result in conflicts between reporters. One reporter went so far as to (3)_____ the news using another reporter's discovery. Arguments over such issues as sharing interview time and stealing story angles are not rare. Competition is so great that the author of this article lied to the mother of a (4)_____ victim in order to get an interview. He later decided it is wrong to lie for the sake of sensationalism, though he believes journalists may use deceit to dig up the truth. And he has discovered that insensitivity isn't always necessary to get a sensational story. Once, the family of a murder victim (5)_____

_____.

Discussion Questions

1. Which of the examples Teague includes in his article do you think gives the most powerful proof of his thesis? Why?

2. Do you think a news reporter should have the legal right to take people's pictures or use what they say without their permission or knowledge? Why or why not?
3. Do you think there are any news stories that should not be shown on television under any circumstances? If so, what are some examples, and why shouldn't these stories be shown?
4. Teague blames reporters themselves for some of the insensitivity of TV news. Who else might be to blame? Why?

Paragraph Assignments

1. Think of a news story on TV that, in your opinion, should not have been shown (or at least not shown in such gory detail). In a paragraph, describe this story in detail, and then explain why it went too far. Was it too violent? Did it invade the privacy of people who should have been left alone? Could it give some insane people the idea of doing something similar? Your topic sentence could be something like this: "The news story about _____ should never have been permitted on the air."

2. Teague argues that being untruthful is sometimes necessary to get the news. Do you think lying is ever justified? Write a paragraph in which you give reasons for your opinion. You might want to write about situations such as the following:

   - A friend asks, "Do you like my new suede jacket?"—and you don't.
   - The most boring person in the college asks if you are on your way to the cafeteria for lunch and, if so, may he join you?
   - A police officer can trick a suspect into confessing by telling him— untruthfully—that the suspect's partner has already confessed.
   - A dying woman asks her doctor, "Will I get well?"

Essay Assignments

1. Teague points out that the intense competition among reporters is responsible for much of the insensitivity of TV news. Is intense competition usually bad or good? Write about one or more situations in which intense competition has negative—or positive—results. Support your point with specific examples of what can happen when people compete fiercely for the same goal. For example, you might want to write about competition for grades, a job, a date, a political or class office, or places on a team. A possible thesis for your essay might be "Competition has helped me get in good enough shape to make the basketball team, raise my grade in accounting, and become employee of the month at Clockwork Enterprises."

2. Teague suggests that TV reporters must often be insensitive. What other jobs besides reporting demand a certain amount of insensitivity to gruesome details and people's feelings? Think of three occupations that would fit this description, and write an essay explaining why people in these jobs need to be less sensitive than other people. Among the jobs to consider for this assignment are

   - doctor or nurse
   - soldier
   - judge
   - funeral director
   - police officer
   - teacher

   As an alternative, write an essay telling why people in these jobs should be more sensitive.

5

Back from Death?
Susan Seliger

Preview

The scene is a hospital room. The patient in the bed has stopped breathing. Doctors work feverishly to revive her, and, moments later, she wakes up. Later, she tells the story of the few minutes she was "dead." Others have told similar stories. What did they see? And what do these experiences mean? Read Susan Seliger's article, and decide for yourself.

Words to Watch

void (1): empty space
permeated (1): completely filled
realms (2): regions
uncanny (4): weird
dubbed (10): called
panoramic (10): including everything
repertoire (17): supply of knowledge
celestial (20): heavenly
skeptical (27): doubting
spontaneously (28): without warning
beachhead (29): secure position
conclusive (34): final
effecting (36): bringing about
serenity (36): calmness

"I had a heart attack, and I found myself in a black void, and I knew I was dying. . . . I could see a gray mist, and I was rushing toward it. . . . Beyond the mist I could see people. . . . The whole thing was permeated with the most gorgeous light—a living, golden-yellow glow, a pale color, not like the harsh gold color we knew on earth. As I approached more closely, I felt certain that I was going through that mist. It was such a wonderful, joyous feeling; there are just no words in human language to describe it. Yet it wasn't my time to go through the mist, because instantly from the other side appeared my Uncle Carl, who had died many years earlier. He blocked my path, saying: "Go back. Your work on earth has not been completed. Go back now." I didn't want to go back, but I had no choice, and immediately I was back in my body. I felt that horrible pain in my chest, and I heard my little boy crying, 'God, bring my mommy back to me.'"

This experience, related by a woman who nearly died, is one of many from *Life After Life*, a book written by Dr. Raymond Moody, an Augusta, Ga., physician. Moody says he has heard so many similar accounts, from persons of totally dissimilar religious and educational backgrounds, that he no longer can "dismiss out of hand the notion that there could be other realms of existence."

Dr. Elisabeth Kübler-Ross, a Chicago psychiatrist widely known for her work with the dying, goes even further. She has announced that she is convinced "beyond a shadow of a doubt that there is life after death." She says that "hundreds of cases of this kind have not been scientifically verified. We've just been afraid to admit it."

Not all researchers share these convictions about a hereafter. Others who have studied near-death experiences note that other conclusions can be drawn from the survivors' accounts. But there is no disagreement about the uncanny similarity of visions and feelings that different people describe after coming close to death or being declared "clinically dead" and then revived.

A Great Sense of Relief

Moody says that nearly every survivor says ordinary language is inadequate to describe the extraordinary experience. Often the survivors have heard themselves pronounced dead by doctors or spectators at the scene of an accident. This, many say, is followed by a great sense of release, peace, even euphoria.

One man who suffered a severe head injury and who was clinically dead (heart and breathing stopped, blood pressure undetectable, and body temperature falling) recalled for Moody:

> "At this point of injury there was a momentary flash of pain, but then all the pain vanished. I had the feeling of floating in a dark space. The day was bitterly cold, yet while I was in that blackness all I felt was warmth and the most extreme comfort I have ever experienced. . . . I remember thinking, 'I must be dead.' "

Pleasant music or a buzzing noise often is heard. Survivors then recount a sensation of moving out of their bodies and floating like a feather toward the ceiling, where they can look down on their own bodies. One elderly woman who had a heart attack recalls:

"I felt almost as though I were a piece of paper that someone had blown up to the ceiling. I watched them reviving me from up there. . . . I heard one nurse say, 'Oh my God! She's gone!' while another one leaned down to give me mouth-to-mouth resuscitation. I was looking at the back of her head while she did this. . . . As I saw them below beating on my chest and rubbing my arms and legs, I thought, 'Why are they going to so much trouble? I'm just fine now.'"

Flashback to Childhood

Many people, Moody says, remark upon a sensation of being whisked away rapidly through a small, dark space like a cave or a tunnel. At the end there is a bright, "indescribable" light, often dubbed "the being of light," or given religious names such as God or Jesus because it seems to have a consciousness that can communicate. This light may trigger or lead people through a panoramic survey of their lives at amazing speed and in vivid sensuous detail.

Dr. Russell Noyes, a professor of psychiatry at the University of Iowa College of Medicine who has just published a study of 104 near-deaths, reports this account from a young woman who survived an automobile accident:

"My life passed before me in a way that took me back to my childhood. I remember the smell of pudding my mother used to make, the smell of the old house, and feelings I had then. . . ."

Sometimes relatives who are dead appear to come into view, according to Moody. They may beckon the near-death person across a barrier that cannot be crossed, or tell the person to go back now, back to life.

A former philosophy professor with a second degree in medicine, Moody is the first to point out that "what I've shown is not proof. I haven't collected a random sample or done a number of things that would make it 'scientific.'"

Moody says that he has been swamped ever since his book came out last July with calls from persons who have had near-death experiences and want to talk about them with a sympathetic person.

Such experiences are common, says Moody, who asks rhetorically, "So why don't we hear about it?" His answer: "Doctors don't ask patients." Either it doesn't occur to them, or they're afraid to, Moody contends. "Doctors as a group have a high level of anxiety about death."

Fear of Talking

But even more important, most people until very recently have been reluctant to discuss their experiences for fear of being thought insane.

Those who agreed to talk to researchers usually insisted that their identities be kept confidential. An exception is Sheldon Ruderman of Oakland, Calif., who described to *The Observer* his two near-death experiences, one 7 and the other 16 years ago. But even he wouldn't tell anybody about them until recently, when he heard a few others revealing their stories. Says Ruderman: "I'd come into all this a scientist type and an atheist. . . . When you go through an experience like this [he felt as if he had slipped out of his body, watched doctors operating on him to remove cancerous tissue, roamed about the room unseen, feeling 'free and elated'] and it's not part of the cultural repertoire you know, you think you're crazy. You just don't allow these experiences in."

Now Ruderman himself counsels dying cancer patients in California, who have told him stories that parallel his own. He observes: "All a patient has to do is hear someone say, 'Yeah, I understand,' and he'll say, 'Wow, I'm not crazy!' Then he'll spill his guts out to you."

Outside One's Body

But Dr. Charles Garfield, at the Cancer Research Institute of the University of California in San Francisco, contends that not much has been heard of near-death experiences because they are not common. He believes that it is misleading to suggest that everyone will have such an experience. "People are talking about this subject to a public that is thirsting for it," Garfield says. "It's not really fair. Soon you'll get 6,000 old gramdmas in Des Moines, Iowa, starting a cult."

Garfield has worked for many years with cancer patients and with cardiac patients who were "dead" and then revived. "Most didn't remember much," he says. But he adds: "A number said they heard celestial music. A number said they had out-of-body experiences where they drifted out of the physical boundaries of the body and watched the drama from a different perspective."

Garfield says, "I've heard talk of reunions, being freed, mentioning names of dead relatives. I wish I could conclude what I'd like to—that they're having some contact with [the relatives]. But right now I'm stuck with the words."

Death Without Anxiety

Kübler-Ross, who has been counseling dying patients for two decades, believes such stories aren't just words. But she says it was not easy to announce that she is convinced there is life after death, even though a recent Gallup poll reports that 73 percent of Americans share her belief.

She feared losing her colleagues' respect. But now she says that she feels she is not alone.

Because of the advances in high-speed rescue and resuscitation techniques, more clinically dead persons are being brought back to life. And a growing number of researchers are interviewing the survivors afterward.

After interviews with more than a thousand patients, Kübler-Ross says: "The common denominators before they die are they are at peace; they are fully awake; when they float out of their bodies, they are without fear, pain, or anxiety; and they have a sense of wholeness."

Kübler-Ross says that not everyone dies with a peaceful facial expression. But for the most part, she explains, the stories that near-death patients tell make death sound so beautiful that she has been afraid that publicizing them will encourage suicides.

Not Just Hallucinations

"Many of my patients talked with people who had died before them," Kübler-Ross contends. "My own father, a businessman, started to talk to his father." These are not hallucinations, she insists, adding: "I've seen patients hallucinating. [But] many of these [near-death] patients have *not* been on medication, *not* had hallucinations."

Kübler-Ross notes that "skeptical scientists say this is simply thought projection." But she contends: "It cannot be, because when I asked 5- or 6-year-olds who have had this experience whom they see, not one has seen Mommy or Daddy. It was always a dead person."

Kübler-Ross says that she believes Robert Monroe of Charlottesville, Va., has the explanation for this. Monroe contends that the out-of-body experience is the projection of "the second body," or "the soul," as he puts it, into the same state of being or "energy system" that humans enter after death. Though he says these experiences can occur spontaneously in times of extreme stress, such as facing death, he insists that people can also learn how to have them at will. Monroe is working in an elaborately equipped clinic near his home to train others to duplicate these out-of-body projections.

Monroe says that he began a program in Kansas City, Kansas, with Kübler-Ross as an adviser, to train terminally ill patients "to go into these out-of-body states so they can know where they're going when they die and establish a beachhead there, as it were." Monroe adds hastily that he already has more applicants than his staff can handle.

Monroe has no medical training. He got interested in out-of-body projections 18 years ago when, he says, one happened to him without warning. He had never even heard of such experiences before that, he says. Though initially frightened, he became determined to find out the how and why of the experience by trying to repeat the process. He says that he has now had many such excursions in which he has talked with the dead. "I don't believe there's life after death; I *know* it," he says.

Very Similar Experiences

Noyes, the Iowa professor, thinks that some researchers go too far in reaching personal conclusions about a hereafter. "I don't believe one can take this sort of experience as evidence of life after death," he says. "There are a lot of conclusions one can draw."

Noyes notes, for example, that people undergo very similar experiences whether they actually are close to death or simply faced with a sudden threat that makes them think they are about to die. Albert Heim, a geology professor, bears out this view in an 1892 study on what it might be like to die from a fall. He interviewed 30 persons who had survived falls in the Alps. A man named Sigrist, who fell backward from the peak of Karpfstock, reported:

> "The fall was . . . entirely unaccompanied by the sort of anxious feeling one often has in dreams. Instead I believed myself to be floating downward in the most pleasant way, and I had the fullest consciousness during the fall. Without pain and anxiety I surveyed the situation, the future of my family, and the arrangement I had already made for their security, with a rapidity of which I had never before been capable . . . I painlessly lost consciousness upon the most powerful impact on the cushion of snow covering the crag below. . . . I cannot think of a milder, finer way to die."

No Proof of Hereafter

Noyes contends that while such experiences may give us some insight into what it is like to die, they say nothing conclusive about a hereafter.

The out-of-body experiences, Noyes says, are projections that the brain makes to negate death, to pretend we are only witnessing it as a spectator. He cites Freud: "Our own death is indeed unimaginable, and whenever we make the attempt to imagine it we can perceive that we really survive as spectators. Hence . . . at bottom no one believes in his own death, or to put the same thing another way, in the unconscious every one of us is convinced of his own immortality."

The mind works quickly, as a survival response, Noyes adds, to enable a person to save himself or herself if possible. If not, facing no future, the mind focuses on the past—the panoramic flashbacks. "We may take comfort from the fact that, suddenly confronted by death, we might find within ourselves the resources for coping with that frightful prospect. In such an urgent moment, strength might be found for effecting our rescue, but, failing in that, to face life's end with serenity, even acceptance."

This does not mean, Noyes adds, that he has made up his mind personally one way or the other. "All I can tell you is what patients tell me," he says. "They are filled with curiosity, wonderment. We'll just have to wait and see."

Charles Garfield, the California researcher, agrees that we will have to wait and see—if not until our own deaths then "until we develop more sophisticated ways of detecting whether there is really communication with the dead," as many of his patients believe.

"Who knows?" he shrugs. "We were forced to the conclusion that the earth is round. We were forced to the conclusion that the earth is not the center of the universe. We've been forced to accept things that seemed more ridiculous than this."

First Impressions

Freewrite for ten minutes on one of the following.

1. Did you enjoy reading this selection? Why or why not?
2. Do you believe in life after death? Why or why not? If you do, what do you think it will be like?
3. Why do you think stories of people who have been "brought back to life" interest so many people?

Vocabulary Check

Circle the letter of the word or phrase that best completes each of the following four sentences.

1. The word *verified* in "Dr. Elisabeth Kübler-Ross . . . is convinced 'beyond a shadow of a doubt that there is life after death.' She says that 'hundreds of cases of this kind have now been scientifically verified' "(paragraph 3) means
   a. laughed at.   c. doubted.
   b. lost.   d. proved.
2. The word *euphoria* in "This, many say, is followed by a great sense of release, peace, even euphoria" (paragraph 5) means
   a. serious illness.   c. lost time.
   b. great happiness.   d. intense sorrow.
3. The words *common denominators* in "The common denominators before they die are they are at peace; they are fully awake; when they float out of

their bodies they are without fear, pain, or anxiety; and they have a sense of wholeness"(paragraph 24) mean
   a. share qualities.
   b. distractions.
   c. greatest problems.
   d. worst experiences.
4. The word *negate* in "The out-of-body experiences . . . are projections that the brain makes to negate death, to pretend we are only witnessing it as a spectator" (paragraph 35) means
   a. frighten.
   b. remember.
   c. praise.
   d. deny.

Circle the letter of the word (or form of the word) from "Words to Watch" that best completes each of the following four sentences.

5. From the top of the cliff we had a _____ view of the entire valley.
   a. dubbed
   b. skeptical
   c. panoramic
   d. permeated

6. Maria is certainly a very _____ person; she questions much of what she reads and hears.
   a. skeptical
   b. spontaneous
   c. euphoric
   d. celestial

7. Sabrina's ability to guess the winning number so often is absolutely _____ .
   a. panoramic
   b. void
   c. skeptical
   d. uncanny

8. The death of Grandfather's dog left a _____ in his life.
   a. void
   b. repertoire
   c. beachhead
   d. panorama

Reading Check

Central Point and Main Ideas

1. Which sentence best expresses the central point of the selection?
   a. Modern research proves that there is definitely life after death.
   b. Though reports of near-death experiences suggest that there is life after death, some researchers are not sure.
   c. Some researchers feel that near-death experiences are only imagination or wishful thinking.
   d. Researchers are not interested in stories of near-death experiences.
2. Which sentence best expresses the main idea of paragraph 20?
   a. Some of Garfield's patients have reported pleasant experiences while "dead."
   b. Garfield has worked with cancer and cardiac patients for many years.
   c. A number of patients who have been revived reported hearing music.
   d. Most of Garfield's patients have died.

Key Supporting Details

3. Researchers agree that
   a. there is life after death.
   b. many people who have been near death have had similar experiences.
   c. federal funding should be provided to study near-death experiences.
   d. there is no life after death.
4. _____ TRUE OR FALSE? A Gallup poll has found that most Americans believe in life after death.
5. Young children who have had near-death experiences report seeing
   a. a parent.
   b. someone who has died.
   c. a favorite television personality.
   d. a classmate.

Inferences

6. Near-death experiences suggest that people who are already dead
   a. are lonely.
   b. know when living people will die.
   c. are worse off than living people.
   d. wish they could come back to life.
7. We can infer from this article that in the future
   a. everyone will be convinced that there is life after death.
   b. scientists will continue to do research on near-death experiences.
   c. people will completely lose interest in the question of life after death.
   d. everyone will be able to communicate with the dead.

The Writer's Craft

8. The author supports her ideas by using
   a. stories of other people's personal experiences.
   b. quotations from researchers.
   c. evidence from surveys.
   d. all of the above.
9. The author begins and ends the article with
   a. statistics.
   b. definitions.
   c. facts.
   d. quotations.
10. In paragraph 27, the word *but* in the sentences "Kubler-Ross notes that 'skeptical scientists say this is simply thought projection.' But she contends: 'It cannot be, because when I asked 5- or 6- year-olds who have had this experience whom they see, not one has seen Mommy or Daddy. It was always a dead person'" introduces a
    a. statistic.
    b. contrast.
    c. summary.
    d. list.

Summarizing Activity

Complete the following summary of "Back from Death?" by filling in each blank with one or more words.

    According to the book *Life After Life* by Dr. Raymond Moody, near-death glimpses into what seems to be a hereafter have convinced some researchers that there might be life after (1) _____. Others recognize the similarity in such experiences but are not convinced that a hereafter exists. People who have been near death report experiencing wonderful feelings of (2) _____, out-of-body sensations, and flashbacks to (3) _____. While Moody's approach isn't scientific, he and others, such as psychiatrist Dr. Elisabeth Kübler-Ross, believe that near-death experiences are common and that people want to discuss them but are afraid of being thought (4) _____. On the other hand, Dr. James Garfield, a cancer researcher, says that we haven't heard more about near-death experiences because they are uncommon. Dr. Russell Noyes of the University of Iowa says that near-death experiences can be interpreted in many different ways, and he and Garfield conclude that (5) _____

_____

Discussion Questions

1. Which "near-death" story did you consider the most convincing? The least convincing? Why?
2. Why do you think Seliger begins her article with the story of the heart-attack victim? What does the opening paragraph have to do with her central point?
3. Why are so many people afraid of death? Might anything in this selection change their feelings? What would it take to convince you that death is pleasant?
4. What might be some of the dangers of believing that death is just a painless, even pleasant, doorway into an afterlife?

Paragraph Assignments

1. In a paragraph, describe what happens in a typical near-death experience, so that people who have never heard of one could understand what it is. Use specific details from "Back from Death?" Your topic sentence might be like this one: "Many near-death experiences are amazingly similar."
2. You might not have had a near-death experience, but you might have had a strange experience while you were sick, feverish, overtired, recovering from surgery, or the like. Write a paragraph describing such an experience. What did you see? Hear? Feel? How did you feel afterwards?

Essay Assignments

1. Everyone needs to believe in something—if not in life after death, then in some other important idea. Write about a belief that is important to you, one that has given you strength and hope. Explain how it has supported and encouraged you through some difficult times. Below are some beliefs that others have depended on. You may use one of them if you too have found it helpful.

   - People are basically good and decent.
   - If life hands you a lemon, make lemonade.
   - A winner never quits; a quitter never wins.
   - There's always a second chance.
   - God will provide.
   - It could have been worse.
   - Live for today.
   - The past is past, so put it behind you.
   - Nothing ventured, nothing gained.

   Your thesis statement could be something like this: "My belief that things turn out for the best helped me survive a serious car accident, the loss of my first job, and the death of my grandmother."

2. According to this selection, people near death seem to leave their bodies and can see what is happening around them. If you could be present at and see and hear what happened at your own funeral, what would you like to hear people saying about you? Write an essay about three things you would like to be remembered for after your death. You might, for example, write about your good qualities, your accomplishments, or your relationships with your loved ones.

Families and Children

Batter Up
Bill Cosby

Preview

"*Nothing* is harder for a parent than getting your kids to do the right thing," writes Bill Cosby, noted humorist, star of his own wildly successful television series, and real-life father of five children. In this selection from his 1986 best-seller, *Fatherhood*, Cosby describes what happened when one of these children disobeyed his rules.

Words to Watch

reason (1): logic
feat (1): accomplishment
reversion (9): return
underground (11): secret organization fighting against those in power
animal husbandry (18): science of breeding and raising animals
eloquence (25): ability to speak persuasively
barbaric (28): uncivilized
righteousness (36): moral behavior
pondering (36): thinking carefully about
reservoir (36): storage area
maintaining (39): keeping
designated hitter (40): in baseball, someone who bats instead of the pitcher

Let me repeat: *nothing* is harder for a parent than getting your kids to do the right thing. There is such a rich variety of ways for you to fail: by using threats, by using bribery, by using reason, by using example, by using blackmail, or by pleading for mercy. Walk into any bus terminal in America and you will see men on benches poignantly staring into space with the looks of generals who have just surrendered. They are fathers who have run out of ways to get their children to do the right thing, for such a <u>feat</u> is even harder than getting my daughter to remember her own telephone number.

I succeeded once. It happened after my son, who was twelve at the time, had sent me on a trip to the end of my rope. He had taken up a new hobby: lying; and he was doing it so well that he was raising it to an art. Disturbing letters were coming from school—disturbing to me, not to him, for he was full of the feeling that he could get away with anything; and he was right.

"No longer are we going to *ask* you to do something," I told him one day, "we're going to *tell* you that you'd better do it. This is the law of our house: you do what we *tell* you to do. Thomas Jefferson will pardon me, but you're the one American who isn't ready for freedom. You don't function well with it. Do you understand?"

"Yes, Dad," he said.

A few days later, I called from Las Vegas and learned from my wife that this law of the house had been broken. I was hardly taken by surprise to learn that the outlaw was my son.

"Why didn't you do what you were told?" I said to him on the phone. "This is the second time I've had to tell you, and your mother's very upset. The school also says you're not coming in with the work."

"Well, I just don't feel like doing it," he said.

"Very well. How does this idea strike you? When I come home on Thursday, I'm going to kick your butt."

Now I know that many distinguished psychologists feel that kicking butt is a <u>reversion</u> to the Stone Age. But kids may have paid more attention in the Stone Age. When a father said, "No shrinking heads this week," his boy may have listened.

On Thursday, I came home, but I couldn't find the boy. He didn't make an appearance at dinner, and when I awoke the next morning, he still wasn't there. So I assembled my staff and solemnly said, "Ladies, where is my son?"

"He's around here *somewhere*," one of my daughters said. They were the French <u>underground</u> hiding one of their heroes from the Nazis.

At last, just before dinner, he entered the house, tired of wandering in the wilderness.

"Young man," I said, "I told you that when I came home, I would kick your behind."

"Yes, Dad," he replied.

"And you know why, don't you?"

"Yes, Dad."

"Then let's go over to the barn."

He may have been slow in his studies, but by now he must have suspected that I wasn't planning a lesson in <u>animal husbandry</u>. When we reached the barn, I said, "Son, we are now going to have a little talk about breaking the law and lying."

As the boy watched me roll up my sleeves, his usual cool gave way to fear, even though I was a father with absolutely no batting average: I had never before hit him or any of the other children. Was I making a mistake now? If so, it would just be mistake number nine thousand, seven hundred, and sixty-three.

"Dad, I know I was wrong," he said, "and I'm really sorry for what I did. I'll never do it again."

"I appreciate your saying that," I said, "and I love you; but I made a promise to you and you wouldn't respect me if I broke it."

"Oh, Dad, *I'd* respect you—I'd respect you like crazy!"

"Son, it's too late."

"It's *never* too late!"

He was reaching heights of legal eloquence, which didn't help him because I've often wanted to hit lawyers, too.

"Just turn around," I said. "I want you to know that this is a form of punishment I truly do not believe in."

"I hate to see you go against your *principles*, Dad."

"I can make an exception. I also won't say that this will hurt me more than it will hurt you. That would be true only if I turned around and let you hit *me*. This is simply a barbaric form of punishment, but it happens to match your barbaric behavior."

And then I hit him. He rose up on his toes in the point position and the tears began.

"Now do you understand my point about never lying again?" I said.

"Oh *yes*, Dad!" he said. "I've never understood it better."

"Fine. Now you can go."

He turned around to leave and I hit him again. When he turned back to me with a look of having been betrayed, I said, "I'm sorry; I lied. Do you ever want me to lie to you again?"

"No, Dad," he said.

And to this day, he has not lied again to me or my wife. Moreover, we received a letter from his school taking credit for having done a wonderful job on our son. I'm glad I had been able to supplement this work by the school with my own parent-student conference in the barn.

Could I have done anything else to put him on the road to righteousness? My wife and I spent long hours pondering this question. The problem was that the reservoir was empty: we had tried all the civilized ways to redirect him, but he kept feeling he could wait us out and get away with anything. And we loved him too much to let him go on thinking that.

The week after our trip to the barn, a friend of mine, Dr. Eddie Newman, said something that clicked with the boy.

"My boy is having his problems being a serious student," I told Eddie.

"Well, your studying is very important," Eddie said, while the boy sat smiling a smile that said: an old person is about to hand out some Wisdom. Could this please be over fast? "You know, a jet plane burns its greatest energy taking off; but once it reaches its cruising altitude, it burns less fuel. Just like studying. If you're constantly taking off and landing, you're going to burn more fuel as opposed to taking off and staying up there and <u>maintaining</u> that altitude."

A few days later, I ran into my son in the house. (He was around a lot more now that he knew the <u>designated hitter</u> had retired.)

"How's school?" I said.

Without a word, he raised his arm and laid his palm down and flat like a plane that had leveled off. He suddenly knew it was the only way to fly.

There are many good moments in fathering, but few better than that.

First Impressions

Freewrite for ten minutes on one of the following.

1. Did you enjoy reading this selection? Why or why not?
2. Were you ever spanked or hit by a parent? If so, what effect did this punishment have on you?
3. What are some of the *rewards* of being a parent?

Vocabulary Check

Circle the letter of the word or phrase that best completes each of the following four sentences.

1. The word *poignantly* in "Walk into any bus terminal in America and you will see men on benches poignantly staring into space with the looks of generals who have just surrendered" (paragraph 1) means
   a. happily.   c. proudly.
   b. hungrily.   d. pathetically.
2. The word *supplement* in "Moreover, we received a letter from his school taking credit for having done a wonderful job on our son. I'm glad I had been able to supplement this work by the school with my own parent-student conference in the barn" (paragraph 35) means
   a. cause trouble for.   c. leave out.
   b. add to.   d. profit on.
3. The word *redirect* in "we had tried all the civilized ways to redirect him, but he kept feeling he could wait us out and get away with anything" (paragraph 36) means
   a. guide.   c. reward.
   b. dress.   d. pay.

60 FAMILIES AND CHILDREN

4. The words *cruising altitude* in "You know, a jet plane burns its greatest energy taking off; but once it reaches its cruising altitude, it burns less fuel" (paragraph 39) mean
   a. runway.
   b. normal flying level.
   c. final destination.
   d. crash landing.

Insert each of the following words (or forms of words) from "Words to Watch" where it belongs in one of the four sentences below.

    maintain   pondered   reservoir   reverted

5. When I brought my newborn daughter home from the hospital, my jealous nine-year-old son _____ to babyish behavior and began sucking his thumb.
6. Unless I _____ a C average, I'll be kicked off the swimming team.
7. Although I _____ for several weeks, I still couldn't decide which refrigerator to buy.
8. During the recent heat wave, the water supply in our town's _____ was running dangerously low.

Reading Check

Central Point and Main Ideas

1. Which sentence best expresses the central point of the selection?
   a. Raising a child is not difficult.
   b. Strict discipline can improve a child's behavior.
   c. Children often lie to their parents.
   d. Few parents have the courage to punish their children.
2. Which sentence best expresses the main idea of paragraph 1?
   a. A parent's most difficult job is teaching children how to do what is right.
   b. Parents sometimes bribe their children to behave properly.
   c. Parents never know what is best for their children.
   d. Parents who are failures end up in bus terminals.
3. Which sentence best expresses the main idea of paragraph 39?
   a. Old people know more than younger people.
   b. Forming regular study habits works better than studying irregularly.
   c. Jet planes burn a great deal of fuel.
   d. Taking off and landing are the worst parts of a pilot's job.

Key Supporting Details

4. Cosby's son was punished because
   a. he had forgotten his telephone number.
   b. he had not been doing his chores at home.

c. he had disobeyed his parents' rules.
d. he had run away from home.

5. _____ TRUE OR FALSE? Cosby had never hit any of his children before.
6. Cosby decided to hit his son because
    a. none of his other methods of discipline had worked.
    b. his wife had refused to punish the boy.
    c. the school had threatened to expel Cosby's son unless his grades improved.
    d. Cosby felt his son did not respect him.

Inferences

7. We can assume that Bill Cosby hit his son a second time because
    a. he was really angry with his son and wanted to hurt him badly.
    b. he enjoyed punishing his children.
    c. he had missed the first time.
    d. he wanted to teach his son that lying can hurt people.
8. From paragraphs 40 through 42, we can conclude that Cosby's son
    a. is more afraid of his father now than he used to be.
    b. is studying more regularly than he used to.
    c. is still telling lies.
    d. has decided to be a pilot when he grows up.

The Writer's Craft

9. _____ TRUE OR FALSE? Cosby probably chose the title "Batter Up" for his article in order to suggest his son would rather play baseball than study.
10. The tone of this selection can be described as
    a. objective.
    b. self-pitying.
    c. amusing.
    d. angry.

Outlining Activity

Complete the following outline of "Batter Up" by writing the letters of the missing items where they belong.

Items Missing from the Outline

a. From then on, Cosby's son told the truth at home and became a better student as well.
b. The boy broke this rule immediately, so Cosby told his son to expect a beating when he got home.
c. As his son turned to leave, Cosby hit him again.

62 FAMILIES AND CHILDREN

Central point: Cosby's son's behavior improved after Cosby punished him.

A. When Cosby's twelve-year-old son began telling lies, Cosby ordered the boy to obey his parents.

B. _____

C. Just before dinner, Cosby took his son to the barn and hit him once.

D. Then he told the boy he could leave the barn.

E. _____

F. Cosby apologized immediately and asked his son if he ever wanted to be lied to again.

G. _____

Discussion Questions

1. Do you feel Cosby was right to hit his son? Why or why not?
2. If you had a child who disobeyed you, what would you do to make him or her behave? If you were the child, what would you want your parent to do to you? Why?
3. Which do you think has a bigger effect on our behavior, home or school? Why?
4. Do you think it's better for children to be forced to obey all their parents' rules, or should they be permitted to break a rule now and then? Which of these approaches—strictness or permissiveness—works better on adults?

Paragraph Assignments

1. Cosby ends his essay with the words, "There are many good moments in fathering, but few better than that." Write a paragraph about a "good moment" you experienced as a parent or as a child, spouse, student, employee, athlete, team or club member, or member of your community. Your topic sentence could be something like this: "My best moment as a _____ was the time I _____
   _____."

2. Although Cosby was unsure about how to solve the problem with his son, the solution he finally chose worked well. Write about a time you were unsure about how to solve a problem but finally found a good solution. For example, you could write about how you broke up with a boyfriend or girlfriend, how you got a job, how you were able to do better in work or at school, how you lost (or gained) weight, or how you saved money. Tell what the problem was, why it was difficult to solve, what you decided to do, and how things turned out.

Essay Assignments

1. Write an essay about a time when, like Bill Cosby, you kept your promise even though it was difficult for you to do so. First, describe the situation. Then explain what promise you kept and why it was difficult for you to do so. Then tell what happened as a result. Your thesis statement could be similar to one of the following:

   Even though I didn't have the time and energy, I agreed to have all our relatives to Thanksgiving dinner because I had promised I would.
   I kept my promise to donate blood in spite of being terrified of needles.

2. According to Cosby, a parent's hardest job is getting a child to do what is right. What are some other things that are difficult for a parent—or any authority figure (such as a boss, coach, or instructor)? Choose one or more of the following and write an essay explaining, by giving examples, why each of them would be hard for someone in charge to do:

   - saying no
   - letting a child, team member, or employee make his or her own decisions
   - accepting a child's friends
   - giving advice on moral issues
   - not giving in to demands
   - getting someone to do an unpleasant job

What Do Children Owe Their Parents?
Ann Landers

Preview

"I don't owe anybody anything," teenagers sometimes claim. According to Ann Landers, the famous advice columnist, they are mistaken. But what, exactly, do teenagers owe their parents? And what do older children owe? The answers Ann Landers gives to these questions may surprise you.

Words to Watch

punitive (2): punishing
injunction (4): command
bestow (6): give
brittle (6): easily broken
stemming from (6): arising out of
chronic (6): continuing over time
obsolescence (6): becoming out of date
muster (11): gather up
gumption (14): boldness
exploit (14): take advantage of
outset (15): beginning
incontinent (17): unable to control bodily waste functions
implore (17): beg

"What is your mother doing these days?" I asked a friend who recently returned from a visit with her family in New York. "Mother is very busy doing what she does best," was the reply. "She's the East Coast distributor for guilt."

I often hear this sentiment expressed by young marrieds, who are irritated and resent their invisible burden. There's a tremendous amount of guilt around these days, and many of the victims don't know if it is being laid on them by self-centered, punitive parents—or if they really are rotten kids.

What do children owe their parents, anyway? Not just married children, but all children—from six years of age to 66. No one can speak for everyone, but since this question has been raised by many people groping for answers, I shall try to respond.

First, let's start with teenagers. Here are the basics: You owe your parents consideration, loyalty, and respect. The Biblical injunction "Honor thy father and thy mother" is simple and clear. "But what if they are drunks and abusive and failures, not only as parents but as human beings? Are we still supposed to 'honor' them? Do we still owe them consideration, loyalty, and respect?" This question is often put to me. "Yes," is my answer. Honor them because they gave you life. Give them consideration and loyalty for the same reason.

Consideration is a word that needs no definition, but loyalty as it relates to the family is sometimes vague. What does it mean? It means hanging in there when things go wrong. It means keeping family matters inside the family. The child who speaks ill of his parents and runs them down to outsiders says more about himself than he says about them.

Respect is difficult to bestow when it hasn't been earned—and sad to say, some parents have not earned it. If you feel your parents have not earned your respect, try to find it in your heart to substitute understanding and compassion. Granted, this is a great deal to ask of a teenager, but if you can do it, it will help you grow as a person. Look beyond the brittle facade and you'll see people who are bitterly ashamed of their inability to measure up. They're insecure and shaky—struggling with unresolved problems stemming from their childhood. To fail as a parent is extremely painful. They suffer a lot. But most parents are not drunks; nor are they abusive. They are plain, ordinary people with good intentions and feet of clay—trying desperately to survive in a dangerous, untidy world. They are out there every day, on the front lines, battling inflation, obesity, chronic fatigue, obsolescence, and crabgrass.

Nearly 48% of the work force in America today is female. This means great numbers of mothers are wearing two hats, or three. They're working at part-time (or full-time) jobs, trying to run a house, raise children, and participate in community activities. What do children owe parents who fit this description? Here are the fundamentals. They owe them prompt and honest answers to the following questions:

- Where are you going?
- Who are your companions?
- How do you plan to get there?
- When will you be home?

Teenagers frequently write to complain that their parents want to pick their friends. Do they have a right to do this? The answer is, "No." I never fail to point out, however, that when parents are critical of a teenager's friends, they usually have a good reason. Bad company can be bad news. But in the final analysis, the choice of friends should be up to the individual. If he or she makes poor selections, he or she will have to pay for it.

Parents have the right to expect their children to pick up after themselves and perform simple household chores. For example, every member of the family over six years of age should clean the bathtub and the sink so they will be in respectable condition for the next person. He or she should also run errands and help in the kitchen if asked—in other words, carry a share of the load without feeling persecuted. The days of "hired help" are, for the most part, gone. And this is good. Boys as well as girls should be taught to cook and clean, do laundry, and sew on buttons. This is not "sissy stuff." It makes for independence and self-reliance.

What do teenagers and college students owe their parents in terms of time and attention? There's no pat answer. Some parents are extremely demanding; others are loose hangers. Some children can't wait to move out of the house; others must be pushed out. A college student shouldn't be expected to write home every day, but certainly a postcard once a week isn't asking too much if parents wish this. A phone call (collect, of course) on Sunday should not be impossible to manage if parents want it. What about vacations? Do children owe it to their parents to come home, rather than go to Fort Lauderdale or to a ski resort? Yes, they do, if the parents want them home and are footing the bills for education and transportation.

What do working children who live at home owe their parents in terms of financial compensation? The following letter is typical of what I read at least two dozen times a week:

Dear Ann Landers:

Our daughter is 26 years old. She chose business school over college and is now number-one secretary to the president of a large firm. We are pleased that Terry still lives with us and doesn't want an apartment of her own, but I feel we are being taken advantage of.

Terry has no savings account. She buys expensive clothes, has her own car, vacations in Europe, and doesn't give us one cent for room and board. She pays the telephone bill, because the long-distance calls are hers. I do her laundry, clean her room, fix her breakfast every morning, and dinner whenever she wants it.

Our home is paid for and Terry knows we are not hard up for money, but it would be awfully nice to have a little extra coming in. My husband says not to 'rock the boat' or she might move. What do you say? If you believe she should pay—how much? Thanks for your help, Ann.

A Pittsburgh Mom

I replied,

Dear Mom:

Terry should give you 20% of her paycheck. If she thinks she can get lodging, breakfast, laundry, and maid-service elsewhere for less—let her try it.

The fact that you are not hard up for money is no excuse for your daughter's selfishness. Share this letter with your husband; and I hope together you will <u>muster</u> up the courage to talk to Terry promptly.

When sons and daughters marry, things change considerably. Even though parents have a tendency to forever think of their children as "children," they should be granted a totally different status when they establish a family unit of their own. Should Mom be forever and always the No. 1 woman in Sonny's life? Not at all. A loving mother willingly relinquishes that place to her daughter-in-law. She remembers how she felt about her husband's mother when she married. By the same token, a kind and thoughtful daughter-in-law will be considerate of her husband's mother so she will not feel displaced. Life's cycles have an ironic way of evening up the score. The woman who finds herself with a mother-in-law problem might do well to think ahead a few years when her son will marry and she will become the mother-in-law.

Getting down to specifics, what do married children owe their parents in terms of time and attention? According to my readers, this is a major problem among marrieds in their 30's and 40's. Here are some questions from this week's mailing:

From Lubbock, Texas:

My mother telephones me at least four times a day. She wants to know if the children ate a good breakfast, who wore what at a party last night, what am I fixing for supper, has my husband's boss said anything about a raise . . . ?

From Nashville, Tennessee:

My husband's mother asks me every two weeks if I am pregnant yet. She keeps reminding me that I'm not getting any younger and she would give anything to have a grandchild. The woman is getting on my nerves.

From Richmond, Virginia:

My husband's parents are in their mid-70's. He spends at least five hours every Saturday driving them to the supermarket, the dentist, the doctor, the pharmacy, the optometrist, the greenhouse, the dry cleaners, and so on. My in-laws have two daughters who live in town, but they never bother them—my husband is the one they run ragged. Does he owe them this kind of service?

From San Diego, California:

My mother is 64, a widow, attractive, and well-read. When we have guests for an evening, she's hurt if she isn't included. I love her dearly, but Mom has strong opinions and I have the feeling our friends resent her. Am I obligated to include her because she is my mother?

There are no rules to cover every situation, but here are suggestions that can be tailored to fit a great many:

- Countless people are also victims of friends who have black-cord fever—also known as telephonitis. The best protection against these types is to develop a technique for getting off the phone after a reasonable period of time. The victim should have prepared sentences handy and read them when the need arises. Sample: "Sorry, dear. I have a million things to do this morning and I must hang up now. We'll talk again soon."
- People have no right to complain about being trapped or taken advantage of if they don't have the <u>gumption</u> to assert themselves. I tell them repeatedly, "No one can <u>exploit</u> you without your permission." This includes refusing to answer "nun-uvyer-bizniz" type questions. Sample comeback: "Now why in the world would you be interested in that?"

- No woman owes her in-laws grandchildren. Any person who pressures a woman to "give us a grandchild" should be put in her place.
- Running errands and chauffeuring aged parents can be time- and energy-consuming, but it may be essential when no alternatives exist. If there are other children (or nieces and nephews) who might help out, they certainly should be asked to do so. Where time is more valuable than money, a paid driver may relieve a lot of tension.
- Including parents in social activities is not essential, and parents should not expect it. No excuses are necessary.

Perhaps the most anxiety-producing problem is one that hits in the late 40's or early 50's—about the same time some adults are going through the mid-life crisis: what to do with Mama when Papa dies. Or, if Mama goes first, what should be done with Papa? Circumstances alter cases. Some mamas wouldn't live with their children on a bet. The same goes for some papas. Many factors should be considered at the outset—first, how would Grandma or Grandpa fit in with the family? Is she or he too bossy? Would there be trouble in the kitchen? Would the children feel that too many people are telling them what to do? Finances are another major consideration. Does the surviving parent have sufficient money to maintain his or her own place? The issue of health is also important. Is Mama or Papa well enough to live alone? The answers to these questions should be carefully reviewed before a decision.

Strictly from a standpoint of morality and decency, do you owe your parent a place in your home if he or she would like to move in? I say, "No." If parents need housing or care, it goes without saying you should provide it, but you do not owe them a place under your roof if it would create dissension and conflict in your family. The ideal solution is to keep the surviving parent in his or her own home if it is economically feasible. When money is a problem, all the children should ante up and share the cost. (Often this is easier said than done.) Endless family fights have resulted because brother George or sister Mabel say they can't help out with the old folks because they have kids in college. Yet they go to Florida or Arizona every winter, belong to the country club, and drive new cars.

The most serious crisis arises when Mama or Papa becomes ill or too old to take care of themselves. Nursing homes are expensive, and many old people don't want to go there. What then? Some heroic women have taken in a parent or an in-law (or both) at tremendous personal sacrifice. This can be the most physically exhausting and emotionally draining job in the world, since old folks tend to be senile, incontinent, ill-tempered, and in need of constant watching. Implore daughters and daughters-in-law not to feel guilty if they are unable to do it. The woman who does make this sacrifice, in my opinion, deserves a place at God's right hand, come reckoning time.

In the final analysis, none of us goes through life debt-free. We all owe something to somebody. But the most noble motivation for giving is not prompted by a sense of duty—it flows freely from unselfish love. 18

First Impressions

Freewrite for ten minutes on one of the following.

1. Did you enjoy reading this selection? Why or why not?
2. Do you ever read advice columns such as the one Ann Landers writes? Do you think these columns contain good advice? Why or why not?
3. Did your parents ever make you feel guilty about anything? If so, what? Did their technique work?

Vocabulary Check

Circle the letter of the word or phrase that best completes each of the following four sentences.

1. The word *facade* in "Look behind the brittle facade and you'll see people who are bitterly ashamed" (paragraph 6) means
    a. false front.   c. sadness.
    b. candy.   d. inner self.
2. The word *relinquishes* in "Should Mom be forever and always the No. 1 woman in Sonny's life? Not at all. A loving mother willingly relinquishes that place to her daughter-in-law" (paragraph 12) means
    a. keeps back.   c. gives up.
    b. fights for.   d. stands in.
3. The word *dissension* in "you do not owe them a place under your roof if it would create dissension and conflict in your family" (paragraph 16) means
    a. strong disagreement. c. harmless fear.
    b. great generosity.   d. shared goals.
4. The word *feasible* in "The ideal solution is to keep the surviving parent in his or her own home if it is economically feasible" (paragraph 16) means
    a. difficult.   c. wrong.
    b. possible.   d. careful.

Circle the letter of the answer that best completes each of the following four items. Each sentence uses a word (or form of a word) from "Words to Watch."

5. When Billy brought home a bad report card, his mother took *punitive* action;
    a. she gave him ten dollars.
    b. she made him stay in the house for a week.

6. The twig was very *brittle*—
   a. nothing could break it.
   b. it snapped at the slightest touch.
7. The workers in our company feel *exploited* because the management pays them
   a. very high salaries.
   b. nothing for overtime.
8. When the doctor told Martha her illness was *chronic*, she knew she would
   a. have it for the rest of her life.
   b. never have it again.

Reading Check

Central Point and Main Ideas

1. Which sentence best expresses the central point of the selection?
   a. Children of all ages owe their parents something.
   b. Parents and children would get along better if they just ignored their problems.
   c. All parents deserve their children's respect.
   d. Parents have ways of making their children feel guilty.
2. Which sentence best expresses the main idea of paragraph 15?
   a. Many questions must be answered when an elderly parent is widowed.
   b. People sometimes are dealing with a mid-life crisis when one of their parents dies.
   c. It's important for children to ask if Grandma or Grandpa will fit in with the family before inviting them to share their home.
   d. Elderly people have more problems than young people do.

Key Supporting Details

3. According to Landers, teenagers should *not*
   a. be allowed to pick their own friends.
   b. criticize their parents to outsiders.
   c. have to write home from college once a week.
   d. tell their parents where they are going.
4. _____ TRUE OR FALSE? Landers thinks bad parents are ashamed of their failures.
5. Landers feels that married children owe their parents
   a. grandchildren.
   b. a daily phone call.
   c. help with errands when necessary.
   d. invitations to social events.

Inferences

6. The author implies in paragraph 11 that parents should accept money from working children who live at home
   a. because it is the best way to get them to move out.
   b. only if they need it.

FAMILIES AND CHILDREN

   c. only if the children are over 21.
   d. as a fair exchange for room, board, and laundry.
7. _____ TRUE OR FALSE? Landers implies that it is often people's own fault when others take advantage of them.

The Writer's Craft

8. In the article, Landers uses letters from her readers
   a. to make the writers feel ashamed of themselves.
   b. because the people who wrote them are friends of hers.
   c. to show the kinds of problems real people face.
   d. so that readers have a chance to give her advice for a change.
9. Landers has organized her essay according to
   a. the difficulty of the problems.
   b. the kinds of solutions.
   c. the ages of children.
   d. the dates when she got the letters.
10. To conclude her essay, the author uses
    a. a prediction.
    b. a series of questions.
    c. an anecdote.
    d. a summary and final thought.

Outlining Activity

Complete the following outline of "What Do Children Owe Their Parents?" by writing the letters of the missing items where they belong.

Items Missing from the Outline:

   a. Not grandchildren
   b. Married children
   c. Money for food and lodging
   d. Financial help if necessary
   e. Honest answers to parents' questions

   Central point: What children owe their parents depends on the ages and situations of the children, but all children owe their parents something.

   A. Teenagers
      1. Consideration, loyalty and respect
      2. _____
   B. Working children
      1. _____
      2. Money for laundry and maid service

C. _____
   1. Time and attention
   2. _____
D. Children with elderly parents
   1. Care, but not necessarily in children's homes
   2. _____

Discussion Questions

1. Which parts of Landers' advice do you agree with? Which letter (or letters) would you have answered differently than she did?
2. Assume that you are a parent whose child has chosen a friend you do not approve of. How would you handle this situation?
3. What do you think college students living at home owe their parents?
4. If you had children of your own, what do you think they would owe you? Why?

Paragraph Assignments

1. Landers writes in paragraph 18 that "none of us goes through life debt-free. We all owe something to somebody." Think of a person who has been important to you, someone to whom you owe something. Write a paragraph in which you tell who this person is, what he or she has done for you, and what you feel you owe in return. Use a topic sentence such as "If it hadn't been for Miss Lee, my high school guidance counselor, I would never have decided to go to college."
2. Write a one-paragraph letter to Ann Landers describing a real or imagined problem in your life (or in a friend's life) and asking for advice. Use specific details, and provide one or two clear examples to illustrate the problem. You might even suggest some solutions and ask what Landers thinks of them. Choose a problem similar to one of the following:

   - telling a co-worker he or she has made a mistake
   - refusing to lend money to a friend
   - getting rid of unwanted house guests
   - coping with friends who insist on telling you their problems
   - dealing with an overly demanding boss

Essay Assignments

1. Would you raise your children the same way you were raised? Write an essay comparing and contrasting the way you would raise (or are raising) your children with the way you were brought up. In your essay, argue that children either should or should not be raised as you were. Support your points with explanations and specific examples. You might use a

thesis such as "When I have children, I hope I can spend as much time with them, listen as carefully to their problems, and show them as much affection as my parents did for me."

2. In paragraph 8, Landers writes that if a teenager makes a poor choice of friends, "he or she will have to pay for it." Write an essay about a time when you chose a friend and later regretted it. Tell what the friend was like, what he or she did to you, and how you felt afterwards. If you learned a useful lesson from the experience, explain what it was. As an alternative, write about someone who proved to be a true friend. Devote a separate paragraph of your essay to each quality you admire in your friend.

Students in Shock

John Kellmayer

Preview

People say that the college years should be the best ones. If so, why are so many college students miserable? These days more students than ever are experiencing intense emotional problems; some even commit suicide. In this article, educator John Kellmayer explains what is causing the misery and reveals how schools are trying to help.

Words to Watch

warrant (6): call for
anorexia (6): an abnormal lack of appetite which can result in serious illness or death
bulimia (6): an abnormal craving for food that leads to heavy eating and then intentional vomiting
inflicted (7): caused (something harmful)
stability (9): permanence
devastating (9): very destructive
magnitude (11): great importance
meditation (13): deep thought
relevant (14): on the topic
unique (15): one of a kind

If you feel overwhelmed by your college experiences, you are not alone—many of today's college students are suffering from a form of shock. Going to college has always had its ups and downs, but today the "downs" of the college experience are more numerous and difficult, a fact that the schools are responding to with increased support services.

Lisa is a good example of a student in shock. She is an attractive, intelligent twenty-year-old college junior at a state university. Having been a straight-A student in high school and a member of the basketball and softball teams there, she remembers her high school days with fondness. Lisa was popular then and had a steady boyfriend for the last two years of school.

Now, only three years later, Lisa is miserable. She has changed her major four times already and is forced to hold down two part-time jobs in order to pay her tuition. She suffers from sleeping and eating disorders and believes she has no close friends. Sometimes she bursts out crying for no apparent reason. On more than one occasion, she has considered taking her own life.

Dan, too, suffers from student shock. He is nineteen and a freshman at a local community college. He began college as an accounting major but hated that field. So he switched to computer programming because he heard the job prospects were excellent in that area. Unfortunately, he discovered that he had little aptitude for programming and changed majors again, this time to psychology. He likes psychology but has heard horror stories about the difficulty of finding a job in that field without a graduate degree. Now he's considering switching majors again. To help pay for school, Dan works nights and weekends as a sales clerk at K-Mart. He doesn't get along with his boss, but since he needs the money, Dan feels he has no choice except to stay on the job. A few months ago, his girlfriend of a year and a half broke up with him.

Not surprisingly, Dan has started to suffer from depression and migraine headaches. He believes that in spite of all his hard work, he just isn't getting anywhere. He can't remember ever being this unhappy. A few times he considered talking to somebody in the college psychological counseling center. He rejected that idea, though, because he doesn't want people to think there's something wrong with him.

What is happening to Lisa and Dan happens to millions of college students each year. As a result, roughly one-quarter of the student population at any time will suffer from symptoms of depression. Of that group, almost half will experience depression intense enough to warrant professional help. At schools across the country, psychological counselors are booked up months in advance. Stress-related problems such as anxiety, migraine headaches, insomnia, anorexia, and bulimia are epidemic on college campuses.

Suicide rates and self-inflicted injuries among college students are higher now than at any other time in history. The suicide rate among college youth is fifty percent higher than among nonstudents of the same age. It is estimated that each year more than five hundred college students take their own lives.

College health officials believe that these reported problems represent only the tip of the iceberg. They fear that most students, like Lisa and Dan, suffer in silence.

There are three reasons today's college students are suffering more than in earlier generations. First is a weakening family support structure. The transition from high school to college has always been difficult, but in the past there was more family support to help get through it. Today, with divorce rates at a historical high and many parents experiencing their own psychological difficulties, the traditional family is not always available for guidance and support. And when students who do not find <u>stability</u> at home are bombarded with numerous new and stressful experiences, the results can be <u>devastating</u>.

Another problem college students face is financial pressure. In the last decade tuition costs have skyrocketed—up about sixty-six percent at public colleges and ninety percent at private schools. For students living away from home, costs range from five thousand dollars to as much as twelve thousand a year and more. And at the same time that tuition costs have been rising dramatically, there has been a cutback in federal aid to students. College loans are now much harder to obtain and are available only at near-market interest rates. Consequently, most college students must work at least part-time. And for some students, the pressure to do well in school while holding down a job is too much to handle.

A final cause of student shock is the large selection of majors available. Because of the <u>magnitude</u> and difficulty of choosing a major, college can prove a time of great indecision. Many students switch majors, some a number of times. As a result, it is becoming commonplace to take five or six years to get a degree. It can be depressing to students not only to have taken courses that don't count towards a degree but also to be faced with the added tuition costs. In some cases these costs become so high that they force students to drop out of college.

While there is no magic cure-all for student shock, colleges have begun to recognize the problem and are trying in a number of ways to help students cope with the pressures they face. First of all, many colleges are upgrading their psychological counseling centers to handle the greater demand for services. Additional staff is being hired, and experts are doing research to learn more about the psychological problems of college students. Some schools even advertise these services in student newspapers and on campus radio stations. Also, upperclassmen are being trained as peer counselors. These peer counselors may be able to act as a first line of defense in the battle for students' well-being by spotting and helping to solve problems before they become too big for students to handle.

In addition, stress-management workshops have become common on college campuses. At these workshops, instructors teach students various techniques for dealing with stress, including biofeedback, <u>meditation</u>, and exercise.

Finally, many schools are improving their vocational counseling services. By giving students more <u>relevant</u> information about possible majors and career choices, colleges can lessen the anxiety and indecision often associated with choosing a major.

If you ever feel that you're "in shock," remember that your experience is not <u>unique</u>. Try to put things in perspective. Certainly, the end of a romance or failing an exam is not an event to look forward to. But realize that rejection and failure happen to everyone sooner or later. And don't be reluctant to talk to somebody about your problems. The useful services available on campus won't help you if you don't take advantage of them.

First Impressions

Freewrite for ten minutes on one of the following.

1. Did you enjoy reading this selection? Why or why not?
2. Have you or someone you know ever been a victim of "student shock"? If so, describe what happened.
3. Which group do you think faces more pressures, young adults who go to college or young adults who do not attend college? Why?

Vocabulary Check

Circle the letter of the word or phrase that best completes each of the following four sentences.

1. The word *prospects* in "he switched to computer programming because he heard the job prospects were excellent" (paragraph 4) means
   a. failures.
   c. candidates.
   b. possibilities.
   d. limitations.
2. The word *aptitude* in "he discovered that he had little aptitude for programming and changed majors again" (paragraph 4) means
   a. natural ability.
   c. theory.
   b. health.
   d. hatred.
3. The word *bombarded* in "[they] are bombarded with numerous new and stressful experiences" (paragraph 9) means
   a. helped.
   c. amused.
   b. comforted.
   d. attacked.

4. The word *skyrocketed* in "In the last decade tuition costs have skyrocketed—up about sixty-six percent at public colleges and ninety percent at private schools" (paragraph 10) means
   a. slowed.
   b. dropped.
   c. stayed the same.
   d. risen rapidly.

Circle the letter of the word (or form of the word) from "Words to Watch" that best completes each of the following four sentences.

5. Annie prides herself on her _____ way of dressing; nobody else has outfits anything like hers.
   a. relevant.
   b. anorexic
   c. unique
   d. stable

6. Rita may be suffering from _____. She is so thin that her family and friends are worried about her.
   a. anorexia
   b. magnitude
   c. stability
   d. meditation

7. The police knew Oscar's wounds were not self-_____ because his hands had been tied.
   a. unique
   b. stable
   c. warranted
   d. inflicted

8. One of the most _____ experiences of Bill's childhood was his mother's leaving one morning and never coming back.
   a. stable
   b. devastating
   c. warranted
   d. anorexic

Reading Check

Central Point and Main Ideas

1. Which sentence best expresses the central point of the selection?
   a. Going to college is a depressing experience for many students.
   b. College life has become more stressful, so schools are increasing support services.
   c. Lisa and Dan have not enjoyed college because their lives have been filled with stress.
   d. Colleges should increase their counseling services.

2. Which sentence best expresses the main idea of paragraph 3?
   a. Lisa is experiencing difficult emotional problems.
   b. Lisa can't decide on a major.
   c. Lisa feels she has lost all her good friends.
   d. Lisa cries frequently.

3. Which sentence states the main idea of paragraph 10?
   a. Sentence 1
   b. Sentence 2
   c. Sentence 4
   d. Sentence 7

FAMILIES AND CHILDREN

Key Supporting Details

4. _____ TRUE OR FALSE? A college student is more likely to commit suicide than a nonstudent of the same age.

5. According to paragraph 12, which of the following methods are *not* being used by colleges to reduce stress?
   a. upgraded psychological counseling
   b. lowered tuition
   c. research into the psychological problems of students
   d. peer counseling

Inferences

6. _____ TRUE OR FALSE? From the article we can conclude that students who can turn to their families for support are less likely to suffer from "student shock."

7. The author implies that some students who suffer from extreme depression
   a. should drop out of college.
   b. are reluctant to get professional help.
   c. can always handle it on their own.
   d. have never done well in school.

The Writer's Craft

8. Kellmayer concludes his essay by
   a. making a frightening prediction.
   b. quoting an expert on psychology.
   c. asking a tough question.
   d. giving advice.

9. The word *also* in "Some schools even advertise these services in student newspapers and on campus radio stations. Also, upperclassmen are being trained as peer counselors" (paragraph 12) signals
   a. a contrast.
   b. an addition.
   c. a time.
   d. a conclusion.

10. The author supports his point that college life has become more difficult for students with
    a. anecdotes, statistics, and reasons.
    b. quotations from experts.
    c. information taken from a survey of college dropouts.
    d. personal experiences.

Outlining Activity

Complete the following outline of "Students in Shock" by writing the letters of the missing items where they belong.

Items Missing from the Outline

a. Increased services at colleges
b. Improved vocational counseling
c. Greater financial pressure
d. Suicide and self-inflicted injuries
e. Examples of students in shock

Central point: Stress-related problems are increasing on college campuses for several reasons, and schools have responded.

A. Introduction

B. _____
   1. Lisa
   2. Dan
C. Symptoms of "student shock"
   1. Depression and other stress-related problems
   2. _____
D. Reasons for today's increased "student shock"
   1. Weakened family
   2. _____
   3. Confusion over majors

E. _____
   1. More psychological research and counseling
   2. Stress-management workshops
   3. _____
F. Conclusion

Discussion Questions

1. How would you define "student shock"? How common is it at your college?
2. What do the stories about Lisa and Dan add to this article? What would be lost if these anecdotes were eliminated?
3. Does your college have facilities to help students in shock? If so, what are they? In what other ways do you think colleges should help troubled students?
4. Can you think of any ways that "student shock" could be prevented or reduced by students themselves? By their families or friends?

Paragraph Assignments

1. Kellmayer gives two examples of students who have experienced "student shock," Lisa and Dan. Write a paragraph describing someone you know who has experienced the pressures, anxiety, depression, or other problems associated with "student shock." (Do not use the person's real name.) Write about what caused these feelings and what the student is doing as a result. Your topic student could be similar to this: "_____" is another example of a student in shock."

2. Students are not the only victims of "shock." Anyone in an unfamiliar situation can feel pressured and hopeless. Write a paragraph on the specific causes of "shock" for one of the following:

    - the "new kid on the block" (someone who's just moved into a school or neighborhood)
    - a newly hired worker
    - a new or recently traded member of a team
    - a newlywed
    - a new supervisor or boss

   Explain what pressures this person would feel and what he or she might do to reduce them.

Essay Assignments

1. We all feel stress now and then, but most of us have ways to reduce it. How do you deal with stress? Write an essay describing the ways you have found to combat stress in your daily life. Explain what you do, and tell how each approach helps you relax. One possible thesis sentence for this essay is "When I'm feeling stress, I can usually relax by exercising, watching one of my favorite television programs, or going to the mall."

2. Kellmayer discusses three causes of "student shock," but he leaves out some others. For instance, he could have written about the problems of fitting in with people at a new place, the pressure to experiment with drugs or to drink illegally, sexual pressures, or the pressure of facing too much freedom, among others. In an essay, explain some pressures college students face that Kellmayer doesn't mention. Use a separate paragraph for each pressure, and give examples of how these pressures can affect students.

When My Brother Was Slain

Ben Fong-Torres

Preview

When Ben Fong-Torres, a journalist and music critic, chatted one day with his older brother Barry, he had no idea that the conversation would be their last. A few days later, Barry was shot down in his Chinatown apartment, a victim of gang violence. In this article, originally written for *Parade*, Fong-Torres tries to come to terms with his brother's death. In the process, he realizes some important truths about his heritage.

Words to Watch

abounded (3): was fully supplied
estrangement (4): being cut off
crystallized (6): took form
assailants (6): attackers
dominant (8): strongest
semblance (11): appearance
indelible (14): not able to be removed
perennially (14): permanently
irrationally (15): crazily
vicariously (15): as if sharing someone else's experience
celluloid (15): movie film
vigilante (15): taking the law into one's own hands
wistful (16): sadly longing
eloquent (18): expressive
yin-yang (18): in traditional Chinese thought, two opposite forces which interact to influence everything

It was nearly 13 years ago that I last saw Barry, my older brother. He came by my apartment in San Francisco with some food from our parents across the bay in Oakland. We sat around and chatted, and it stuck me as ironic. We lived in the same town, but now that we were well established in our careers—he, at 29, was a probation officer and youth worker; I, at 27, was a magazine editor and writer—we saw very little of each other.

He had just returned from Lake Tahoe, where he had taken Dad for Father's Day. They had won a couple hundred dollars. He smiled, "That kind of makes up for what happened at my apartment," he said. Someone had broken in a couple of days before, he said, but had taken only a few antique rifles and guns. His fine collector's swords and jade pieces, a TV set, stereo equipment, cameras, skis and a bike—all had been left alone. Barry shrugged, mystified.

I asked about Chinatown. These were troubled times, and that part of San Francisco abounded with gangs and violence. Barry had taken a leave of absence from his probation work to become director of a youth center there. He said he wanted to do something for "his people." And, though frustrated by the conflicts, he told me he wanted to stay just a little longer.

I started complaining about our parents. I was still going through a mildly hippie phase and (how absolutely American) had had a fight with them over the length of my hair. Barry was no stranger to estrangement from our folks. After all, we had both, in our ways, rebelled against the strict, traditional Chinese upbringing we'd had. Barry was dating girls who weren't Chinese, and he had studied not law or medicine, which most Chinese parents seemed to encourage, but criminology. Still, he had worked hard at the family restaurants; he had gone to the University of California at Berkeley; and he was always available to help our parents, who don't speak or write English, do various chores. In short, he was a good "number one son," so important to the Chinese family structure.

And now he was sounding just like one, as he counseled me with words I hadn't heard from him before. "Just be patient," he said. "Just go along with them. They're the way they are, and the best thing to do is to give in a little." Barry sounded like a young man who had come home not only to Chinatown but also to his identity. He was telling me that I should understand the Chinese way. I remember thinking that he didn't sound like the Barry I had grown up with.

A few days later, the edgy mysteries of our last visit somehow crystallized even as our lives were suddenly shattered. At about 11:30 p.m. on June 26, 1972, Barry was shot down in his apartment. The next morning, the front page story began: "A brilliant and respected youth worker has become the tenth known victim in a series of Chinatown gangland slayings." Barry, it was made clear, was not a member of any gang himself. There were, reportedly, two <u>assailants</u>; the case was never solved. Although I was a journalist, I couldn't investigate: my parents forbade me from getting involved. And I was bound to obey. After all, as Barry had just reminded me, I am, more than anything else, a Chinese-American.

Don't get me wrong. Our family is American, and not without a bit of struggle. My father, born in a village of dirt-floor hovels in Guangdone Province in southeast China, slept on wooden planks, using bricks for pillows, and dreamed of doing better. As a teenager, his dreams turned to America, and he labored through his teenage years in Manila, saving money and eventually buying official papers bearing a non-Chinese name that made it easier for him to enter the United States.

My mother was born in another Guangdone village. She has one <u>dominant</u> memory of her life as a young girl. "What I wanted most was to come to the United States," she once told me. "I heard that life was much, much better than in the village." It was, but it took much hard work. And it resulted in a dual identity for their five children. Growing up and going to school, we knew we were American, but we spoke Cantonese at home as well as English; in the evenings, we went to "Chinese school."

Our parents, understandably, clung to the ways of the country they had left behind; their work, they said, did not afford them the time to learn good English, and so we would have to accommodate them. Besides, they said, we should not forget that we were, first and foremost, Chinese. As such, we had different priorities. The understanding—once we were old enough to understand—was that, just as they had sacrificed for us, we would sacrifice for them.

The obligation begins with work. If the family has a business, the child automatically is part of that business. Our family business was the restaurant. I was raised in the New Eastern Cafe in Chinatown, Oakland. At age 8, I was shelling prawns and stripping snow peas; as soon as I could take an order and carry a dish, I was a waiter.

Through our high school years and into college, Barry and I worked at various restaurants almost every evening, weekend and summer. We missed out on any <u>semblance</u> of social life. We stayed up late to squeeze in our homework. We covered for each other for the very occasional night off. We were often angry and frustrated, but business was such that we couldn't afford any overhead, and there was no use complaining. "Party? What for? Plenty of time to have fun later—when you grow up." Then, having grown up: "When you get married." I didn't escape until I became an editor on my college daily newspaper at San Francisco State and had to move across the bay. And even then, I felt guilty about not being at the restaurant.

In the end, there is no real escape from one's heritage. Thinking back, we saw beyond the boredom and frustration and came to appreciate what we got. We learned to be responsible. And, although there are few outward displays of affection in Chinese families, we earned our parents' respect for sticking by them.

The stuff of lower-class life—cardboard swords, paper bags as baseball gloves, cardboard boxes on fences for basketball—may have been embarrassing then; now, it serves to remind me that my parents didn't have much while raising five children. All they had were our futures. And, in Barry's case, they were robbed even of that. Thirteen years later, all they have of him are bittersweet anniversaries—on May 8, of his birth; on June 26, of his death. And, of course, memories.

But I have something more. For 13 years, there have been few days when I haven't thought of Barry. And though the pain has lessened over those years, there are <u>indelible</u> thoughts and images, not connected as much with my brother as with his death. Whenever I think of him, he is still my older brother; somehow, right now, he is ageless yet <u>perennially</u> two years older than I. He is wiser. He has kept me forever younger.

In the aftermath of his murder, I was numbed. I witnessed the major events of that summer in a warped daze. I remember thinking of Barry missing the high drama of the Watergate hearings; I thought just of him when the terrorists struck at the Munich Olympics. I remember acting <u>irrationally</u>. I collected and devoured newspaper stories about gangs. Reading the articles, I stopped at every name, wondering. I watched crime shows on TV and lived <u>vicariously</u> through the likes of Peter Falk, whose Columbo always managed to nail the killer, and of Charles Bronson, whose various characters made it their personal mission in life to exterminate the scum of the earth. I've never wanted anything more than answers and justice. But, yes, sometimes, lost in the <u>celluloid vigilante</u> heroics of a Bronson or Clint Eastwood, I thought about the sweetness of revenge.

I looked on people as possible surrogate older brothers. I remember the brother of a girlfriend. A roommate. But that was just <u>wistful</u> nonthinking. I came to realize that, by Chinese tradition, I was now the older brother of the family, and I had obligations and responsibilities, among them not to dwell on the past.

Still, I think of Barry almost every day. Anything will trigger it: talking with any member of the family, hearing or reading the name "Barry," any trip into or through the neighborhood where he last lived, a glimpse of an antique sword in a store window, a song by Elton John called "Daniel" (". . . my brother, you are older than me, do you still feel the pain?"). I was unable to listen to Bach, especially to pieces that were on one of Barry's favorite albums, *A New Sound From the Japanese Bach Scene*. We played it at his wake. With the turntable unattended, the record played repeatedly, so that "Minuet in G," "Air on a G String" and other melodies got embedded in my mind—a soundtrack of our loss. Since then, whenever I come across those compositions, I have to tune out or walk away.

Our family was never religious, but after Barry was gone, I found myself looking into the heavens and talking with him, with his soul. I did—and do—this usually on visits to the Mountain View Cemetery, high over Oakland. The talk is easy, loving, sometimes <u>eloquent</u>, in a balanced, <u>yin-yang</u> way. I tell him the news of the family, the ups and downs, and I think about how he might fit in, might affect those events. Sometimes, standing at Mountain View, I believe he still does.

Barry's death ultimately inspired the bridging of a lifelong language barrier between my folks and me. With help from a family friend, I was able to interview them about their lives in China, their courtship by mail, the beginnings of our family in Oakland. I still haven't asked them about Barry. If he enters my mind almost every day, he must enter theirs almost every hour. The family of any victim of senseless, sudden death knows that it isn't easy being a survivor. But all one can do is survive and look for what lessons there are.

After years of uninterest in my identity as a Chinese, I had occasion to visit China two springs ago, and I immersed myself in that country. I visited my parents' villages and met relatives I never knew I had. On their walls, I saw framed photos of myself and the rest of our family. We are forever connected.

And, in China, in a moment of paying respects to deceased family members, I of course thought of Barry. I remember thinking about him on the ferry from Hong Kong to Macao, our gateway into China. I felt as if I'd somehow taken him to China with me, to a home he'd never seen. On the deck, my fellow travelers were dancing joyously to a song by the Doobie Brothers. In my head, another tune fought through the disco beat, a tune I'd been resisting for years. As we spotted the mountains of China in the distance, the tune took hold in my consciousness. It was a quiet little thing by Bach. And it was really quite lovely.

FAMILIES AND CHILDREN

First Impressions

Freewrite for ten minutes on one of the following.

1. Did you enjoy reading this selection? Why or why not?
2. Have you ever lost or been separated from someone who meant a great deal to you? If so, write about the loss and how it made you feel.
3. How has your family background influenced you? Write about your own family or ethnic (religious, racial, national, or cultural) heritage.

Vocabulary Check

Circle the letter of the word or phrase that best completes each of the following four sentences.

1. The word *ironic* in "it struck me as ironic. We lived in the same town, but now that we were well established in our careers . . . we saw very little of each other" (paragraph 1) means
   a. made out of very strong metal.
   b. opposite to what might be expected.
   c. tiring.
   d. fortunate.

2. The word *surrogate* in "I looked on people as possible surrogate older brothers. . . . But that was just wistful nonthinking. . . . I was now the older brother of the family" (paragraph 16) means
   a. weak.
   b. undesirable.
   c. angry.
   d. substitute.

3. The word *embedded* in "the record played repeatedly, so that . . . 'Air on a G String' and other melodies got embedded in my mind" (paragraph 17) means
   a. barely heard.
   b. firmly placed.
   c. forgotten.
   d. ignored.

4. The word *immersed* in "After years of uninterest in my identity as a Chinese, I had occasion to visit China two springs ago, and I immersed myself in that country. I visited my parents' villages and met relatives I never knew I had" (paragraph 20) means
   a. betrayed.
   b. confused.
   c. deeply involved.
   d. hurt.

Circle the letter of the word (or form of the word) from "Words to Watch" that best completes each of the following four sentences.

5. This blood stain seems to be _____; I have scrubbed as hard as I could, but it won't come out.
   a. eloquent
   b. vicarious
   c. indelible
   d. estranged

6. Through television, we can _____ live many lives, from a doctor's to a murderer's.
   a. vicariously
   b. indelibly
   c. eloquently
   d. irrationally

7. The candidate's _____ speech convinced many citizens to vote for her.
   a. estranged
   b. crystallized
   c. eloquent
   d. indelible

8. With a (an) _____ glance at the home she was leaving forever, Rebecca sighed, closed the car door, and drove away.
   a. abounded
   b. wistful
   c. indelible
   d. perennial

Reading Check

Central Point and Main Ideas

1. Which sentence best expresses the central point of the selection?
   a. Barry, the author's older brother, was murdered almost thirteen years before this article was written.
   b. The author has never accepted the reality of Barry's death.
   c. The author and his family often disagreed.
   d. In the process of adjusting to Barry's death, the author learned to accept his family.
2. Which sentence states the main idea of paragraph 7?
   a. Sentence 1
   b. Sentence 2
   c. Sentence 3
   d. Sentence 4
3. Which sentence best expresses the main idea of paragraph 17?
   a. The author could not listen to music after Barry's death.
   b. Music can remind us of the past.
   c. Many sights and sounds make the author think of Barry.
   d. One of Barry's favorite albums was played at his wake.

Key Supporting Details

4. Barry worked in Chinatown because
   a. he had always worked there.
   b. he was assigned there as a probation officer.
   c. he belonged to a gang there.
   d. he wanted to do something for the Chinese people.
5. The author could not investigate his brother's death because
   a. he was too frightened.
   b. his parents would not allow him to get involved.

c. his editor would not assign him to the story.
d. only the police could investigate a murder.
6. Ben and Barry worked in their family's restaurants because
   a. they wanted to earn money for college.
   b. they loved the work.
   c. their parents expected them to help in the family business.
   d. they had no social life.

Inferences

7. We can conclude from paragraphs 19 and 20 that the author
   a. still does not want to talk with his parents.
   b. has no interest in what his parents think about Barry.
   c. feels nothing can be learned from Barry's death.
   d. has become more familiar with his heritage.

8. _____ TRUE OR FALSE? In Chinese-American families older sons have special responsibilities.

The Writer's Craft

9. In paragraph 15, the author supports the sentence "I remember acting irrationally" with
   a. examples.
   b. statistics.
   c. a single incident.
   d. quotations.

10. _____ TRUE OR FALSE? The events described in the article are given in the order in which they actually happened.

Outlining Activity

Complete the following outline of "When My Brother Was Slain" by writing the letters of the missing items where they belong.

Items Missing from the Outline
   a. Ben's acceptance of his Chinese-American heritage
   b. The author's parents' decision to come to America
   c. Barry's last visit to the author
   d. Barry's tragic death
   e. Ben's reaction to Barry's death

   Central point: Adjusting to his brother's death not only became less painful to the author in time but also helped him accept his Chinese heritage.

   A. _____

   B. _____

C. _____

D. Barry and Ben's childhood

E. _____

F. _____

Discussion Questions

1. How has his brother's death affected Fong-Torres? How has he changed in the thirteen years since his brother died?
2. What do we learn about Chinese-American life from reading this article? Which parts of Fong-Torres' life are Chinese, and which parts are American?
3. Do all children rebel against their parents? Is rebellion against authority a necessary part of growing up? Why or why not?
4. What are some things people can do to increase their understanding of or pride in their family heritage?

Paragraph Assignments

1. Ben Fong-Torres says that while he was still complaining about his parents, his older brother Barry was sounding more and more like the typical "'number one son' so important to the Chinese family structure" (paragraph 4). In a paragraph, explain what's special about being the older, younger, middle, or only child in your family or in a family you know about. Use a topic sentence such as "Being the youngest child in my family has meant that I can't get away with anything."
2. Just as Ben Fong-Torres associates certain pieces of music with his late brother, we all tend to associate songs, places, and particular objects with events or people in our lives. Write a paragraph about the special memories or feelings you associate with a certain object, song, or place. Give details and examples so that your readers can understand why the object, song, or place is important to you.

Essay Assignments

1. Not many of us have experienced a loss as sudden and painful as the one described in this article. But all of us have had losses of some kind—the loss of a beloved family member, a job, a pet, a home, and so on. Write an essay about a time in your life when you experienced some sort of loss. How did it happen? How did you adjust? Among the possible central points for this assignment are the following:

   Losing my job as a _____ led to a new and better job.
   Memories of my grandfather are a bittersweet part of my life.

2. In paragraph 12, Fong-Torres writes that "In the end, there is no real escape from one's heritage." How important has your family's ethnic or religious background been in your life? Write an essay about the ways in which you have either accepted or rejected your heritage. Use reasons and specific examples to support your central point.

Living the Simple Life
Carolyn Lewis

Preview

What are your dreams for the future? If you're like most people, you probably fantasize about earning a large income or getting an important job. Yet some people reject high-pressure occupations, even if they pay well. Carolyn Lewis's uncompetitive sons have done just that. In this article, written for the "My Turn" column in *Newsweek*, Lewis describes her reactions to her sons' choice of the simple life.

Words to Watch

starkly (1): completely
singular (2): remarkable
esthetic (also spelled *aesthetic*) (3): based on a love of beauty
vistas (3): views
spawning (4): giving birth to
malaise (6): discomfort
usurious (11): at an overly high rate
abhor (11): hate
barter (12): trade
serenity (12): calmness
vagaries (13): chance behavior
notoriety (15): being widely known for something unfavorable
strove (15): tried hard
be reconciled to (15): accept
intractability (17): difficulty

My two sons live lives <u>starkly</u> different from my own. They make their homes in small rural places, and theirs are the lives of voluntary simplicity.

1

They have chosen work that gives service to others, requires no harm in the name of greater good. They share a <u>singular</u> lack of interest in accruing possessions. Their clothes would make Brooks Brothers shudder, and they drive automobiles that are both ancient and uncomely.

They till the earth around their modest houses to grow vegetables, trees and flowers. They are entertained by shared festivities with neighbors, wives and children. They have records for music, books for learning, and each lives close enough to the sea to enjoy the <u>esthetic</u> pleasures of blue <u>vistas</u> and open sky.

This curious phenomenon—of ambitious, competitive, urban parents <u>spawning</u> gentle, unambitious, country offspring—is not unique to my own experience. I observe it all around me and listen with amusement to the puzzled comments of middle-aged parents faced with this unexpected generational shift.

"We gave him everything, and he chooses to weave blankets in Maine," they say accusingly. Or, "We invested in Andover and Harvard, and he cuts trees in Oregon." The refrain is sorrowful, even embarrassed, as though our children have somehow turned against us by choosing to live in ways different from our own.

But I confess that every time I return to the big city after visiting my children, I am haunted by a psychic <u>malaise</u>. I go through my days comparing this with that, and more and more the *that* is looking better.

What my sons have is a world that is small enough to be readily understood, where those responsible wear a human face. When I talk about the big city where I live, in the only terms that can grasp its enormity—about groups and studies, trends and polls—my sons smile sweetly and speak of the people who live around the corner, have specific names and definitive problems. Theirs are flesh-and-blood realities instead of my pale, theoretical formulations. They remind me that the collective humanity I measure and label is far less interesting and vital than the individual who, mercifully, in the end will defy categorization.

When I ask him how he likes living in a town of 500 people three hours away from the nearest large city, my son Peter says: "Just fine. You see, I know who I am here."

That statement resonates in my brain. It's true; he has a definable space to call his own. He has warming relationships with family and neighbors. He has what E. F. Schumacher would call "good work."

On the other hand, he certainly cannot be labeled rich. His income is hardly the kind that makes the GNP go into a tailspin. When the sophisticated instruments of measurement are applied to his life—husband, wife, two children (family of four earning so much)—they mark him low income.

I, by comparison, living in my overpriced city apartment, walking to work past putrid sacks of street garbage, paying usurious taxes to local and state governments I generally abhor, I am rated middle class. This causes me to wonder, do the measurements make sense? Are we measuring only that which is easily measured—the numbers on the money chart—and ignoring values more central to the good life?

For my sons there is, of course, the rural bounty of fresh-grown vegetables, line-caught fish and the shared riches of neighbors' orchards and gardens. There is the unpaid baby-sitter for whose children my daughter-in-law baby-sits in return, and neighbors who barter their skills and labor. But more than that, how do you measure serenity? Sense of self? The feeling that, in order to get ahead, you don't have to trample on somebody else's skull?

I don't want to idealize life in small places. There are times when the outside world intrudes brutally, as when the cost of gasoline goes up or developers cast their eyes on untouched farmland. There are cruelties, there is bigotry, there are all the many vices and meannesses in small places that exist in large cities. Furthermore, it is harder to ignore them when they cannot be banished psychologically to another part of town or excused as the vagaries of alien groups—when they have to be acknowledged as "part of us."

Nor do I want to belittle the opportunities for small decencies in cities—the eruptions of one-stranger-to-another caring that always surprise and delight. But these are, sadly, more exceptions than rules and are often overwhelmed by the awful corruptions and dangers that surround us.

In this society, where material riches and a certain notoriety are considered admirable achievements, it takes some courage to say, no thanks, not for me. The urban pleasures and delights—restaurants, museums, theater, crowds in the streets—continue to have an urgent seductiveness for many young people. For parents like myself, who strove to offer our children these opportunities and riches, it is hard to be reconciled to those same children spurning the offer and choosing otherwise.

Plainly, what my sons want and need is something different—something smaller, simpler and more manageable. They march to a different drummer, searching for an ethic that recognizes limits, that scorns overbearing competition and what it does to human relations, and that says simply and gently, enough is enough.

Is my sons' solution to the complexity and seeming intractability of modern problems the answer for everyone? Of course not. Some of us have to stay in the cities, do what we can, fight when it is necessary, compete in order to survive. Maybe if we are diligent, we can make things a little better where we are.

But to choose small places, modern ambitions and values that are tolerant and loving is surely an admirable alternative. It may in the end be the only alternative we have to an urban culture in which we have created so much ugliness, and where we seem to inflict so much pain on each other through neglect, selfishness and failure of will.

First Impressions

Freewrite for ten minutes on one of the following.

1. Did you enjoy reading this selection? Why or why not?
2. In what ways are you living up to the dreams or ambitions that your parents had for you? In what ways are you not?
3. How would you describe "the good life"? What would it be like?

Vocabulary Check

Circle the letter of the word or phrase that best completes each of the following four sentences.

1. The word *accruing* in "theirs are the lives of voluntary simplicity. . . . They share a singular lack of interest in accruing possessions. . . . they drive automobiles that are . . . ancient" (paragraphs 1 and 2) means
   a. aging.
   b. piling up.
   c. sharing.
   d. spoiling.
2. The word *putrid* in "I, by comparison, living in my overpriced city apartment, walking to work past putrid sacks of street garbage" (paragraph 11) means
   a. valuable.
   b. rotten-smelling.
   c. clean-looking.
   d. unreal.
3. The word *spurning* in "For parents like myself, who strove to offer our children these opportunities and riches, it is hard to be reconciled to those same children spurning the offer and choosing otherwise" (paragraph 15) means
   a. rejecting.
   b. accepting.
   c. requiring.
   d. explaining.
4. The word *diligent* in "Some of us have to stay in the cities, do what we can, fight when it is necessary, compete in order to survive. Maybe if we are diligent, we can make things a little better where we are" (paragraph 17) means
   a. hard-working.
   b. ignorant.
   c. greedy.
   d. lazy.

Circle the letter of the answer that best completes each of the following four items. Each sentence uses a word (or form of a word) from "Words to Watch."

5. Joanne had a feeling of *malaise* as soon as she entered the roomful of people. She was very shy,
   a. but she knew everyone there.
   b. and she didn't know anyone there.
6. We decided that the credit card's rates were *usurious*, so we
   a. paid cash for everything.
   b. used it for all our charges.
7. I *abhor* liver. Whenever I see it on the menu, I
   a. order it.
   b. order something else.
8. I enjoy *serenity*. That's why, when I have free time, I prefer to go
   a. to an amusement park.
   b. to the woods.

Reading Check

Central Point and Main Ideas

1. Which sentence best expresses the central point of the selection?
   a. A good education is wasted on some young people today, although some parents are too stubborn to accept this fact.
   b. Expensive clothes are not important.
   c. The small towns where Lewis's sons live are more interesting than large cities.
   d. Lewis's sons were right to choose simple, rural lives.
2. Which sentence best expresses the main idea of paragraph 13?
   a. Small towns have their problems too.
   b. Prejudice is harder to ignore in a small town than in a big city.
   c. High gasoline prices affect rural areas more than cities.
   d. Real estate developers always ruin a community.
3. Which sentence best expresses the main idea of paragraph 17?
   a. Modern problems are harder to solve than the problems of the past.
   b. Competition is necessary in cities.
   c. The simple, rural life is not for everyone.
   d. Hard work is important.

Key Supporting Details

4. Lewis's son Peter
   a. makes his own clothes.
   b. has a new car.
   c. lives in a small town.
   d. earns a high salary.
5. _____ TRUE OR FALSE? Lewis says that many young people are still attracted to the restaurants, museums and theaters in cities.

98   FAMILIES AND CHILDREN

    6. Lewis admires her sons' choice of
       a. dangerous jobs.
       b. colleges.
       c. cutthroat competition.
       d. modest ambitions.

Inferences

    7. The author implies that most parents
       a. never criticize their children.
       b. easily accept whatever their children choose to do.
       c. live in cities.
       d. want their children to choose ways of life similar to their own.

    8. _____ TRUE OR FALSE? Lewis implies that her job pays more than her sons' jobs do.

The Writer's Craft

    9. The pattern of organization used in paragraph 7 is
       a. comparison and contrast.
       b. time order.
       c. space order.
       d. least important to most important.

    10. The tone of Lewis's article is
       a. bitter.
       b. approving.
       c. humorous.
       d. joyous.

Outlining Activity

Complete the following outline of "Living the Simple Life" by writing the letters of the missing items where they belong.

Items Missing from the Outline

    a. Though each style of living has its good and bad points, the simple life might be better.
    b. They live close to nature and grow their own food.
    c. There is garbage in the streets.
    d. One son explains that in a small town, he knows who he is.

    Central point: Lewis's sons have chosen a different and perhaps better lifestyle than their mother's.

      A. Her sons live simply in small towns.
        1. They make very little money and do not own expensive things.
        2. _____

3. The neighbors know each other and help each other out.
4. _____
B. Lewis lives a middle-class life in a large city.
1. _____
2. Taxes are high.
C. _____
1. In a small town, the outside world can still interfere, and bad people are harder to avoid.
2. In a large city, there are more opportunities and more things to do, and not everyone is cruel.
3. Still, the simple life and its solid values are an attractive substitute for people who no longer enjoy the city.

Discussion Questions

1. What do you think Lewis means by "voluntary simplicity" (paragraph 1)? In what ways have her sons chosen to simplify their lives?
2. Which style of living would you prefer, Lewis's or her sons'? What are the advantages and disadvantages of each?
3. Do parents who put their children through college have a right to be disappointed or angry if their children choose a job that doesn't require a college degree—say, that of a lumberjack or weaver or house painter—instead of one that does?
4. What are some ways that college students could make their lives simpler and better? How might you benefit from simplifying your life?

Paragraph Assignments

1. Lewis respects and admires some of the choices her sons have made. Write a paragraph describing some of the things you think your parents admire (or should admire) about you. You could discuss your personal qualities, such as honesty and courage, as well as your accomplishments. Use a topic sentence such as "My willingness to help other people and my sense of humor are the qualities my parents should most admire in me."
2. Do your values differ from those of your mother or father? If so, write a paragraph in which you compare how you and your parents feel about one or more of the following:

- honesty
- education
- religion
- money
- independence
- conformity

FAMILIES AND CHILDREN

- hard work
- relaxation

If you and your parents share the same values, explain what they are. In either case, use examples and details to show what you mean.

Essay Assignments

1. Which would you prefer, living in the city or living in the country? Write an essay in which you either attack or defend life in the city or life in the country. Give convincing reasons and use specific examples to support your central point. Use a thesis statement such as one of the following:

    City life gives me what I need: friends, job opportunities, and entertainment.
    I agree with Lewis when she says that cities are ugly and painful places.

2. Lewis lists three reasons why her son Peter likes living in a small town: he has "a definable space to call his own," "warming relationships with family and neighbors," and "good work." What would you like your living conditions, relationships, and work to be in the future? Write about what you hope your life will be like five or ten years from now. You could discuss topics such as the following:

    - where you'd like to be living and in what kind of place (house or apartment)
    - what important relationships—marriage? children? friends? relatives?—would be part of your life
    - what kind of job you'd have or what you would do

Sports and Leisure

Fun. Oh Boy, Fun. You Could Die from It

Suzanne Britt Jordan

Preview

Have you ever been to a party at which everybody was trying hard to have fun—and failing? Perhaps people stood around with silly smiles on their faces, their jokes becoming louder but less funny. Before long the guests probably began looking for their coats. Not just at parties, but in everything we do, we seem to believe that having fun is more important than anything else. But how often do we really have fun? Not very often, according to Suzanne Britt Jordan, who suggests that we may have been looking for it in the wrong places.

Words to Watch

beneficial (4): helpful
fetish (5): something that is worshiped
by Jove (5): an expression of surprise
traipsing (8): wandering
licentiousness (9): immorality
capacity (12): ability to do or hold something
damper (13): something that depresses
reverently (13): with great respect
mirth (13): great amusement
blaspheme (13): speak evil of something holy
horizon (14): line where the sky and earth seem to meet

Fun is hard to have.

Fun is a rare jewel.

Somewhere along the line people got the modern idea that fun was there for the asking, that people deserved fun, that if we didn't have a little fun every day we would turn into (sakes alive!) puritans.

"Was it fun?" became the question that overshadowed all other questions: good questions like: Was it moral? Was it kind? Was it honest? Was it <u>beneficial</u>? Was it generous? Was it necessary? And (my favorite) was it selfless?

When the pleasure got to be the main thing, the fun <u>fetish</u> was sure to follow. Everything was supposed to be fun. If it wasn't fun, then <u>by Jove</u>, we were going to make it fun, or else.

Think of all the things that got the reputation of being fun. Family outings were supposed to be fun. Sex was supposed to be fun. Education was supposed to be fun. Work was supposed to be fun. Walt Disney was supposed to be fun. Church was supposed to be fun. Staying fit was supposed to be fun.

Just to make sure that everybody knew how much fun we were having, we put happy faces on flunking test papers, dirty bumpers, sticky refrigerator doors, bathroom mirrors.

If a kid, looking at his very happy parents <u>traipsing</u> through that very happy Disney World, said, "This ain't fun, ma," his ma's heart sank. She wondered where she had gone wrong. Everybody told her what fun family outings to Disney World would be. Golly gee, what was the matter?

Fun got to be such a big thing that everybody started to look for more and more thrilling ways to supply it. One way was to step up the level of danger or <u>licentiousness</u> or alcohol or drug consumption so that you could be sure that, no matter what, you would manage to have a little fun.

Television commercials brought a lot of fun and fun-loving folks into the picture. Everything that people in those commercials did looked like fun: taking Polaroid snapshots, swilling beer, buying insurance, mopping the floor, bowling, taking aspirin. We all wished, I'm sure, that we could have half as much fun as those rough-and-ready guys around the locker room, flicking each other with towels and pouring champagne. The more commercials people watched, the more they wondered when the fun would start in their own lives. It was pretty depressing.

Big occasions were supposed to be fun. Christmas, Thanksgiving and Easter were obviously supposed to be fun. Your wedding day was supposed to be fun. Your wedding night was supposed to be a whole lot of fun. Your honeymoon was supposed to be the epitome of fundom. And so we ended up going through every Big Event we ever celebrated, waiting for the fun to start.

It occurred to me, while I was sitting around waiting for the fun to start, that not much is, and that I should tell you just in case you're worried about your fun <u>capacity</u>.

I don't mean to put a <u>damper</u> on things. I just mean we ought to treat fun <u>reverently</u>. It is a mystery. It cannot be caught like a virus. It cannot be trapped like an animal. The god of <u>mirth</u> is paying us back for all those years of thinking fun was everywhere by refusing to come to our party. I don't want to <u>blaspheme</u> fun anymore. When fun comes in on little dancing feet, you probably won't be expecting it. In fact, I bet it comes when you're doing your duty, your job, or your work. It may even come on a Tuesday.

I remember one day, long ago, on which I had an especially good time. Pam Davis and I walked to the College Village drug store one Saturday morning to buy some candy. We were about 12 years old (fun ages). She got her Bit-O-Honey. I got my malted milk balls, chocolate stars, Chunkys, and a small bag of M & M's. We started back to her house. I was going to spend the night. We had the whole day to look forward to. We had plenty of candy. It was a long way to Pam's house but every time we got weary Pam would put her hand over her eyes, scan the <u>horizon</u> like a sailor and say, "Oughta reach home by nightfall," at which point the two of us would laugh until we thought we couldn't stand it another minute. Then after we got calm, she'd say it again. You should have been there. It was the kind of day and friendship and occasion that made me deeply regretful that I had to grow up.

It was fun.

First Impressions

Freewrite for ten minutes on one of the following.

1. Did you enjoy reading this selection? Why or why not?
2. What do you do for fun? What makes it fun? When it isn't fun, why isn't it?
3. Who do you think have more fun, children or adults? Explain.

Vocabulary Check

Circle the letter of the word or phrase that best completes each of the following four sentences.

1. The word *puritans* in "people got the modern idea that . . . if we didn't have a little fun every day we would turn into (sakes alive!) puritans" (paragraph 3) means
   a. shy people who fear strangers.
   b. serious people who avoid pleasure.
   c. people who like to cook.
   d. people who can't make decisions quickly.
2. The word *epitome* in "Big occasions were supposed to be fun. Christmas, Thanksgiving and Easter were obviously supposed to be fun. . . . Your

honeymoon was supposed to be the epitome of fundom" (paragraph 11) means
   a. perfect example.   c. opposite.
   b. worst kind.   d. end.

3. The word *scan* in "Pam would put her hand over her eyes, scan the horizon like a sailor and say, 'Oughta reach home by nightfall'" (paragraph 14) means
   a. ignore.   c. touch.
   b. copy.   d. look at.

4. The word *regretful* in "It was the kind of day . . . that made me deeply regretful that I had to grow up. It was fun" (paragraph 14) means
   a. happy.   c. prayerful.
   b. surprised.   d. sorry.

Circle the letter of the word (or form of the word) from "Words to Watch" that best completes each of the following four sentences.

5. Some people make a _____ of cleanliness—they cannot tolerate even a single speck of dust.
   a. fetish   c. blasphemy
   b. capacity   d. horizon

6. The judge urged Ryan to give up his _____ and live a moral life.
   a. reverence   c. horizon
   b. licentiousness   d. damper

7. In some cultures, the wisdom of old age is deeply respected, and old people are treated _____ .
   a. licentiously   c. reverently
   b. blasphemously   d. mirthfully

8. Melvin's father put a _____ on the party by insisting we turn the music down, so we all went to Elena's house.
   a. fetish   c. benefit
   b. mirth   d. damper

Reading Check

Central Point and Main Ideas

1. Which sentence best expresses the central point of the selection?
   a. Having fun should be the most important thing in our lives.
   b. Fun is rarer than we think, and it tends to come when we don't expect it.
   c. We put happy faces on things to show how much fun we're having.
   d. Disney World should be fun.

2. Which sentence best expresses the main idea of paragraph 6?
   a. Everyone should stay fit.
   b. People should enjoy going to school.
   c. We expect many activities to be fun.
   d. Work is not really fun.
3. Which sentence best expresses the main idea of paragraph 10?
   a. Taking Polaroid pictures is fun.
   b. Television influences viewers too much.
   c. Television ads can depress people by making them wonder when the fun will start in their own lives.
   d. In television commercials, the guys flicking towels at each other in the locker room are having fun.

Key Supporting Details

4. Fun, writes Jordan, became so important that people started to look for more thrilling sources of fun, such as
   a. watching more television.
   b. celebrating Thanksgiving.
   c. buying candy.
   d. using more alcohol and drugs.
5. The author feels that instead of looking for fun everywhere, we ought to
   a. avoid fun.
   b. work harder at our jobs.
   c. treat fun with respect.
   d. watch more television commercials.

Inferences

6. Jordan implies that big occasions
   a. are more fun for children.
   b. are more fun for adults.
   c. are not as much fun as going to Disney World.
   d. are not as much fun as we expect them to be.
7. We can conclude from this selection that the author
   a. goes to many parties.
   b. had an unhappy childhood.
   c. thinks that fun is overemphasized in our society.
   d. has never been on family outings or to Disney World.
8. By "It may even come on a Tuesday" (paragraph 13) Jordan implies that
   a. most people dislike Tuesdays because they are too far from the weekend.
   b. Tuesday is the best day of the week.
   c. Tuesday is her day off.
   d. we don't need to wait for a weekend to have fun.

The Writer's Craft
9. One paragraph in which the author uses repetition to make her point is
   a. paragraph 6.
   b. paragraph 7.
   c. paragraph 8.
   d. paragraph 14.
10. To conclude her article, Jordan uses
    a. a summary of her main ideas.
    b. a personal experience and her opinion of it.
    c. a plea for a change in the way people define fun.
    d. a prediction of what fun will be like in the future.

Summarizing Activity

Complete the following summary of "Fun. Oh Boy, Fun. You Could Die from It" by filling in each blank with one or more words.

People have gotten the idea that the main goal of life is to have fun. Our emphasis on fun has led to participation in more exciting and more dangerous activities, such as drinking and using (1) _____. Television ads have supported the idea that life is all fun by showing people having fun in many unlikely ways. These ads can (2) _____ viewers who wonder when the fun will start in their own (3) _____. In addition, people have been disappointed by big events, which are also supposed to be fun. Jordan feels that not much about life is really fun. She believes fun is a mystery that should be treated with respect and that it is more likely to come when people aren't (4) _____ it. An example of her idea of fun is a day she spent (5) _____
_____.

Discussion Questions

1. Do you think school or work can be fun? Why or why not?
2. Why do you think Jordan calls twelve a "fun age" (paragraph 14)? What was fun to you when you were twelve? Can twelve-year-olds have fun in ways that older people can't?
3. Jordan writes that the search for fun became so important "that everybody started to look for more and more thrilling ways to supply it" (paragraph 9). What are some of these "thrilling ways"? Do you agree that people turn to these "thrills" because they are searching for fun?
4. Do you think our society emphasizes fun too much? If so, explain.

Paragraph Assignments

1. Write a paragraph about an experience in your childhood or in the more recent past that you definitely would label "fun." To help your reader experience the fun you had, include vivid details describing what you did and how you and others felt about the experience and each other. Your topic sentence could be something like "I really had fun when I _____."

2. In her final example, Jordan suggests that children or adolescents may find ways to have fun more easily than adults, who seem to have to work hard at having fun. Do agree? In a paragraph, give reasons to explain why fun comes more easily to children than to adults. Or, if you prefer, tell why adults have more fun than children. Include examples of things children can do that adults might feel silly doing, such as play tag, finger paint, or build sand castles. Or describe things adults can do that children are not permitted to do, such as shop or travel by themselves or set their own hours.

Essay Assignments

1. Jordan implies that experiences which we hope or expect to be fun often turn out not to be fun at all. Write an essay about a time you expected to have fun but did not. Or, as an alternative, write about something that was just as much fun as you expected it to be. You might write about a family outing or vacation (such as a trip to Disney World), about a "big occasion" (like a prom, a concert, a Christmas holiday, or a honeymoon), or about a meal or an evening out with friends. Tell in detail what you had hoped would happen and how things actually turned out. Your thesis might be similar to one of these:

    Our senior class trip to _____ turned out to be anything but the pleasurable experience we had thought it would be.
    My engagement party was one of the happiest occasions of my life.

2. Jordan says that for some people to have fun, they must increase "the level of danger" (paragraph 9). Write an essay in which you describe some of the risky ways people you know have fun, such as by playing practical jokes, climbing mountains, or gambling. In your final paragraph, write about whether what these people do is really worth doing. Do the risks always lead to fun? Is the fun worth the risks?

Rudeness at the Movies
Bill Wine

Preview

Some of today's movie audiences are not content to sit quietly and watch the show—they want to be in the show. In this article, columnist and film critic Bill Wine uses humor to reveal how these people's thoughtless actions can spoil moviegoing for the rest of us.

Words to Watch

spritzes (4): sprays
engulfed (9): swallowed up
Paul Bunyanesque (10): like Paul Bunyan, a fictional giant
galling (14): irritating
invariably (16): always
superfluous (16): unnecessary
infectiousness (18): ability to be spread
prescient (20): knowing what will happen beforehand
waxing (21): becoming
provocation (23): urging
gregarious (25): sociable
eccentric (26): peculiar
Fascist (29): right-wing dictator

Is this actually happening or am I dreaming?

I am at the movies, settling into my seat, eager with anticipation at the prospect of seeing a long-awaited film of obvious quality. The theater is absolutely full for the late show on this weekend evening, as the reviews have been ecstatic for this cinema masterpiece.

Directly in front of me sits a man just an inch or two taller than Kareem Abdul-Jabbar. His date, sitting on his left, sports the very latest in fashionable hairdos, a gathering of her golden locks into a shape that resembles the Tacony-Palmyra bridge when it's open.

On his right, a woman <u>spritzes</u> herself liberally from a perfume bottle her popcorn-munching husband got her for Valentine's Day, something called Essence of Elk.

The row in which I am sitting quickly fills up with members of Cub Scout Troop 432, on an outing to the movies because rain has cancelled their overnight hike. Their leader explains to them the rules in tonight's Best Sound Made from an Empty Good-'n'-Plenty's Box competition, about to begin.

Directly behind me, a man and his wife are ushering three other couples into their seats. I hear the woman say to the couple next to her: "You'll love it. You'll just love it. This is our fourth time and we enjoy it more and more each time. Don't we, Harry? Tell them about the pie-fight scene, Harry. Wait'll you see it. It comes just before you find out that the daughter killed her boyfriend. It's great."

The woman has more to say—much more—but she is drowned out at the moment by the wailing of a two-month-old infant in the row behind her. The baby is crying because his mother, who has brought her triplets to the theater to save on exorbitant babysitting costs, can breast-feed only two at a time.

Suddenly, the lights dim. The music starts. The credits roll. And I panic.

I scream and plead with everyone around me to do whatever they can to allow me to enjoy the movie. All I ask, I wail, is to be able to see the images and hear the dialogue and not find out in advance what is about to happen. Is that so much to expect for three-and-a-half bucks, I ask, now <u>engulfed</u> by a cloud of self-pity. I begin weeping unashamedly.

Then, as if on cue, the <u>Paul Bunyanesque</u> chap slumps down in his seat, his wife removes her wig, the Elk lady changes her seat, the Scouts drop their candy boxes on the floor, the play-by-play commentator takes out her teeth, and the young mother takes Manny, Moe, and Jack home.

Of course I am dreaming, I realize, as I gain a certain but shaky consciousness. I notice that I am in a cold sweat. Not because the dream is scary, but from the shock of people being that cooperative.

I realize that I have awakened to protect my system from having to handle a jolt like that. For never—NEVER—would that happen in real life. Not on this planet.

I used to wonder whether I was the only one who feared bad audience behavior more than bad movie-making. But I know now that I am not. Not by a long shot. For the most frequent complaint I have heard in the last few months about the moviegoing experience has had nothing to do with the particular film itself.

No. What folks have been complaining about goes on in the audience. And that has been what seems like an epidemic of <u>galling</u> inconsiderateness and outrageous rudeness.

It is really not that difficult to forgive a person's excessive height, or malodorous perfume, or perhaps even an inadvisable but understandable need to bring very young children to adult movies.

But the talking: that is not at all easy to forgive. For it is inexcusable, really. Talking—loud, constant, and <u>invariably</u> <u>superfluous</u>—seems to be standard operating procedure on the part of many movie patrons these days. And it is almost as bothersome and obnoxious as would be the screaming of the word "Fire!" in the proverbial crowded theater.

It is true, I admit, that after a movie critic has seen several hundred movies in the ideal setting of an almost-empty screening room with no one but other politely silent movie critics around him, it does tend to spoil him for the packed-theater experience.

And something is lost viewing a movie in almost total isolation. Which the movie distributors acknowledge with their reluctance to screen certain audience-pleasing movies for small groups of critics. Especially with comedies, the <u>infectiousness</u> of laughter is an important ingredient of movie-watching pleasure.

But it is a decidedly uphill battle to enjoy a movie—no matter how suspenseful or hilarious or moving it is—with a non-stop gabber sitting within earshot. And they come in sizes, ages, sexes, colors and motivations of every kind.

Some chat as if there is no movie playing. Some greet friends as if at a picnic. Some alert those around them to what is going to happen, either because they have seen the film before and know, or because they are self-proclaimed experts on the predictability of plotting and want to be seen as <u>prescient</u> geniuses.

Some describe in graphic terms exactly what is happening as if they were doing the radio commentary for a sporting event on radio. ("Ooh, look, he's sitting down. Now he's looking at that green car. A banana—she's eating a banana.") Some audition for Gene Shalit's job by <u>waxing</u> witty as they critique the movie right before your very ears.

And all act as if it is their Constitutional or God-given right. As if their admission price allows them to ruin the experience for anyone and everyone else in the building. But why?

Good question. I wish I knew. Maybe rock concerts and ball games—both environments which condone or even encourage hootin' and hollerin'—have conditioned us to voice our approval and disapproval and just about anything else we can spit out of our mouths at the slightest <u>provocation</u> when we are part of an audience.

But my guess lies elsewhere. The villain, I'm afraid, is the tube. We have seen the enemy and it is television. For we have gotten conditioned over the last few decades to spending most of our screen-viewing time in front of a little box in our living rooms and bedrooms.

And when we watch that piece of furniture, regardless of what is on it—be it commercial, be it Super Bowl, be it soap opera, be it funeral procession, be it prime-time sitcom, be it Shakespeare play—we chat. Boy, do we chat. Because TV viewing tends to be an informal, <u>gregarious</u>, friendly, casually interruptible experience, we talk whenever the spirit moves us. Which is often.

And we have learned to live with that, and to see as <u>eccentric</u> anyone who demands total silence and attention from other family members during the viewing of any televison offering whatever. I mean, you can watch if you want to, we tell them, but I'm sure as hell gonna talk if I want to.

All of which is fine. But we have carried this behavior, which is perfectly acceptable in the family living room, right to our neighborhood movie theater, where we are doing unto our neighbors what we wouldn't mind that they do unto us—AT HOME.

And it is turning lots of people off to what used to be a truly pleasurable experience: sitting in a jammed movie theater and watching a crowd-pleasing movie. And that is a first-class shame.

Nobody wants <u>Fascist</u>-like ushers, yet that may be where we're headed of necessity. Let's hope not. But something's got to give.

For movies during this Age of Television may or may not be better than ever. About audiences, however, there is no question.

They are worse.

First Impressions

Freewrite for ten minutes on one of the following.

1. Did you enjoy reading this selection? Why or why not?
2. Do you think Wine is right about today's moviegoers, or is he unfair to them? Why?
3. How do you feel when someone is rude to you? What do you do about it?

Vocabulary Check

Circle the letter of the word or phrase that best completes each of the following four sentences.

1. The word *ecstatic* in "The theater is absolutely full for the late show on this weekend evening, as the reviews have been ecstatic for this cinema masterpiece" (paragraph 2) means
   a. very enthusiastic.   c. missing.
   b. cautious.   d. disappointing.

2. The word *exorbitant* in "his mother . . . has brought her triplets to the theater to save on exorbitant babysitting costs" (paragraph 7) means
   a. too loud.   c. boring.
   b. too high.   d. interesting.
3. The word *malodorous* in "It is really not that difficult to forgive a person's excessive height, or malodorous perfume" (paragraph 15) means
   a. pleasant.   c. bad-smelling.
   b. expensive.   d. hard-to-smell.
4. The word *condone* in "Maybe rock concerts and ball games—both environments which condone or even encourage hootin' and hollerin'—have conditioned us to voice our approval and disapproval" (paragraph 23) means
   a. punish.   c. fear.
   b. forbid.   d. overlook.

Insert each of the following words (or forms of words) from "Words to Watch" where it belongs in one of the four sentences below.

        galling   gregarious   prescient   superfluous

5. To make your writing less wordy, rewrite until every _____ word has been eliminated.
6. Opposites really do attract sometimes; in several of the couples I know, one partner is quiet and prefers to be alone, while the other is very _____.
7. Jackie's snoring wouldn't be so _____ if it weren't so loud.
8. Palm readers like to think they are _____, but I have never met one who knew anything about my future.

Reading Check

Central Point and Main Ideas

1. Which sentence best expresses the central point of the selection?
   a. Going to the movies used to be more fun than it is today.
   b. The rude behavior of today's audiences is ruining the movies.
   c. People like to talk while watching television.
   d. Ushers must control the behavior of movie audiences.
2. Which sentence best expresses the main idea of paragraph 16?
   a. Most people talk too much.
   b. Some loud talking during movies is acceptable.
   c. Talking during a movie is unforgivable.
   d. Screaming "Fire!" in a theater is wrong.
3. Which sentence best expresses the main idea of paragraph 27?
   a. Good behavior is learned at home.
   b. Most people don't mind the behavior of movie audiences.

114   SPORTS AND LEISURE

  c. Audiences mistakenly behave at the movies as they do when watching television at home.
  d. Behavior that is acceptable in the family living room is also acceptable at the movies.

Key Supporting Details

4. _____ TRUE OR FALSE? The Cub Scouts in Wine's dream are playing with empty candy boxes.
5. The author feels that watching television
  a. has affected the behavior of movie audiences.
  b. should be done in silence.
  c. is usually done in silence.
  d. is a good model for watching movies in theaters.

Inferences

6. _____ TRUE or FALSE? The author implies that teenagers are the rudest members of movie audiences.
7. In the last four paragraphs of the article, the author implies that unless audiences become quieter,
  a. movie theaters will be closed.
  b. everyone will watch less television.
  c. movies will get worse.
  d. ushers will have to force talkers to leave.
8. _____ TRUE OR FALSE? The author would always prefer to watch a movie in a screening room with other critics.

The Writer's Craft

9. The tone of the first twelve paragraphs is
  a. formal.
  b. exaggerated.
  c. sad.
  d. forgiving.
10. In paragraphs 23 through 26, the author
  a. discusses the effects of rudeness at the movies.
  b. explains the causes of rudeness at the movies.
  c. illustrates rudeness at the movies.
  d. illustrates other types of rudeness.

Summarizing Activity

Complete the following summary of "Rudeness at the Movies" by filling in each blank with one or more words.

The author was sitting in a movie theater in which his ability to (1) _____ the movie was greatly threatened—by tall people, noisy people, and strong perfume. Then everyone suddenly stopped annoying him.

That's when he realized that he had been (2) _____, for real-life audiences, he claims, are consistently uncooperative. He feels that while some

of the annoying behavior of moviegoers is acceptable, (3) _____ in a movie is unforgivable because it ruins the movie for others. The main reason for this rude behavior, he says, may be that people are used to talk-

ing while they are (4) _____ in their own homes. But something has to be done about such behavior in a movie theater because (5)

_____

_____ .

Discussion Questions

1. Do you agree with Wine's theory about why some people are rude at the movies? What might be some other causes for this behavior?
2. Certain movies seem to bring out the worst in people. Which ones? Why?
3. Wine uses humorous exaggeration to make many of his points. For example, he claims that the man in front of him is "just an inch or two taller than Kareem Abdul-Jabbar [a basketball player who is seven feet, four inches tall]." What are some other examples of such exaggeration?
4. In what activities besides moviegoing can rudeness make life harder for us?

Paragraph Assignments

1. Assume that you are the manager of a movie theater who has been receiving complaints from patrons about excessive talking and other inconsiderate behavior that has spoiled their moviegoing. Write a paragraph to your patrons—possibly to be put on a sign in the theater lobby—trying to convince them to be more considerate of those sitting near them. Your paragraph might begin something like this: "Movies are wonderful entertainment, and the management of Movie Magic Cinemas wants every patron to enjoy our movies. For the sake of everyone in the audience, we ask our patrons to follow a few guidelines for courteous viewing."
2. In spite of the distractions Wine mentions in this selection, people still go to the movies. Why? In a paragraph, explain why people still pay to see movies in theaters instead of—for example—staying home and watching television or renting movies to show on their VCR's. One possible reason for going out to a movie is to get out of the house for a change. Think of several others to add to your paragraph.

Essay Assignments

1. Write an essay about a time someone was rude to you. Explain what happened, how you reacted, and how you felt about it. Conclude by explaining why your response was a good one or by telling what you wish you had done. As an alternative, write about a time someone was unusually considerate. Your thesis statement could be similar to one of the following:

   I consider my mother-in-law's asking me if I'm pregnant yet to be inexcusable rudeness.

   I'll never forget the time a total stranger gave me bus fare after my wallet had been stolen.

2. Write an essay about several situations or places besides a movie theater where people are apt to be rude and inconsiderate. Like Wine, use specific examples of how people behave. Try to persuade your reader that the behavior you are describing is a real problem and should be stopped. You might write about some of the following situations or any others you can think of:

   - waiting in line at the supermarket
   - waiting in line for tickets to a concert
   - shopping at a department store during a sale
   - riding in a crowded bus
   - driving during rush hour

13

Strike Out Little League
Robin Roberts

Preview

What could be more wholesome than Little League baseball? Unfortunately, when young children play an organized sport, unexpected problems can arise. In an essay written for *Newsweek*, Robin Roberts, who pitched for the Philadelphia Phillies for fourteen years and was later elected to the Baseball Hall of Fame, points out some fundamental problems with Little League. Roberts also proposes some changes that would benefit both the players and their parents.

Words to Watch

restrict (2): limit
disrupt (3): break up
stability (4): steadiness
eligible (4): qualified
farce (4): ridiculous joke
incompetent (5): not capable
retards (6): slows down
fundamentals (7): basics
alternatives (14): other choices

In 1939, Little League baseball was organized by Bert and George Bebble and Carl Stotz of Williamsport, Pa. What they had in mind in organizing this kids' baseball program, I'll never know. But I'm sure they never visualized the monster it would grow into.

At least 25,000 teams, in about 5,000 leagues, compete for a chance to go to the Little League World Series in Williamsport each summer. These leagues are in more than fifteen countries, although recently the Little League organization has voted to restrict the competition to teams in the United States. If you judge the success of a program by the number of participants, it would appear that Little League has been a tremendous success. More than 600,000 boys from 8 to 12 are involved. But I say Little League is wrong—and I'll try to explain why.

If I told you and your family that I wanted you to help me with a project from the middle of May until the end of July, one that would totally disrupt your dinner schedule and pay nothing, you would probably tell me to get lost. That's what Little League does. Mothers or fathers or both spend four or five nights a week taking children to Little League, watching the game, coming home around 8 or 8:30 and sitting down to a late dinner.

These games are played at this hour because the adults are running the programs, and this is the only time they have available. These same adults are in most cases unqualified as instructors and do not have the emotional stability to work with children of this age. The dedication and sincerity of these instructors cannot be questioned, but the purpose of this dedication should be. Youngsters eligible for Little League are of the age when their concentration lasts, at most, for five seconds—and without sustained concentration, organized athletic programs are a farce.

Most instructors will never understand this. As a result, there is a lot of pressure on these young people to do something that is unnatural for their age—so there will always be hollering and tremendous disappointment for most of these players. For acting their age, they are made to feel incompetent. This is a basic fault of Little League.

If you watch a Little League game, in most cases the pitchers are the most mature. They throw harder, and if they throw strikes, very few batters can hit the ball. Consequently, it makes good baseball sense for most hitters to take the pitch. Don't swing. Hope for a walk. That could be a player's instruction for four years. The fun is in hitting the ball; the coach says don't swing. That may be sound baseball, but it does nothing to help a young player develop his hitting. What would seem like a basic training ground for baseball often turns out to be a program of negative thoughts that only retards a young player.

I believe more good young athletes are turned off by the pressure of organized Little League than are helped. Little Leagues have no value as a training ground for baseball fundamentals. The instruction at that age, under the pressure of an organized league program, creates more doubt and eliminates the naturalness that is most important.

If I'm going to criticize such a popular program as Little League, I'd better have some thoughts on what changes I would like to see.

First of all, I wouldn't start any programs until the school year is over. Any young student has enough of a schedule during the school year to keep busy.

These programs should be played in the afternoon—with a softball. Kids have a natural fear of a baseball; it hurts when it hits you. A softball is bigger, easier to see and easier to hit. You get to run the bases more, and there isn't as much danger of injury if one gets hit with the ball. Boys and girls could play together. Different teams would be chosen every day. The instructors would be young adults home from college, or high-school graduates. The instructor could be the pitcher and the umpire at the same time. These programs could be run on public playgrounds or in schoolyards.

I guarantee that their dinner would be at the same time every night. The fathers could come home after work and relax; most of all, the kids would have a good time playing ball in a program in which hitting the ball and running the bases are the big things.

When you start talking about young people playing baseball at 13 to 15, you may have something. Organize them a little, but be careful; they are still young. But from 16 on, work them really hard. Discipline them, organize the leagues, strive to win championships, travel all over. Give this age all the time and attention you can.

I believe Little League has done just the opposite. We've worked hard with the 8- to 12-year-olds. We overorganize them, put them under pressure they can't handle and make playing baseball seem important. When our young people reach 16, they would appreciate the attention and help from the parents, and that's when our present programs almost stop.

The whole idea of Little League baseball is wrong. There are alternatives available for more sensible programs. With the same dedication that has made the Little League such a major part of many of our lives, I'm sure we'll find the answer.

I still don't know what those three gentlemen in Williamsport had in mind when they organized Little League baseball. I'm sure they didn't want parents arguing with their children about kids' games. I'm sure they didn't want to have family meals disrupted for three months every year. I'm sure they didn't want young athletes hurting their arms pitching under pressure at such a young age. I'm sure they didn't want young boys who don't have much athletic ability made to feel that something is wrong with them because they can't play baseball. I'm sure they didn't want a group of coaches drafting the players each year for different teams. I'm sure they didn't want unqualified men working with the young players. I'm sure they didn't realize how normal it is for an 8-year-old boy to be scared of a thrown or batted baseball.

For the life of me, I can't figure out what they had in mind.

First Impressions

Freewrite for ten minutes on one of the following.

1. Did you enjoy reading this selection? Why or why not?
2. What do you remember about participating in sports and games as a child? What did you enjoy? What didn't you enjoy?
3. Should young children be encouraged to play competitive sports? Why or why not?

Vocabulary Check

Circle the letter of the word or phrase that best completes each of the following four sentences.

1. The word *visualized* in "What they had in mind in organizing this kids' baseball program, I'll never know. But I'm sure they never visualized the monster it would grow into" (paragraph 1) means
   a. criticized.   c. forgot.
   b. pictured.   d. frightened.
2. The word *sustained* in "their concentration lasts, at most, for five seconds—and without sustained concentration organized athletic programs are a farce" (paragraph 4) means
   a. new.   c. long-lasting.
   b. poor.   d. interrupted.
3. The word *sound* in "it makes good baseball sense for most hitters to take the pitch. Don't swing. Hope for a walk.... That may be sound baseball, but it does nothing to help a young player develop his hitting" (paragraph 6) means
   a. noisy.   c. crazy.
   b. good.   d. quick.
4. The word *strive* in "But from 16 on, work them really hard. Discipline them, organize the leagues, strive to win championships" (paragraph 12) means
   a. resist the urge.   c. relax more.
   b. try hard.   d. leave town.

Circle the letter of the answer that best completes each of the following four items. Each sentence uses a word (or form of a word) from "Words to Watch."

5. Our dinner party for my boss was a *farce*—
   a. I spilled gravy on her lap, and my dog ate the dessert.
   b. everything went smoothly, and the dinner was delicious.
6. Harvey is convinced he's *incompetent* at word processing because
   a. he just wrote a twenty-page paper on his computer.
   b. he always destroys what he's working on.

7. My daughter *disrupted* our lunch by
   a. preparing the sandwiches.
   b. coming in twice to complain about her little brother.
8. There is no *stability* in Ronnie's home because
   a. his parents are getting a divorce.
   b. his parents have been married for twenty years.

Reading Check

Central Point and Main Ideas

1. Which sentence best expresses the central point of the selection?
   a. Little League ruins family dinner schedules.
   b. Many Little League coaches are unqualified.
   c. Little League should be changed because it does players more harm than good.
   d. Eight- to twelve-year-olds are too young to play baseball.
2. Which sentence best expresses the main idea of paragraph 6?
   a. Pitchers are the most mature players among Little Leaguers.
   b. Players in Little League improve their skills more quickly than players in pickup games do.
   c. Little League does not improve players' batting skills.
   d. Little League coaches don't know how to win games.
3. Which sentence best expresses the main idea of paragraphs 8 through 11?
   a. Little League needs to be made safer for children.
   b. Certain changes could make Little League more rewarding for the entire family.
   c. Little League games should be played at times convenient for children.
   d. Young children are too busy to play baseball during the school year.

Key Supporting Details

4. _____ TRUE OR FALSE? Roberts believes that youngsters aged 16 and over should be given more opportunities to play baseball.
5. According to the author, a major fault of Little League is that
   a. the children are not mature enough to do well at competitive sports.
   b. children are forced to participate.
   c. the instructors are too young.
   d. there are better things for children to do than play baseball.

Inferences

6. _____ TRUE OR FALSE? Roberts suggests that children would enjoy playing baseball more if they were under less pressure.
7. By suggesting that "Different teams would be chosen every day" (paragraph 10), the author implies that
   a. winning should be less important than simply taking part.

122   SPORTS AND LEISURE

    b. no one would be allowed to play two days in a row.
    c. organizing different teams is a way to find perfect lineups.
    d. Little League participation should be limited to one day a week.

The Writer's Craft

8. The first and last paragraphs of this article
    a. are both anecdotes about Robin Roberts' experiences in baseball.
    b. are both summaries.
    c. are tied together by references to the people who founded Little League.
    d. quote baseball statistics.
9. In paragraph 15, the author adds emphasis through
    a. a series of questions.
    b. repetition.
    c. direct appeals to the reader.
    d. very short sentences.
10. For which of the following readers did Roberts probably write this article?
    a. Little League players' parents.
    b. Little League players themselves.
    c. Major league baseball players.
    d. Professional sportswriters.

Summarizing Activity

Complete the following summary of "Strike Out Little League" by filling in each blank with one or more words.

    In spite of its seeming success, Little League baseball needs to be improved. The program disturbs both adult schedules and the family dinner hour. The (1) _____ in charge lack the training and emotional stability to work with young children, and they stress winning rather than growth. Young players, who don't have good concentration, are only disappointed and held back by this approach. Little League should be made less (2) _____, less disruptive, and less threatening to eight- to twelve-year-olds. The program should be run on afternoons only in the (3) _____ when it can't compete with school activities. (4) _____ should replace the baseballs that young children fear. Competitive activities can be added little by little for (5)

Discussion Questions

1. Do you think all of Roberts' criticisms of Little League are justified? Do you know if any of his suggestions have actually been followed? Which (if any) of his suggestions in your opinion should not be followed?
2. As Roberts points out, Little League has successfully attracted many participants. If it is as harmful as he says, how can you account for the large number of youngsters who go out for the teams?
3. Have you ever considered being a coach? Did reading this article change your ideas about coaching? If so, how?
4. In what other situations besides Little League do you think success is emphasized too much? What are the effects on the people involved?

Paragraph Assignments

1. According to Roberts, Little League discourages more good young athletes than it encourages. What activity have you been involved with that turned out to be less helpful than you thought it would be? For example, have you taken a class that confused you more than it taught you? Or have you been a member of an organization that simply did not accomplish its purpose? Write a paragraph about how an activity you participated in did not work out as you thought it would. Your topic sentence might be something like the following:

   My experience with Scouting turned out to be disappointing.
   My job at a fast food restaurant was not as easy as I thought it would be.

2. Write a paragraph describing an experience that helped you or someone you know improve skills or gain self-confidence. You could write about a situation such as the following:

   - learning to drive
   - taking over household chores
   - tutoring or being tutored
   - gaining more responsibility at work
   - being in a skit or a play

   In your paragraph, explain what the experience was like and how it changed you or the person you are writing about.

Essay Assignments

1. Roberts suggests that a good Little League coach should be patient, should know how to teach baseball skills, and should understand children's abilities and needs. Choose another person in authority—for example, a teacher, a parent, a boss, or a member of the clergy—and write an essay on several qualities this person should have. Your thesis statement

could be something like "An effective boss should be patient, flexible, and organized."

2. In this selection, Roberts does two things—he tells what's wrong with Little League and then goes on to say how it might be improved. Write an essay in which you suggest improvements that could be made in a group or organization that you are familiar with: a class, your family, an athletic organization, a church group, and so on. The central point of this essay might be similar to "There are several ways my sociology class could be a better learning experience for students." Topic sentences for some paragraphs supporting that central point could be similar to the following:

First of all, it would be better if the teacher didn't waste so much time at the beginning of class.

Also, students would probably learn the material better if more of the quizzes were announced ahead of time instead of being surprises.

Finally, it would be very helpful if the teacher made more detailed comments on tests and papers.

Remember to support your topic sentences with specific examples and details.

Television Addiction
Marie Winn

Preview

When we hear the word "addict," we usually think of someone hooked on drugs or alcohol. Yet people who watch a great deal of television may fit Marie Winn's definition of an addict. Winn, author of the book *The Plug-In Drug*, from which this passage is taken, argues that television viewing, like other dangerous addictions, can be hazardous to people's health.

Words to Watch

wryly (1): humorously
surge (1): sudden increase
denote (1): mean
essence (3): basic nature
organism (3): living creature
potentially (4): possibly
distorted (4): unnaturally twisted
craves (4): strongly desires
deferred (7): put off
enervated (8): weakened
ruefully (9): regretfully
endeavor (9): task
renders (10): makes

The word "addiction" is often used loosely and <u>wryly</u> in conversation. People will refer to themselves as "mystery book addicts" or "cookie addicts." E. B. White writes of his annual <u>surge</u> of interest in gardening: "We are hooked and are making an attempt to kick the habit." Yet nobody really believes that reading mysteries or ordering seeds by catalogue is serious enough to be compared with addictions to heroin or alcohol. The word "addiction" is here used jokingly to <u>denote</u> a tendency to overindulge in some pleasurable activity.

People often refer to being "hooked on TV." Does this, too, fall into the lighthearted category of cookie eating and other pleasures that people pursue with unusual intensity, or is there a kind of television viewing that falls into the more serious category of destructive addiction?

When we think about addiction to drugs or alcohol, we frequently focus on negative aspects, ignoring the pleasures that accompany drinking or drug-taking. And yet the <u>essence</u> of any serious addiction is a pursuit of pleasure, a search for a "high" that normal life does not supply. It is only the inability to function without the addictive substance that is dismaying, the dependence of the <u>organism</u> upon a certain experience and an increasing inability to function normally without it. Thus a person will take two or three drinks at the end of the day not merely for the pleasure drinking provides, but also because he "doesn't feel normal" without them.

An addict does not merely pursue a pleasurable experience and need to experience it in order to function normally. He needs to repeat it again and again. Something about that particular experience makes life without it less than complete. Other <u>potentially</u> pleasurable experiences are no longer possible, for under the spell of the addictive experience, his life is peculiarly <u>distorted</u>. The addict <u>craves</u> an experience and yet he is never really satisfied. The organism may be temporarily sated, but soon it begins to crave again.

Finally a serious addiction is distinguished from a harmless pursuit of pleasure by its distinctly destructive elements. A heroin addict, for instance, leads a damaged life: his increasing need for heroin in increasing doses prevents him from working, from maintaining relationships, from developing in human ways. Similarly an alcoholic's life is narrowed and dehumanized by his dependence on alcohol.

Let us consider television viewing in the light of the conditions that define serious addictions.

Not unlike drugs or alcohol, the television experience allows the participant to blot out the real world and enter into a pleasurable and passive mental state. The worries and anxieties of reality are as effectively <u>deferred</u> by becoming absorbed in a television program as by going on a "trip" induced by drugs or alcohol. And just as alcoholics are only inchoately aware of their addiction, feeling that they control their drinking more than they really do ("I can cut it out any time I want—I just like to have three or four drinks before dinner"), people similarly overestimate their control over television watching. Even as they put off other activities to spend hour after hour watching television, they feel they could easily resume living in a different, less passive style. But somehow or other while the television set is present in their homes, the click doesn't sound. With television pleasures available, those other experiences seem less attractive, more difficult somehow.

A heavy viewer (a college English instructor) observes: "I find television almost irresistible. When the set is on, I cannot ignore it. I can't turn it off. I feel sapped, will-less, <u>enervated</u>. As I reach out to turn off the set, the strength goes out of my arms. So I sit there for hours and hours."

The self-confessed television addict often feels he "ought" to do other things—but the fact that he doesn't read and doesn't plant his garden or sew or crochet or play games or have conversations means that those activities are no longer as desirable as television viewing. In a way a heavy viewer's life is as imbalanced by his television "habit" as a drug addict's or an alcoholic's. He is living in a holding pattern, as it were, passing up the activities that lead to growth or development or a sense of accomplishment. This is one reason people talk about their television viewing so <u>ruefully</u>, so apologetically. They are aware that it is an unproductive experience, that almost any other <u>endeavor</u> is more worthwhile by any human measure.

Finally it is the adverse effect of television viewing on the lives of so many people that defines it as a serious addiction. The television habit distorts the sense of time. It <u>renders</u> other experiences vague and curiously unreal while taking on a greater reality for itself. It weakens relationships by reducing and sometimes eliminating normal opportunities for talking, for communicating.

And yet television does not satisfy, else why would the viewer continue to watch hour after hour, day after day? "The measure of health," writes Lawrence Kubie, "is flexibility . . . and especially the freedom to cease when sated." But the television viewer can never be sated with his television experiences—they do not provide the true nourishment that satiation requires—and thus he finds that he cannot stop watching.

First Impressions

Freewrite for ten minutes on one of the following.

1. Did you enjoy reading this selection? Why or why not?
2. Do you know a TV addict (yourself or someone else)? If so, describe what the person watches and how it affects him or her.
3. Have you ever lived for a few days or weeks without a television set? *Could* you? What would you do instead of watching TV?

Vocabulary Check

Circle the letter of the word or phrase that best completes each of the following four sentences.

1. The word *sated* in "The organism may be temporarily sated, but soon it begins to crave again" (paragraph 4) means
   a. satisfied.
   b. shiny.
   c. hungry.
   d. troubled.
2. The word *induced* in "The worries and anxieties of reality are as effectively deferred by . . . a television program as by . . . a 'trip' induced by drugs or alcohol" (paragraph 7) means
   a. prevented.
   b. shortened.
   c. cured.
   d. caused.
3. The word *inchoately* in "alcoholics are only inchoately aware of their addiction, feeling that they control their drinking more than they really do" (paragraph 7) means
   a. completely.
   b. quickly.
   c. recently.
   d. partly.
4. The word *adverse* in "it is the adverse effect of television viewing . . . that defines it as a serious addiction. The television habit distorts the sense of time. It renders other experiences vague and . . . . weakens relationships" (paragraph 10) means
   a. weak.
   b. educational.
   c. harmful.
   d. poetic.

Circle the letter of the answer that best completes each of the following four items. Each sentence uses a word (or form of a word) from "Words to Watch."

5. I *crave* ice cream, so I eat some
   a. rarely.
   b. every day.
6. My family decided to *defer* our trip to Disneyland
   a. with a credit card.
   b. until next summer.
7. "Mrs. Gold," said Charles *ruefully*,
   a. "I'm sorry, but I left my homework at home."
   b. "I'm so happy you gave me an A for the semester."
8. I felt so *enervated* after my workout that I
   a. ran five more miles.
   b. collapsed on the living room couch.

Reading Check

Central Point and Main Ideas

1. Which sentence best expresses the central point of the selection?
   a. Rehabilitation programs should be set up for TV addicts.
   b. Television viewing can become a serious addiction.

c. Television addicts don't do many things they feel they should be doing.
d. All addictions are harmful.
2. Which sentence best expresses the main idea of paragraph 4?
   a. Addicts seek pleasurable experiences.
   b. Addicts can choose from a wide variety of pleasurable experiences.
   c. Addicts need to repeat the pleasurable experiences on which they are dependent.
   d. Addicts can lead normal lives in spite of their addictions.
3. Which sentence best expresses the main idea of paragraph 5?
   a. Serious addictions are destructive.
   b. Heroin addicts cannot live normal lives.
   c. Addicts are never satisfied.
   d. Most addictions are harmless.

Key Supporting Details

4. According to the author, an addiction to television
   a. is as harmful as an addiction to mystery novels.
   b. is easy for the addict to control.
   c. doesn't interfere with the addict's other interests.
   d. weakens the addict's personal relationships.

5. _____ TRUE OR FALSE? Television addicts can turn off their TV sets whenever they want to.

Inferences

6. Winn implies that television addicts
   a. learn a great deal from watching television.
   b. are not educated people.
   c. feel more energetic after watching their favorite programs.
   d. are not in control of their lives.

7. _____ TRUE OR FALSE? The author implies that television addiction cannot be cured.

8. From the article, we can conclude that the author thinks that
   a. nobody should watch television.
   b. in limited amounts, television is as worthwhile as reading and having conversations.
   c. there aren't many television addicts.
   d. unlike watching TV, activities such as gardening and having conversations lead to personal development.

The Writer's Craft

9. The author introduces her article by
   a. discussing harmless addictions.
   b. explaining the importance of serious addictions.
   c. telling a story about one television addict.
   d. asking a series of questions about addiction.

10. The tone of this essay is
    a. humorous.
    b. serious.
    c. friendly.
    d. cruel.

Summarizing Activity

1. Circle the letter of the statement that summarizes the introduction of "Television Addiction" (paragraphs 1 and 2).
    a. People often misuse the word "addiction."
    b. Addiction to television may be in the same category as addiction to drugs or alcohol.
    c. Being "hooked on TV" is like being addicted to mysteries or cookies.
2. Circle the letter of the statement that summarizes the supporting details in paragraphs 3 through 5.
    a. Addiction has many positive as well as many negative aspects.
    b. Alcoholics do not feel normal if they are not drinking.
    c. Serious addicts harm themselves because they cannot feel normal unless they repeat their addictive behavior.
3. Circle the letter of the statement that summarizes the supporting details in paragraphs 6 through 10.
    a. All college English instructors watch too much television.
    b. Television addicts ignore the real world and neglect other activities.
    c. TV addicts don't have time to plant gardens or play games.
4. Circle the letter of the statement that summarizes the conclusion of this selection (paragraph 11).
    a. Television should be outlawed.
    b. Television addicts simply cannot escape from the set although they keep trying to control their addiction.
    c. Television addicts continue to watch because the programs do not satisfy their need.

Discussion Questions

1. The word "addiction" is usually reserved for dependence on substances that are physically harmful. Do you agree that excessive TV watching is an addiction? Why or why not?
2. Do you know children who watch too much TV? If you were the parent of such a child, what would you do to prevent him or her from becoming a television addict?
3. What activities could be substituted for television watching? Which of them might become equally addictive—but in a good, not a bad, way? Which of them would bring people closer together instead of separating them?

4. Winn argues that TV blots out the real world and brings us an unreal world in its place (paragraph 7). Do you agree? Are there any ways in which television acquaints us with the *real* world?

Paragraph Assignments

1. Winn emphasizes the harmful aspects of TV viewing, but there are, of course, good things to say about television. In a paragraph, discuss one or more important benefits television provides for you. Use a topic sentence such as "Watching the news every night keeps me up to date with what's going on in the world." Support your topic sentence with convincing examples.
2. If you were limited to having either a radio or a television set, which would you choose? Why? In a paragraph, state the main reason for your choice, and support that reason with convincing examples. For example, you might prefer a radio because you could listen to music whenever you wanted. Or you might select the TV set so you could continue to watch a favorite program.

Essay Assignments

1. If you are "addicted" to a particular television program, write about your addiction. When did you first begin to watch this program, and what drew you to it? Which of its features do you find pleasurable and habit-forming? Has it influenced the rest of your life? Your thesis statement for this essay could be similar to this one, "_____ (name of program) has been a big part of my life for several reasons." As an alternative, write about the TV addiction of someone you know.
2. Winn defines serious addiction as pleasurable, habit-forming, and harmful; she points out that a serious addiction causes people to neglect other activities and lose touch with the real world. Using some of Winn's ideas, write an essay showing how another activity usually not considered dangerous is in fact an addiction. Consider activities such as the following:

    - collecting baseball cards
    - eating junk food
    - talking on the telephone
    - reading romance novels
    - listening to music
    - shopping
    - playing bingo
    - exercising

    Each of your supporting paragraphs should focus on a different reason why the activity you have chosen is addictive.

Boxing Is a Barbarism Civilization Can Do Without

H. Bruce Miller

Preview

If you've ever watched a boxing match, you've probably felt the excitement that makes this sport so popular. You may also have seen how dangerous boxing can be. Is it too dangerous? In this newspaper article, written after the death of boxer Johnny Owen, H. Bruce Miller gives his answer to this question. See if you agree.

Words to Watch

barbarism (title): cruel custom
sustained (6): received
prevailed (6): won out
anachronism (6): something left from an earlier age
pugilism (7): boxing
conceded (7): admitted
gladiator (7): trained fighter in ancient Rome
premise (8): underlying idea
ancillary (9): less important
raison d'etre (9): a French phrase meaning "reason for being"
degrading (10): humiliating
carnage (12): slaughter
mandatory (13): required
relic (15): surviving trace

Johnny Owen, 24, of Wales, was beaten unconscious the night of Sept. 19 in Los Angeles. A crowd of several thousand witnessed the assault and cheered the perpetrator. Owen was taken to California Hospital

Medical Center, where he remained in a coma for 45 days before dying last Monday.

No charges have been filed in the incident. None will be filed. Owen and the man who killed him, Lupe Pintor, were professional fighters, and the fatal beating of Owen was something our society calls a "sporting event."

I was lucky enough not to witness the bantamweight title match between Pintor and Owen, but 18 years ago, I saw a man get killed in the ring, live, on nationwide television. The memory is still vivid.

The occasion was the March 1962 welterweight title fight between the reigning champion, Benny "Kid" Paret, and Emile Griffith. Griffith had taken the title away from Paret by a knockout in April of 1961, then Paret had regained it on a decision in September, and there was bad blood between the fighters.

The killing took only 20 to 25 seconds at most. In the 12th round, an infuriated Griffith trapped Paret against the ropes and began hammering him with blindingly fast punches to the head. Paret's eyes went glassy and his hands dropped, all power of self-defense gone. Griffith kept throwing punches. Finally the referee, realizing that Paret was staying upright only because Griffith's blows were keeping him pinned against the ropes, pulled Griffith away. Paret sagged to the canvas, and they took him out on a stretcher. He died a few days later without regaining consciousness.

Johnny Owen was the latest of approximately 330 men who have died since 1945 of injuries sustained in the ring. If reason and humanity prevailed, he would be the last. The "sport" of boxing is a barbaric, brutal anachronism that has no place in modern civilized society.

Pugilism has ancient and bloody roots. In the 10th century B.C., the Greek tyrant Theseus made warriors wrap their hands with leather thongs and pummel each other to death for the entertainment of the court. Later patrons refined the art by adding metal studs and spikes to the leather hand-covering, or cestus. The all-time champion of professional boxing is generally conceded to be a gladiator named Theagenes, who won more than 1,400 bouts. None of his opponents got a rematch.

The cestus has been replaced with padded gloves, and fights (at least in most cases) no longer go on to the death, but the essential premise of boxing remains the same as it was in the 10th century B.C.: to batter one's adversary unconscious or otherwise injure him so badly that he cannot continue.

There are, arguably, other sports more dangerous than boxing. Men are maimed and killed in auto racing, in football, in soccer, in baseball, in mountain climbing. But injury is ancillary to these sports. The unique barbarism of boxing is that injury is the central object of the contest, the raison d'etre of the spectacle.

We do not tolerate commercialized combats between animals or between men and animals. We do not allow men to pit fighting cocks or dogs against each other or to confront a bull with a cape and sword. As a society we have decided, correctly, that these exhibitions are inhuman and degrading. But we allow two men to get into a ring and try to pound each other into a coma for 15 rounds, in between commercials for light beer and twin-track razor blades.

Boxing's defenders will tell you the fight game has provided a route out of poverty for blacks and other disadvantaged people. Indeed it has—for a minuscule minority. A handful of professional fighters have ended up rich. Hundreds simply have ended up dead.

The defenders also will point out that pro boxers are fighting voluntarily, that no one makes them get into the ring. That's true, but it doesn't eliminate the barbarity. For the right price, promoters no doubt could find men willing to go at each other in an arena with chain saws—and no doubt could fill the arena with sadistic freaks happy to pay to witness the carnage. Does that mean any civilized nation could or would permit such a horror?

In the wake of the Owen killing, the secretary of the British Boxing Board of Control is talking about doing away with the mandatory eight-count after each knockdown, and the president of the World Boxing Council pledged that the next convention of that body would "study in-depth aspects of preventive medicine and maximum protection for boxers."

Such tokenistic tinkering dodges the essential problem. The only real way to provide "maximum protection for boxers" is to end boxing. The only real way to reform this "sport" is to kill it.

A nation's sports, as much as its science, laws, arts and letters, are a measure of its maturity and the pitch of its moral development. Boxing is a relic of savagery which we should have outgrown long ago.

First Impressions

Freewrite for ten minutes on one of the following.

1. Did you enjoy reading this selection? Why or why not?
2. Have you ever seen a boxing match? If so, how did you feel about what you saw? Did reading this article change any of your feelings about boxing?
3. Have you ever seen anyone get hurt during a sporting event? If so, what happened? How did you feel?

Vocabulary Check

Circle the letter of the word or phrase that best completes each of the following four sentences.

1. The word *pummel* in "Theseus made warriors wrap their hands with leather thongs and pummel each other to death" (paragraph 7) means
   a. beat.   c. frighten.
   b. walk.   d. bore.
2. The word *adversary* in "to batter one's adversary unconscious or otherwise injure him so badly that he cannot continue" (paragraph 8) means
   a. friend.   c. opponent.
   b. referee.   d. fan.
3. The word *maimed* in "There are . . . other sports more dangerous than boxing. Men are maimed and killed in auto racing, in football, in soccer, in baseball, in mountain climbing" (paragraph 9) means
   a. completely healed.   c. seriously injured.
   b. disturbed.   d. congratulated.
4. The word *minuscule* in "Boxing's defenders will tell you the fight game has provided a route out of poverty for blacks and other disadvantaged people. Indeed it has—for a minuscule minority. A handful of professional fighters have ended up rich" (paragraph 11) means
   a. very small.   c. very tired.
   b. very large.   d. very sorry.

Circle the letter of the answer that best completes each of the following four items. Each sentence uses a word (or form of a word) from "Words to Watch."

5. Our football team *prevailed* in the fourth quarter by
   a. kicking the winning 35-yard field goal.
   b. fumbling and allowing the other team to score the winning touchdown.
6. My twelve-year-old brother thinks it's *degrading* when our parents
   a. raise his allowance.
   b. hire a babysitter for him every time they go out.
7. Because attendance in the class is *mandatory*,
   a. not many students show up on Fridays.
   b. the classroom is always full.
8. Among the *relics* of our vacation is
   a. the Grand Canyon.
   b. a souvenir ashtray.

Reading Check

Central Point and Main Ideas

1. Which sentence best expresses the central point of the selection?
   a. Johnny Owen died from boxing injuries.

b. Boxing should be banned.
   c. Some people are trying to make boxing safer.
   d. Boxing has an ancient and bloody history.
2. Which sentence states the main idea of paragraph 7?
   a. Sentence 1
   b. Sentence 2
   c. Sentence 4
   d. Sentence 5
3. Which sentence best expresses the main idea of paragraph 12?
   a. No one forces professional boxers to go in the ring.
   b. For the right price, men would be willing to fight with chain saws.
   c. Even though boxers agree to fight, boxing is still wrong.
   d. Cruel people will always pay to watch violent contests.

Key Supporting Details

4. According to the article, boxing
   a. is the only dangerous sport popular in our country today.
   b. is altogether different today from boxing in the 10th century B.C.
   c. has caused more than three hundred deaths in the last fifty years.
   d. has not changed since Theagenes' time.
5. According to the author, boxing is worse than other dangerous sports because
   a. boxers are paid less than other athletes.
   b. boxers are trying to hurt each other.
   c. people don't get killed in other sports.
   d. many boxers are from poor neighborhoods.
6. _____ TRUE OR FALSE? According to the author, more professional fighters have gotten rich from boxing than have died from it.

Inferences

7. We can conclude from paragraphs 4 and 5 that
   a. Paret and Griffith were friends.
   b. The referee pulled Griffith away in time.
   c. The referee was on Griffith's side.
   d. Griffith wanted to hurt Paret as well as win the fight.
8. _____ TRUE OR FALSE? Miller implies that our society is more civilized about animals fighting for sport than it is about humans fighting for sport.

The Writer's Craft

9. The author gains the reader's attention by beginning his article with
   a. anecdotes.
   b. statistics.
   c. quotations.
   d. a question.

10. In paragraphs 11 and 12, the author
    a. gives his reasons for not opposing boxing altogether.
    b. argues against those who defend boxing.
    c. lists several statistics.
    d. quotes experts.

Outlining Activity

Complete the following outline of "Boxing Is a Barbarism Civilization Can Do Without" by filling in the missing items where they belong.

Central point: Because boxing is brutal and barbaric, it should be outlawed.

A. Some boxers have died of injuries they received in the ring.
   1. Johnny Owen died after having been beaten unconscious during a fight.
   2. _____
   3. Since 1945, about 330 boxers have died from boxing injuries.
B. Ever since its beginnings, boxing has been violent.
   1. _____
   2. Boxing has changed, but its goal is still to injure an opponent so badly that he cannot continue.
C. Today, boxing is the only sport that encourages fighters to hurt each other.
   1. In other dangerous sports, people are injured only by accident.
   2. In the United States, combat between animals and between people and animals has rightly been outlawed, yet boxing is still legal.
D. Those who defend boxing are wrong.
   1. _____
   2. _____
   3. Officials promise to study ways to protect boxers, but the only good way to protect them is to outlaw boxing.

Discussion Questions

1. After reading Miller's article, do you agree that boxing should be outlawed? Why or why not?
2. Who do you think would object most if boxing were outlawed? The fighters? Promoters? Fans? Television executives? For what reasons?

3. What other sports besides boxing might be considered as bad (or almost as bad) as boxing? Why?
4. Why do people enjoy war movies, crime shows, and violent sports? Can watching violence make viewers feel good? If so, in what ways?

Paragraph Assignments

1. Miller tells us that he has never forgotten seeing a man get killed in a boxing match, even though it happened many years ago. What dramatic event have you seen, either in person or on television, that you still remember almost as clearly as if it had just happened? In a paragraph, describe that event, including as many important and interesting details as you can think of. Begin or end your paragraph with a sentence that explains why this memory is still as vivid as it is. Your topic sentence could be similar to one of the following:

   Although it happened nearly ten years ago, I can still see the look on my mother's face as she spoke at her college graduation ceremony.
   My memories of seeing the *Challenger* exploding on television will stay with me as long as I live.

2. Write a defense of boxing, arguing that it should *not* be outlawed. In your defense, include good arguments against Miller's points and other good reasons that boxing should remain legal. If you like, you may argue instead that boxing should be permitted to continue *if* certain changes are made in the rules. In that case, be sure to include the new rules you recommend and tell how you think they would help. Your topic sentence could be similar to "There are several reasons why boxing should not be banned."

Essay Assignments

1. Miller wants the government to protect boxers by banning boxing. Think of one or more other things the government definitely should (or definitely should not) ban. Some of the topics you might consider are the following:

   - dangerous toys
   - handguns
   - marijuana
   - cigarettes
   - pornography
   - prostitution

   In your essay write a separate paragraph on each of the topics you have chosen. Explain how people will be better off if the policy you propose is carried out. Use a thesis such as "The government should put a stop to _____, _____, and _____ for several reasons" or "_____, _____, and _____ are three areas the government should definitely say out of."

2. Write an essay in which you either attack or defend a sport or recreational activity. If you attack it, you might want to argue that it should be banned totally or banned from television or just made safer. If you defend the activity, you might argue that it has a value that many people overlook. Whether you argue for or against the sport or activity, give convincing reasons for your opinion, along with vivid examples to support your reasons. You might wish to write about one of the following activities:

- skateboarding
- football
- wrestling
- car racing
- horse or dog racing
- skydiving
- motorcycle racing
- hockey

Understanding Ourselves

What Is Intelligence, Anyway?
Isaac Asimov

Preview

The oldest joke in the world is about a wise philosopher wandering through a cow pasture. Lost in thought, he stepped into some manure. He had the kind of intelligence that enabled him to think deep thoughts but not the kind that reminded him to look where he was going. Our usual ideas about intelligence are challenged in this essay by the noted science fiction writer Isaac Asimov. If he's right, our old definitions of *smart* and *stupid* will need some careful rethinking.

Words to Watch

buck private (1): the lowest rank in the Army
KP (1): abbreviation for "kitchen police," or cook's assistant in the armed forces
bents (2): talents
vitals (3): internal organs
pronouncements (3): statements by an authority
oracles (3): messages from the gods
devised (4): designed
academician (4): scholar
intricate (4): complicated
absolute (4): unchanging
arbiter (4): judge
indulgently (6): going along with someone's wishes
smugly (6): in a self-satisfied way

What is intelligence, anyway? When I was in the Army, I received a kind of aptitude test that all soldiers took and, against a normal of 100, scored 160. No one at the base had ever seen a figure like that, and for two hours they made a big fuss over me. (It didn't mean anything. The next day I was still a buck private with KP as my highest duty.)

All my life I've been registering scores like that, so that I have the complacent feeling that I'm highly intelligent, and I expect other people to think so, too. Actually, though, don't such scores simply mean that I am very good at answering the type of academic questions that are considered worthy of answers by the people who make up the intelligence tests—people with intellectual bents similar to mine?

For instance, I had an auto repairman once, who, on these intelligence tests, could not possibly have scored more than 80, by my estimate. I always took it for granted that I was far more intelligent than he was. Yet, when anything went wrong with my car, I hastened to him with it, watched him anxiously as he explored its vitals, and listened to his pronouncements as though they were divine oracles—and he always fixed my car.

Well then, suppose my auto repairman devised questions for an intelligence test. Or suppose a carpenter did, or a farmer, or, indeed, almost anyone but an academician. By every one of those tests, I'd prove myself a moron. And I'd *be* a moron, too. In a world where I could not use my academic training and my verbal talents but had to do something intricate or hard, working with my hands, I would do poorly. My intelligence, then, is not absolute but is a function of the society I live in and of the fact that a small subsection of that society has managed to foist itself on the rest as an arbiter of such matters.

Consider my auto repairman, again. He had a habit of telling me jokes whenever he saw me. One time he raised his head from under the automobile hood to say, "Doc, a deaf-and-dumb guy went into a hardware store to ask for some nails. He put two fingers together on the counter and made hammering motions with the other hand. The clerk brought him a hammer. He shook his head and pointed to the two fingers he was hammering. The clerk brought him nails. He picked out the sizes he wanted, and left. Well, doc, the next guy who came in was a blind man. He wanted scissors. How do you suppose he asked for them?"

Indulgently, I lifted my right hand and made scissoring motions with my first two fingers. Whereupon my auto repairman laughed raucously and said, "Why, you dumb jerk, he used his *voice* and asked for them." Then he said, smugly, "I've been trying that on all my customers today." "Did you catch many?" I asked. "Quite a few," he said, "but I knew for sure I'd catch *you*." "Why is that?" I asked. "Because you're so goddamned educated, doc, I *knew* you couldn't be very smart."

And I have an uneasy feeling he had something there.

First Impressions

Freewrite for ten minutes on one of the following.

1. Did you enjoy reading this selection? Why or why not?
2. Who's the most intelligent person you ever met? Why did you think he or she was so intelligent?
3. How do you feel about standardized tests (such as IQ tests)? Have they helped you or hurt you?

Vocabulary Check

Circle the letter of the word or phrase that best completes each of the following four sentences.

1. The word *complacent* in "All my life I've been registering [high scores] . . . so that I have the complacent feeling that I'm highly intelligent, and I expect other people to think so, too" (paragraph 2) means
    a. self-satisfied.
    b. uneasy.
    c. misunderstood.
    d. surprised.
2. The word *hastened* in "Yet, when anything went wrong with my car I hastened to him with it" (paragraph 3) means
    a. answered.
    b. expanded.
    c. shouted.
    d. hurried.
3. The word *foist* in "a small subsection of that society has managed to foist itself on the rest as an arbiter of such matters" (paragraph 4) means
    a. remove.
    b. force.
    c. promise.
    d. steal.
4. The word *raucously* in "Whereupon my auto repairman laughed raucously and said, 'Why, you dumb jerk, he used his voice and asked for them'" (paragraph 6) means
    a. noisily.
    b. late.
    c. secretly.
    d. immorally.

Circle the letter of the answer that best completes each of the following four items. Each sentence uses a word (or form of a word) from "Words to Watch."

5. My video recorder is so *intricate* that
    a. my seven-year-old son can use it.
    b. I can't understand it even after reading the directions.
6. Rhoda is always making *pronouncements* in class.
    a. She should learn not to make so many mistakes with language.
    b. She thinks she's an expert on everything.
7. In order to be a good *arbiter*, a person should be
    a. a wise supporter of one side.
    b. fair to both sides.

WHAT IS INTELLIGENCE, ANYWAY? **145**

8. Steve is *smug* about his athletic ability.
   a. He won three varsity letters every year in high school.
   b. He's so uncoordinated he won't even play softball at the company picnic.

Reading Check

Central Point and Main Ideas

1. Which sentence best expresses the central point of the selection?
   a. Repairmen have little respect for intelligence.
   b. IQ tests don't predict how well a person will do in the Army.
   c. Society measures and labels intelligence incorrectly.
   d. Most of us dislike people who are too smart.
2. Which sentence best expresses the main idea of paragraph 1?
   a. Everyone on the base made a fuss when Asimov scored 160 on an aptitude test.
   b. Doing well on an aptitude test did not change Asimov's job in the Army.
   c. The Army is not a bad place for intelligent people.
   d. Doing well on an Army aptitude test got the author a lot of criticism.
3. Which sentence best expresses the main idea of paragraph 4?
   a. Intelligence tests should be written by carpenters or farmers.
   b. Intelligence is defined by the people who make up the intelligence tests.
   c. The author's training and talent would make him successful in any job.
   d. The author is unskilled in working with his hands.

Key Supporting Details

4. The author always scores well on intelligence tests because
   a. he enjoys taking them.
   b. he is poor at working with his hands.
   c. many others score poorly.
   d. the tests ask the kinds of questions he can answer.
5. The blind man in the auto repairman's joke
   a. was the repairman's favorite customer.
   b. was smarter than Asimov.
   c. bought scissors by making cutting motions with his fingers.
   d. bought scissors by asking for them.

Inferences

6. The author implies that
   a. he does not believe he is intelligent.
   b. academic abilities are no better than other skills.

c. auto repairmen, carpenters and farmers should not take IQ tests.
d. he knows a great deal about cars.
7. The auto repairman said Asimov was "educated" but not "smart." From the selection, we can conclude that the repairman's definition of "smart" is probably
   a. being talented with car repairs.
   b. doing well in school.
   c. having common sense.
   d. having a good sense of humor.
8. _____ TRUE OR FALSE? We can conclude from the article that Asimov respected his auto repairman's skills.

The Writer's Craft

9. Asimov titled this selection "What Is Intelligence, Anyway?" in order to
   a. puzzle the reader.
   b. tell readers the author doesn't know what intelligence is.
   c. show off his own intelligence.
   d. raise the question of whether or not intelligence has been correctly defined.
10. The words *For instance* in "For instance, I had an auto repairman once who, on these intelligence tests, could not possibly have scored more than 80, by my estimate" (paragraph 3) signal
    a. an illustration.
    b. a contrast.
    c. an addition.
    d. a conclusion.

Summarizing Activity

Complete the following summary of "What Is Intelligence, Anyway?" by filling in each blank with one or more words.

When Issac Asimov was in the (1) _____, he scored very well on an aptitude test. Asimov always does well on such tests, but he knows they don't show how smart people really are. Instead, they measure only one kind of (2) _____. Asimov's auto repairman probably wouldn't score well on standardized tests, but (3) _____. If people with different kinds of talent and training wrote the intelligence tests, Asimov would (4) _____. In fact, Asimov's intelligence didn't keep him from falling for (5) _____
_____.

Discussion Questions

1. Do you think Asimov is right about intelligence tests being unfair? If so, what are some things that could be done to make them fairer?
2. Do you think people should have to take tests in order to get jobs? To get into college? If not, what could replace the tests?
3. What are some ways we judge how intelligent people are when we meet them? Are these ways always accurate? Why or why not?
4. At the end of paragraph 6, the repairman says to Asimov, "Because you're so goddamned educated, doc, I *knew* you couldn't be very smart." What is the difference between being educated and being smart? Which is more important?

Paragraph Assignments

1. Do you know anybody who has a kind of intelligence that is not measured by standardized tests? In a paragraph, describe this person. Include specific examples that indicate his or her intelligence. Your topic sentence could be something like the following:

   My neighbor Edna is a genius at making other people feel comfortable.
   My brother-in-law Jerome's gift for playing the violin amazes me.

2. Asimov says he had always assumed that he was much more intelligent than his mechanic. Write a paragraph about someone you have known who falsely assumed he or she was superior to other people. Tell what this person was like, and then describe an incident (like the one in which Asimov failed to answer his mechanic's question correctly) showing that he or she was not so superior after all.

Essay Assignments

1. People with high scores on standardized tests are not always successful. Besides intelligence, what qualities are important for success? Traits to consider include motivation, compassion, ability to get along with people, athletic ability, good mental and physical health, gentleness, courage, and discipline. In an essay, describe the qualities you consider most necessary for success. Your thesis might be similar to the following:

   Intelligence as measured by standardized tests is not the only qualification for success.

   To be truly successful, people should have _____,
   _____, and _____.

2. Which has been more important to you, what you've learned in or outside the classroom? Decide which kind of learning has been more valuable and

think of three lessons you learned in that way. Write a separate paragraph of your essay about each of these lessons. In each paragraph describe what happened and tell what you learned from it. Your topic sentences could be similar to the following:

At work I learned how to get along with people even if they were unpleasant to me.

From my friends I learned the value of talking over my problems instead of keeping them inside.

From my parents I learned that helping others is a source of great satisfaction.

17

Funerals Are Good for People

William M. Lamers, Jr.

Preview

Although we know that everyone will eventually die, accepting death when it happens is always difficult. It is even harder to accept, argues William M. Lamers, Jr., when there is no funeral. In this article, originally published in *Medical Economics*, Lamars, a psychiatrist, explains why he thinks funerals have value.

Words to Watch

macabre (2): gruesome
encephalitis (4): a brain disease
cremation (5): the burning of a corpse
prelude (6): introduction
fester (6): be infected
guerrilla (9): rebel
collaborating (9): cooperating
ruse (9): false excuse
vulnerable to (13): likely to be hurt by
despondent (14): depressed
continuum (18): connected series
turmoil (19): confusion
disservice (21): harm
oversedate (21): give too much calming medicine to
therapeutic (22): healing

While attending a medical meeting about a year ago, I ran into a fellow I'd known in residency. "What are you doing here, Bill?" he asked. "Giving a talk on the responses to death," I replied. "It will cover the psychological value of funerals as well as—"

"Funerals!" he exclaimed. "What a waste they are! I've made it plain to my wife that I don't want a funeral. Why spend all that money on such a macabre ordeal? And why have the kids standing around wondering what it's all about?"

"Look, Jim," I said patiently, "I've seen case after case of depression caused by the inability of patients—young and old—to work through their feelings after a death. I've found that people are often better off if they have a funeral to focus their feelings on. That lets them do the emotional work necessary in response to the loss." My friend still looked doubtful. And, as we parted company, I wondered how many other physicians are also overlooking the psychological value of funerals.

Their value is brought home time and time again in my own practice. Consider the woman who called me recently after making a suicide attempt. She was a divorcee and the mother of three sons, the youngest of whom had died of encephalitis about two months before. She was very much attached to her sons and highly dependent on them emotionally. The youngest had been her pet, and her grief at his loss was overwhelming.

Well-meaning friends persuaded the woman to have an immediate cremation and memorial service rather than go through the pain of a funeral. As a result, within a few hours after the boy's death, his body was cremated. Two weeks later a memorial service was held. The mother went around smiling to show people how well she'd adjusted to the boy's death. There was a small rock'n'roll band and several poetry recitations. It was very pleasant and happy and likely provided some beautiful memories. Yet it was all only frosting on an underbaked cake.

Within a few weeks the mother became extremely depressed. She was afraid to express her true feelings from fear of offending the friends who had planned the memorial service. She didn't want them to feel it wasn't good enough, and she tried to cover up her tremendous unresolved grief. All that was a prelude to her suicide attempt. This woman still had doubts that her son was dead. I'm convinced that, had she gone through a formalized funeral experience and been allowed to vent her grief, her son's death would have held some finality for her. And her feelings wouldn't have healed superficially while the core still continued to fester.

I see constant evidence that the problems resulting from a serious separation—through death, divorce, or other means—can have great psychological impact. If these problems remain unresolved, grave emotional trouble can result later. That's what happened to a patient I saw several years ago. She'd been married and divorced four times, each time to men at least 20 years older than she. And all were men who were gone from home most of the time—sea captains, traveling men, and the like.

She began to develop ulcers, high blood pressure, and had made several suicide attempts. When referred to me, she was about to divorce her fifth husband and marry a sixth. Apparently she also went through psychiatrists as fast as husbands; I was the fourth she'd seen. In consultation she told me she couldn't remember anything before the age of 10. Two or three sessions with her brought no results. Finally, trying to get at her early childhood through the back door, I said, "Tell me about your mother and father." She told me she'd been brought up in Europe and that her father had died in the early days of World War II.

Slowly, more of the story came out. One day, her father came back from the mountains—he was a guerrilla leader—to a triumphant reception in the village. Apparently he was also under strong suspicion of collaborating with the Germans. He'd been home less than an hour when some of his soldiers came and, on a ruse, took him away. Minutes later, my patient painfully recalled, she and her mother were summoned to the village square. There, with no explanation from the villagers, her father was shot before her eyes.

In that village, it was the custom for villagers to file through the home to view the body and express condolences. Then there would be a funeral service, a procession, and a gathering afterwards. In this instance, however, my patient and her mother were carted away to another town. No one knows what happened to the father's body, but there was no funeral. Possibly as a direct result, my patient had never been able to accept emotionally the fact of her father's death.

In my office she finally wept. The extent of her reaction indicated that at last she was beginning to express the feelings that might have been more properly handled about 20 years earlier. From then on, she was gradually able to understand that, in marrying older men who were away most of the time, she'd been searching for her father. Today, she's settled down considerably. But I can't help believing that a funeral, with its acknowledgement of death, would have contributed to her emotional well-being years earlier.

When a death occurs, most people feel a need to do something. And the doing can come out in several ways—in crying, in the funeral and burial, perhaps in informing others that the death has occurred, perhaps in assuring themselves that what was seen and heard was, in fact, a true happening. The funeral makes these things easier by providing the setting in which people can begin to resolve their feelings about death.

Children, of course, are especially vulnerable to the suffering that results from unresolved grief situations. So we do them a tremendous injustice when we don't let them know the facts or we lie—describing "the trip" Grandfather has gone on, for example. We need to answer their questions about death in a straightforward manner and give them the opportunity to talk about death and to express their feelings toward it. Many parents don't seem to understand this. They're not doing their children a favor by sheltering them.

A case in point is that of a 7-year-old girl whose mother brought her to me shortly after the death of the father. The little girl had become <u>despondent</u>, and her mother couldn't understand why. As the mother explained it, she'd done everything to protect her daughter's feelings. She'd kept almost all knowledge of the death from the child and hadn't allowed her to participate in the services or the burial.

Their first visit to me occurred about a week before President John F. Kennedy's assassination. Shortly after the assassination, the mother called to tell me her daughter had run away. Desperately, she asked me what to do, but I couldn't be of much help.

A few days later the girl returned home. She'd been at a friend's house where for the entire weekend she'd watched the Kennedy funeral on TV—a steady, continuous ritual of mourning. When the little girl came home, she told her mother: "Everything's O.K. now. I know what happened to Daddy."

Are there any satisfactory funeral substitutes—a memorial service, for example? In my opinion, there aren't. Though a memorial service is a response to loss and can be extremely satisfying for many, it's not ideal because it lacks several basic elements. First, a memorial service usually doesn't take place when feelings are most intense, which is shortly after the death. Second, members of the family aren't involved in communication, participation, and repeated exposure to the fact that death has occurred. These things force people to acknowledge the reality of loss. Finally, a memorial service doesn't include the presence of the body, which means people aren't given as great an opportunity to fix the fact of death in their minds.

In contrast to the memorial service, which is a one-time gathering, the traditional funeral as we know it in this country is a <u>continuum</u> of things. It includes visitations at the funeral home, usually with the remains lying in state. Frequently, there are religious services there as well as in the church, a procession to the place of burial, and committal service. Afterward, there's often a gathering of close friends and relatives. Throughout these events there's a repeated acceptance of condolences, acknowledgement of the fact of death, sharing of grief feelings, and encouragement for the future.

Since I'm so profuneral, you may wonder how I feel about those attacks on the funeral profession in recent years. Let me make it plain that I don't own a funeral home. Some funeral directors are guilty of abuse and of taking advantage of the public. I contend, however, that they're in the minority and that criticism of the funeral business has been blown out of porportion. In time of need, the majority of the directors provide an effective means of helping families through a lot of turmoil.

What can we, as physicians, do to steer families of dying patients in the right direction? Naturally, we can't actively impose our beliefs on others. In other words, it's unwise to steer a family toward a particular kind of funeral or service. If they prefer to have a memorial service held, then this may well be the most satisfactory for them.

On the other hand, a family that's avoiding the reality of death, trying to seal it over without allowing normal emotional responses to come to the surface, may need guidance. In that case, we doctors have an obligation to point out the possible consequences and to make ourselves available to discuss the situation. We do patients a disservice when we oversedate or overtranquilize them so that they're unaware of what's happening or unable to experience normal feelings of grief.

In short, we should encourage the practice of something as psychologically economical as funerals. They do a therapeutic job, and in most cases they can do it for a lot less money than we psychiatrists could.

First Impressions

Freewrite for ten minutes on one of the following.

1. Did you enjoy reading this selection? Why or why not?
2. Have you ever been to a funeral or memorial service? If so, what do you remember about it? How did you feel?
3. Tell about a loss that affected you a great deal. How long did it take you to get over this loss?

Vocabulary Check

Circle the letter of the word or phrase that best completes each of the following four sentences.

1. The word *vent* in "She was afraid to express her true feelings. . . . [H]ad she gone through a formalized funeral experience and been allowed to vent her grief, her son's death would have held some finality for her" (paragraph 6) means
    a. shut in.   c. ignore.
    b. let out.   d. fool.

2. The word *condolences* in "In that village it was the custom for villagers to file through the home to view the body and express condolences" (paragraph 10) means
   a. hatred.   c. sympathy.
   b. ignorance.   d. pleasure.
3. The word *ritual* in "for the entire weekend she'd watched the Kennedy funeral on TV—a steady, continuous ritual of mourning" (paragraph 16) means
   a. risk.   c. threat.
   b. year.   d. ceremony.
4. The words *impose . . . on* in "Naturally, we can't actively impose our beliefs on others. In other words, it's unwise to steer a family toward a particular kind of funeral or service" (paragraph 20) mean
   a. hide . . . from.   c. deny . . . to.
   b. ignore . . . about. d. force . . . on.

Circle the letter of the answer that best completes each of the following four items. Each sentence uses a word (or form of a word) from "Words to Watch."

5. I used a *ruse* to get an extension on my paper.
   a. I told the instructor I just didn't feel like doing it.
   b. I pretended to have a bad case of the flu.
6. Last night I had a *macabre* dream—
   a. the frog I cut up in biology class came back to haunt me.
   b. my parents gave me a new car for my birthday.
7. The living room was in *turmoil* after the children
   a. played there all morning.
   b. cleaned it up very neatly.
8. Eight hours of sleep is usually *therapeutic* for me; I wake up feeling
   a. tired and stiff.
   b. relaxed and refreshed.

Reading Check

Central Point and Main Ideas

1. Which sentence best expresses the central point of the selection?
   a. Many people never recover from the shock of a loved one's death.
   b. Funerals have become too expensive.
   c. Funerals help people cope with death.
   d. One child learned about death by watching John F. Kennedy's funeral on television.
2. Which sentence best expresses the main idea of paragraph 12?
   a. It is natural for people to cry after a death.
   b. People may need to talk with others after someone has died.
   c. Often people find it hard to accept the fact that someone has died.
   d. Funerals allow people to start coping with their feelings after a death.

3. Which sentence best expresses the main idea of paragraph 17?
   a. A memorial service may be a satisfactory substitute for a funeral.
   b. Memorial services usually take place at a later date than funerals would.
   c. A memorial service is not a satisfactory substitute for a funeral for three reasons.
   d. A memorial service does not include the presence of the body of the person who has died.

Key Supporting Details

4. The woman who was brought up in Europe tried to "find" her father by
   a. marrying older men.
   b. attempting suicide.
   c. attending funerals.
   d. leaving home often.

5. _____ TRUE OR FALSE? The author believes children do not need to be told that a loved one has died.

Inferences

6. In his discussion of a seven-year-old girl who was not told about her father's death, the author implies that
   a. the girl's mother succeeded in protecting her daughter's feelings.
   b. it was surprising that the little girl became depressed.
   c. the girl's mother should have allowed her to attend her father's funeral.
   d. the girl should not have been allowed to watch the Kennedy funeral on television.

7. The author implies that
   a. most people have memorial services, not funerals, when loved ones die.
   b. people who have memorial services instead of funerals want to save money.
   c. all people who don't have funerals for loved ones have psychological problems.
   d. people who attend funerals instead of memorial services seem to get over their losses more quickly.

The Writer's Craft

8. The tone of this article can be described as
   a. angry.
   b. playful.
   c. pessimistic.
   d. concerned.

9. The words *On the other hand* at the beginning of paragraph 21 signal
   a. an addition.
   b. time order.
   c. a contrast.
   d. a conclusion.
10. The evidence that the author uses to support his central point comes from
    a. letters written to the author.
    b. his own observations.
    c. government publications.
    d. statements of experts on death.

Summarizing Activity

Complete the following summary of "Funerals Are Good for People" by filling in each blank with one or more words.

    Funerals help people cope with death, a fact physicians may overlook. Several of the author's patients are good examples of people who were harmed by not attending (1) _____ . A woman whose dead son was given (2) _____ instead of a funeral became very depressed. Another patient (3) _____
_____ .

A seven-year-old girl who was not allowed to attend (4) _____ ran away from home. These and other cases show that there are no adequate substitutes for funerals. When someone dies, doctors should not impose their beliefs on their patients, but they should (5) _____
_____ .

Discussion Questions

1. Are Lamers's arguments convincing? Why or why not?
2. What are some of the feelings you have seen people have when someone close to them dies? How do you think funerals help people deal with these feelings?
3. Do you think children should be told the full truth when a loved one dies? Should they be permitted to attend funerals? If so, at what age?
4. How can we make things easier for friends or relatives who have lost a loved one? What other customs (besides funerals or memorial services) are helpful?

Paragraph Assignments

1. At one time or another, we all feel at least mildly depressed over problems much less important than death. But these problems do cause strong feelings. Write about a time when you felt sad or discouraged. Explain what happened to make you feel that way, how you felt, and how you coped with your feelings. Use a topic sentence such as "When my best friend went to college in another state, I felt lonely and deserted."

2. In paragraphs 17 and 18, Lamers contrasts memorial services with funerals. Write a paragraph in which you contrast two ways of doing something. Your tone may be serious or humorous. Here are some possible topics for this assignment:

    - lecture classes vs. discussion classes
    - surprise birthday parties vs. birthday parties that aren't a surprise
    - writing papers on a typewriter or computer vs. writing them by hand
    - getting to school or work alone vs. going in a car pool
    - buying a new car vs. buying a used one

Essay Assignments

1. Funerals are only one kind of ceremony that people have. Write about three other kinds of ceremonies or customs that are important to you or your family. Consider events such as the following:

    - graduations
    - marriage ceremonies
    - confirmations
    - holiday meals
    - birthday parties
    - sweet 16 parties
    - Bar Mitzvahs
    - anniversary celebrations

    Put each type of event in a separate paragraph. Your thesis sentence could be similar to "_____, _____, and _____ have been significant occasions in my life." Include details that show how important these experiences were for you.

2. Write an essay in which you describe how death—and the grieving and comforting that accompany it—are treated in your family or community. Describe the events that occur and their value for the grieving family. You might organize your essay in time order, covering a single day or perhaps many days. You could write about events such as a wake, a viewing, a gathering of family and friends, or a service at a church, funeral home, or cemetery. As an alternative, write about ways your family or community celebrates the birth of a baby.

The Urge to Conform
Vincent Ryan Ruggiero

Preview

Have you ever tried *not* to do something all your friends were doing? If so, you may already realize that being a noncomformist can be very difficult. In this selection from *Beyond Feelings: A Guide to Critical Thinking*, Vincent Ryan Ruggiero explains just how dangerous it can be to conform to other people's expectations.

Words to Watch

specified (1): stated
crimp in (3): interference with
prefabricated (6): put together beforehand
endorse (7): support
taboos (9): forbidden practices
wrath (9): anger
ironically (11): in a way opposite to what we expect
generate (11): produce
dismay (11): disappointment
dissenting (11): disagreeing
advocates (12): favors
escalate (13): make more intense
traumatic (15): psychologically disturbing

Conformity is behaving the way others around us do. In many ways conformity is good. A child is conforming when he stays away from the hot stove or looks both ways before crossing the street. An automobile driver is conforming when he obeys traffic signs and signals. So is a hospital worker when he sterilizes the operating room. These cases of conformity make living safer. Conformity can also make daily activities more productive. When the employees of a department store arrive at their work places at the <u>specified</u> time each day, the store can open promptly without inconveniencing its customers. When supermarket stock clerks stock the various items in their designated places, customers can shop more efficiently.

Similarly, in a hundred different ways, from using the "up" escalator to go up, to not parking by a fire hydrant, to using the right door to enter a building and the left to exit, conformity makes life less confusing for ourselves and others. And by conforming to the rules of etiquette, we make it more pleasant.

Without a measure of conformity people would never learn to hold a pencil, let alone write. And more complex skills, like flying a plane or operating a computer, would be impossible to acquire. How much non-conformity, after all, does the job of driving a car permit? Can we drive facing sideways or to the rear? Can we accelerate with our left hand and blow the horn with our right foot? Certainly not without some frustration. Yet these limitations are hardly cause for complaint. The safety and comfort such conformity brings us far outweigh the <u>crimp in</u> our creativity.

Not Always Beneficial

Unfortunately, conformity does not always work to our advantage. Sometimes going along with others does not so much increase our safety or serve our convenience as it reinforces our dependency on others. There are situations which require careful evaluation and judgment. In such situations, to conform with the views or actions of others out of conviction, after we have thought and decided, is responsible. But to conform *instead* of thinking and deciding is irresponsible.

As human beings, we are social creatures. We must live with others and relate to them. From our earliest moments of consciousness, we learn the importance of getting along with others. Few things are more painful to a child than separation from the group. Parents sending us to our room, teachers keeping us in while friends went out to play—these were hard punishments to bear. And even more difficult was the rejection of the group itself.

As we grow older, the desire to be included does not go away. It merely takes different forms. We still yearn for the recognition, acceptance, and approval of others. And that yearning is intensified by the bombardment of thousands of advertisements and TV commercials. "Join the crowd—buy this." "Don't be left out—everyone who is someone has one." Young teenagers trying to be sophisticated, and middle-aged people trying to be "cool" and "relevant" have in common the urge to fit some prefabricated image. Conformity promises them *belonging*.

External Pressure

In addition to the urge to conform which we generate ourselves, there is the external pressure of the various formal and informal groups we belong to, the pressure to endorse their ideas and attitudes and to imitate their actions. Thus our urge to conform receives continuing, even daily reinforcement. To be sure, the intensity of the reinforcement, like the strength of the urge and the ability and inclination to withstand it, differs widely among individuals. Yet some pressure is present for everyone. And in one way or another, to some extent, everyone yields to it.

It is possible that a new member of a temperance group might object to the group's rigid insistence that all drinking of alcoholic beverages is wrong. He might even speak out, reminding them that occasional, moderate drinking is not harmful, that even the Bible speaks approvingly of it. But the group may quickly let him know that such ideas are unwelcome in their presence. Every time he forgets this, he will be made to feel uncomfortable. In time, if he values their fellowship, he will refrain from expressing that point of view. He may even refrain from *thinking* it.

This kind of pressure, whether spoken or unspoken, can be generated by any group, regardless of how liberal or conservative, formal or casual it may be. Friday night poker clubs. Churches. Political parties. Committees. Fraternities. Unions. The teenage gang that steals automobile accessories may seem to have no taboos. But let one uneasy member remark that he is beginning to feel guilty about his crimes, and their wrath will descend on him.

Similarly, in high school and college, the crowd a student travels with has certain (usually unstated) expectations for its members. If they drink or smoke, they will often make the member who does not do so feel that he doesn't fully belong. If a member does not share their views on sex, drugs, studying, cheating, or any other subject of importance to them, they will communicate their displeasure. The *way* they communicate, of course, may be more or less direct. They may tell him he'd better conform "or else." They may launch a teasing campaign against him. Or they may be even more subtle and leave him out of their activities for a few days until he asks what is wrong or decides for himself and resolves to behave more like them.

Ironically, even groups pledged to fight conformity can generate strong pressure to conform. As many young people in the 1960s learned to their dismay, many "hippie" communes were as intolerant to dissenting ideas, values, styles of dress and living as the "straight" society they rebelled against.

The urge to conform on occasion clashes with the tendency to resist change. If the group we are in advocates an idea or action that is new and strange to us, we can be torn between seeking their acceptance and maintaining the security of familiar ideas and behavior. In such cases, the way we turn will depend on which tendency is stronger in us or which value we are more committed to. More often, however, the two tendencies do not conflict but reinforce each other. For we tend to associate with those whose attitudes and actions are similar to our own.

"Groupthink"

The urge to conform can cripple thought. Yale psychologist Irving J. Janis intensively analyzed several important actions by U.S. government leaders which later were shown to be foolish. The actions were F. D. Roosevelt's failure to be ready for the Japanese attack on Pearl Harbor, H. S. Truman's decision to invade North Korea, J. F. Kennedy's plan to invade Cuba, and L. B. Johnson's decision to escalate the Vietnam war. In each case he found that the people who made the decision exhibited a strong desire to concur in the group decision. Janis named this conformist tendency "groupthink."

More specifically, Janis identified a number of major defects in decision-making that could be attributed to this conformity. The groups did not survey the range of choices, but focused on a few. When they discovered that their initial decisions had certain drawbacks, they failed to reconsider those decisions. They almost never tested their own thinking for weaknesses. They never tried to obtain the judgments of experts. They expressed interest only in those views that reinforced the positions they preferred, and they spent little time considering the obstacles that would hinder the success of their plans. In each of the cases Janis studied, these defects in thinking cost untold human suffering.

The harm caused by the urge to conform in other areas is perhaps less dramatic, but no less real. Two examples will suggest the extent of that harm. For the past two or three decades many educational psychologists have argued that failure in school is traumatic and students should be passed from grade to grade even if they have not mastered the required knowledge and skills. Many grade and high schools have operated on this principle. The few psychologists and teachers who disputed it were classified as unprogressive. Yet now it is being recognized that the struggle to acquire basic reading, writing, and arithmetic skills is much more traumatic at age eighteen than at age eight.

In the 1960s "speed reading" became very fashionable. Even the President of the United States (J. F. Kennedy), it was revealed, had taken a speed reading course and become more efficient as a result. People began timing themselves and comparing their rates of speed. Speed reading schools multiplied. Reading experts agreed that a slow reader was a poor reader. It took approximately ten years for the realization to develop that slow reading is not necessarily a curse. In 1973 *Reader's Digest* ran an article that would have been scoffed at in 1963—"The Special Joys of Super-Slow Reading."

As was noted at the beginning of the article, some conformity is desirable. But it is foolish to follow the urge to conform blindly. The wise person is *selective* in his conformity. He tries to control his reactions and resist the unreasonable pressures of the group. In important matters he does his own thinking and is willing to risk disagreement with others.

First Impressions

Freewrite for ten minutes on one of the following.

1. Did you enjoy reading this selection? Why or why not?
2. Have you ever gone along with the crowd and later wished you hadn't? If so, what happened?
3. Have you ever joined a group? If so, did you feel pressure to conform?

Vocabulary Check

Circle the letter of the word or phrase that best completes each of the following four sentences.

1. The word *designated* in "When supermarket stock clerks stock the various items in their designated places, customers can shop more efficiently" (paragraph 1) means
    a. wrong.
    b. high.
    c. hidden.
    d. assigned.
2. The word *temperance* in "a new member of a temperance group might object to the group's rigid insistence that all drinking of alcoholic beverages is wrong" (paragraph 8) means
    a. opposed to child abuse.
    b. opposed to abortion.
    c. opposed to liquor.
    d. opposed to drug abuse.
3. The words *refrain from* in "But the group may quickly let him know that such ideas are unwelcome. . . . In time, if he values their fellowship, he will refrain from expressing that point of view" (paragraph 8) mean
    a. begin.
    b. insist on.
    c. avoid.
    d. prefer.

4. The words *concur in* in "the people who made the decision exhibited a strong desire to concur in the group decision. Janis named this conformist tendency 'groupthink'" (paragraph 13) mean
   a. disgrace.
   b. drop out of.
   c. argue with.
   d. agree with.

Circle the letter of the answer that best completes each of the following four items. Each sentence uses a word (or form of a word) from "Words to Watch."

5. Both candidates *advocate* tax increases,
   a. so higher taxes are likely.
   b. so we can probably count on a tax cut.
6. Because our new home was *prefabricated*,
   a. it took an especially long time to build.
   b. it took only two weeks to complete.
7. Due to *escalating* expenses the restaurant
   a. made a big profit.
   b. went out of business.
8. When I came back from vacation, I found, to my *dismay*, that I had
   a. received a big check from my parents.
   b. left the water running and flooded the whole house.

Reading Check

Central Point and Main Ideas

1. Which sentence best expresses the central point of the selection?
   a. The urge to conform helps us live safer, happier lives.
   b. We need to think carefully before deciding to conform.
   c. We must never conform.
   d. We should not belong to groups.
2. Which sentence best expresses the main idea of paragraph 5?
   a. Humans naturally want to belong to groups.
   b. Getting along with others is important.
   c. Parents shouldn't send their children to their rooms.
   d. We might be better off if we didn't have to depend on others.
3. Which sentence best expresses the main idea of paragraph 14?
   a. Conformity always leads to bad judgment.
   b. To avoid poor decisions, people should consult experts.
   c. Conformity can harm decision-making.
   d. Conformists are not willing to reconsider their decisions.

Key Supporting Details

4. According to the author, conformity
   a. helps us learn both basic and complicated skills.
   b. helped end the war in Vietnam.
   c. makes us better thinkers.
   d. keeps people from joining groups.

164 UNDERSTANDING OURSELVES

5. _____ TRUE OR FALSE? In the 1960's, hippie communes did not encourage their members to disagree with the commune rules.

Inferences

6. The author implies that conformity is
   a. likely to lead to poor decisions.
   b. unimportant when driving a car.
   c. unnatural.
   d. rare among government leaders.

7. _____ TRUE OR FALSE? The author implies that it takes will power not to conform.

8. In paragraph 15, the author implies that promoting students who are not ready for the next grade is
   a. better than failing them.
   b. harmful to students.
   c. good only for older students.
   d. becoming more common.

The Writer's Craft

9. The first sentence of this selection
   a. makes a comparison.
   b. tells a story.
   c. gives a definition.
   d. quotes an expert.

10. The author concludes his essay by
    a. asking a thought-provoking question.
    b. making a prediction.
    c. telling a personal story.
    d. stating the central point.

Outlining Activity

Complete the following outline of "The Urge to Conform" by filling in the missing items where they belong. Use the headings in the article as a guide, but put the main ideas in your own words.

Central point: Because conforming is not always beneficial, we should think carefully before following the urge to conform.

A. Introduction: Conformity can make life easier and safer.

B. _____

C. _____
   _____

D. _____
   _____

E. Conclusion

Discussion Questions

1. Have you ever felt pressure to conform (or put pressure on someone else to conform) to a certain kind of thinking or behavior? If so, what form did the pressure take? Did it work?
2. Do you think there is less pressure to conform in college than in high school? Why or why not?
3. Do you think the decisions made by groups are usually better or worse than those made by individuals? Why or why not?
4. In his conclusion, Ruggiero emphasizes the need for a person to think for himself or herself "in important matters." Which are the "important matters" for you—the areas in which you want to make up your own mind?

Paragraph Assignments

1. In the 1980's, a popular anti-drug campaign used the slogan, "Just Say 'No.'" Often, saying "no" isn't so easy, but it may be necessary. Think of a situation in which you would want to say "no" to pressure. You might choose a topic such as saying "no" to drugs or cheating, or refusing to let someone such as a salesperson take advantage of you. Then write a paragraph explaining exactly how you would go about refusing to conform to that pressure. You could begin your paper with a topic sentence similar to "If I were being pressured to _____, I would have several ways of saying 'no.'"

2. In paragraph 16, Ruggiero refers to a *Reader's Digest* article titled "The Special Joys of Super-Slow Reading." Write a paragraph about the joys of another kind of nonconformist experience. You could write about a topic such as the following:
   - walking instead of driving
   - sleeping late instead of getting up early and accomplishing things
   - wearing unfashionable clothes
   - staying home to care for your children instead of working outside of the home (whether you're a woman or a man)
   - owning an unusual pet

Your central point might be that the activity is not what most people would do, but it should be tried because it has rewards they might never guess.

Essay Assignments

1. Ruggiero's discussion of "groupthink" suggests that the more choices we think we have, the better our decisions can be. All of us probably have more options than we realize, but the pressure to conform keeps us from seeing them. Write an essay on one or more decisions you made that were affected by the pressure to conform. Your central point and topic sentences for this essay might be similar to the following:

   Central point: I made three poor decisions because I was overly influenced by the urge to conform.

   I used to skip my two o'clock class because my friends did, but later I regretted it.
   The car my friends urged me to buy turned out to be a lemon.
   At first I chose the major other people said I should instead of considering my own talents and goals.

2. Ruggiero writes in paragraph 6: "As we grow older, the desire to be included does not go away. It merely takes different forms. We still yearn for the recognition, acceptance, and approval of others." Think of situations that show adults' desire for approval, and write an essay about one or more of them. Here are some situations you may write about or that may suggest some other ideas:

   - wanting attention at parties or family gatherings
   - trying to impress bosses or teachers
   - wanting to make a good impression as a new member of an organization
   - wishing children would succeed in ways their parents' friends will notice and even envy
   - trying to impress others with one's belongings

"Learning" to Give Up
Albert Rosenfeld

Preview

"A winner never quits," the saying goes, "and a quitter never wins." Still, quitting may sometimes be very tempting. If it's Friday, you have a ten-page research paper due on Monday, and you haven't even gone to the library yet, you might say to yourself, "Why bother? There's no way I can ever finish. Anyway, I never do well in English." Such thinking, according to the author of the following article from the *Saturday Review*, can have consequences that stretch far beyond the classroom.

Words to Watch

intuitive (1): understood without thinking
valiantly (3): bravely
quiescent (3): motionless
render (6): make
seminal (6): original and influential
alleviation (9): relief
interim (12): meantime
preordained (12): decided in advance
ascribe (14): credit
paradoxical (14): apparently contradictory
inadvertently (14): unintentionally
a priori (15): without testing
validation (18): proof
perseverance (18): not giving up

We all have an intuitive knowledge—supported by personal experience and common sense, reinforced by religious beliefs and folk wisdom—that our attitudes toward life are of critical importance to our enjoyment of it. Whether we overcome our problems or not (or in some crisis situations, whether we even survive or not) may depend on whether or not we have hope, whether we give up or keep on trying.

Over the past few decades, biologists and psychologists have been carrying out some fascinating research that reconfirms how powerfully our mental outlook can affect the outcome of our life situations.

You can, for example, do a simple experiment (as Dr. Curt Richter of Johns Hopkins has done repeatedly) with two rats: hold one rat in your hand firmly so that no matter how <u>valiantly</u> he struggles, he cannot escape. He will finally give up. Now throw that <u>quiescent</u> rat into a tank of warm water. He will sink, not swim. He has "learned" that there is nothing he can do, that there is no point in struggling. Now throw another rat into the water—one that doesn't "know" that his situation is hopeless and that he is therefore helpless. This rat will swim to safety.

Another experiment (done by Dr. Martin E. P. Seligman of the University of Pennsylvania), this time with dogs: suspend a dog in a hammock into which he fits so snugly that he cannot get loose. Give him electric shocks. He will struggle for a while, then just lie there and submit. Later, take the same dog and put him down on one side of a grid that is only half electrified. Though he is perfectly free to get up and move to the unelectrified side, he will sit where he is, enduring the shock, resigned to his fate. Put another dog down in the same spot—a dog that hasn't been taught to be helpless—and he'll move around until he finds an area that doesn't shock him.

Okay. Fine for rats and dogs. But what about people?

Seligman has been one of the pioneering investigators of the ways in which people's perceptions of themselves as being helpless can in fact <u>render</u> them helpless. His <u>seminal</u> book, *Helplessness: On Depression, Development, and Death*, has influenced many other psychologists to pursue this fruitful area of research. Here is a sample Seligman experiment:

Take two groups of college students and put them in rooms where they are blasted with noise turned up to almost intolerable levels. In one room there is a button that turns off the noise. The students quickly notice it, push it, and are rewarded with blissful silence. In the other room, however, there is no turn-off button. The students look for one, find nothing, and finally give up. There is no way to escape the noise (except to leave the room before a previously agreed-upon time period has elapsed), so they simply endure.

Later, the same two groups are put in two other rooms. This time, *both* rooms contain a switch-off mechanism—though not a simple button this time and not as easy to find. Nevertheless, the group that found the button the first time succeeds in finding the "off" switch the second time, too. But the second group, already schooled in the hopelessness of their circumstances, doesn't even search. Its members just sit it out again.

There is an obvious parallel here. In each of the three cases—rats, dogs, and students—the situation had changed decisively, but because their efforts for <u>alleviation</u> didn't work in the first instance, the "helpless" subjects didn't even try the second time.

Yes, you may say, but the students knew that at a given point the experiment would be over and the noise would stop. Otherwise they would have been more highly motivated to keep on looking. Besides, in the first instance, no matter how motivated they may have been, no matter how hard they may have tried, there simply was no way to turn off the noise. Their efforts would have been futile. Aren't many life situations like that—no matter how hard you try, you're doomed to lose?

True enough. In at least one of Richter's rat experiments, for example, he wanted to know how long a rat would keep swimming to try to save itself. The rat swam for 50 hours before it drowned. Were some other rat intelligent and articulate, it might observe this and say: See, what was the point? All that effort for nothing. Wasn't that a foolish rat, to try so hard?

No one suggests there is a guarantee that you'll win if you try. But most of the rats in these experiments did, after all, swim to safety. And even in this one instance, the experimenter might have changed his mind in the <u>interim</u> or been influenced by some outside event to stop the experiment. In most human life situations, the outcome is not rigidly <u>preordained</u>. Many studies in clinical medicine, psychology, and anthropology indicate that seriously ill patients who have hope are more likely to survive than those who don't, that those who are highly motivated tend to last longer—and are happier in the knowledge that they are putting up a fight.

Some population groups are more susceptible to feelings of helplessness than are others; the elderly, for instance; and, as one might suspect, blacks; and women of any color.

In a series of classroom experiments, Dr. Carol Dweck of the University of Illinois found that when girls fail in school, they tend to blame the failure on their inability to master the subject matter. But boys <u>ascribe</u> failure to not trying hard enough. Because girls are considered to be neater, better-behaved, and harder-working, teachers assume that they are already doing the best they can. Because boys are considered to be sloppier and less diligent by nature, teachers tend to tell them, "You can do better. You're just not trying hard enough." The boys believe it.

They do try harder, and do better. Thus, for paradoxical reasons, girls are inadvertently programmed to feel more helpless about improving their situations.

Consider another series of classroom experiments being carried out by Dr. Rita Smith, a former student of Seligman's who is now in the African studies program at Temple University in Philadelphia. She has been comparing the helplessness quotients of black and white children. Though the research is incomplete and the results not yet published, it is already quite apparent to Smith that black children, especially those from poor families, give up much more easily than do white children of similar economic status. If you give the two groups a problem that has no solution (as in the case of Seligman's college students in the room with no turn-off button), the black pupils not only quit trying sooner, but when given a solvable problem next, they are more likely to be convinced a priori that it can't be done—at least not by them. The white kids tend to stay with the problem longer, and they don't assume they can't solve one problem because they failed to solve the other.

Smith attributes these results to the *experience* of black children in a world that does not respond very reliably to their attempts to exercise more control over their lives. The giving-up attitude becomes even more pronounced in the tenth grade than it was in the second grade (the two age groups Smith has been working with). By then, the kids have had eight more years of experience to reconfirm the apparent uselessness of trying.

Whether you look at rats, dogs, or people, it's now abundantly clear that those who try harder do better. Intelligent organisms, says Seligman, automatically know how to help themselves: they keep trying; they have hope. Nor does this healthy tendency have to be learned. In fact, it is so built-in, says Seligman, that even special training doesn't enhance it. But *helplessness*, he is convinced, *must be taught*. Most of us, to one extent or another, are guilty of teaching others helplessness and of permitting ourselves to learn it.

Science has many uses. Experiments such as those described may not provide us with any technological breakthroughs. They do not "conquer" any diseases. But they do give us scientific validation of, and therefore greater confidence in, the value of traditional virtues such as perseverance and hope—which, in these times, is no small service.

Thus through research are our homely truisms doubly confirmed: hope is healthier than despair, perseverance is more sensible than giving up, and helplessness can be self-imposed and therefore self-defeating. The same can be true even in the affairs of nations. One wonders how guilty of defeatism we all, including our statesmen, may be, when we keep saying, "There always have been wars, and there always will be wars; people are no damned good, and you can't change human nature," and so on. Whatever the case in point, the fact that "it didn't work last time" has nothing to do with next time. Next time we may swim to safety. Next time we may find a spot on the grid that doesn't give us a shock. Next time the room may have a turn-off switch.

First Impressions

Freewrite for ten minutes on one of the following.

1. Did you enjoy reading this selection? Why or why not?
2. If you were in one of the experiments described in Rosenfeld's essay, would you have tried to escape—or given up? Why?
3. Is there any situation in your life right now that seems hopeless to you? How close are you to giving up?

Vocabulary Check

Circle the letter of the word or phrase that best completes each of the following four sentences.

1. The word *intolerable* in "they are blasted with noise turned up to almost intolerable levels" (paragraph 7) means
   a. beautiful.   c. cheap.
   b. unbearable.   d. soothing.
2. The word *elapsed* in "The students . . . finally give up. There is no way to escape the noise (except to leave the room before a previously agreed-upon time period has elapsed)" (paragraph 7) means
   a. changed.   c. continued.
   b. lengthened.   d. ended.
3. The word *futile* in "no matter how hard they may have tried, there simply *was* no way to turn off the noise. Their efforts would have been futile" (paragraph 10) means
   a. surprising.   c. appreciated.
   b. rewarded.   d. useless.
4. The word *diligent* in "Because boys are considered to be sloppier and less diligent by nature, teachers tend to tell them, 'You can do better. You're just not trying hard enough'" (paragraph 14) means
   a. lazy.   c. cute.
   b. hard-working.   d. hot-tempered.

Insert four of the following words (or forms of words) from "Words to Watch" where they belong in the sentences below.

alleviate   inadvertently   paradoxical   quiescent   valiant

5. Felice _____ stepped on her date's foot when they started to dance.

6. Samantha made a (an) _____ struggle to continue attending school during her illness.

7. Both loving and hating someone at the same time is _____.

8. With some illnesses, the most doctors can hope for is to _____ the symptoms, not bring about a cure.

Reading Check

Central Point and Main Ideas

1. Which sentence best expresses the central point of the selection?
    a. You can't change human nature.
    b. Research shows that helplessness is learned and can be harmful.
    c. Rats, dogs, and students are similar in the ways they solve problems.
    d. Some people are more motivated than others.
2. Which sentence best expresses the main idea of paragraph 12?
    a. Most of the rats in the experiments swam to safety.
    b. People who have hope and who try are more likely to succeed than those who don't.
    c. Seriously ill patients can't be blamed for giving up.
    d. The outcomes of most situations have been decided in advance.
3. Which sentence best expresses the main idea of paragraph 14?
    a. Dr. Carol Dweck conducted a series of classroom experiments.
    b. Most teachers think girls work harder than boys.
    c. Boys are considered to be sloppier than girls.
    d. Girls are taught to feel more helpless than boys.

Key Supporting Details

4. _____ TRUE OR FALSE? In one of Richter's experiments, a rat that swam for 50 hours finally drowned.
5. According to paragraph 17, the desire to keep trying is
    a. taught.
    b. natural.
    c. unusual.
    d. useless.

Inferences

6. The implied message of this article is that
    a. trying hard guarantees success.
    b. if you don't succeed, you should try again.
    c. scientists conduct too many experiments.
    d. sometimes giving up is the right thing to do.

7. _____ TRUE OR FALSE? We can conclude from the article that people respond to apparently hopeless situations in much the same way animals do.

The Writer's Craft

8. To support his central point, Rosenfeld relies heavily on
   a. scientific research.
   b. statistics.
   c. history.
   d. his own experiences.
9. The purpose of paragraph 5 is to
   a. signal a shift to a new main idea.
   b. shock readers.
   c. provide specific support for the central point.
   d. establish a formal tone.
10. In the last three lines of this selection, Rosenfeld emphasizes his central point by referring to
    a. the experiments he has already described.
    b. world events.
    c. college sports.
    d. commonly accepted truths.

Outlining Activity

Complete the following outline of " 'Learning' to Give Up" by filling in the missing items where they belong.

Central point: Research has shown that repeated failure and lack of encouragement make both animals and humans stop trying.

A. Dr. Curt Richter's experiment with rats in a tank of water
B. Dr. Martin Seligman's experiment with dogs and a partly electrified grid

C. _____

D. Dr. Richter's second experiment with rats

E. _____
F. Dr. Rita Smith's classroom experiments comparing helplessness in black and white children

Discussion Questions

1. What does Rosenfeld mean by "helplessness"? What examples of such helplessness have you seen in yourself and others?
2. The author claims that such groups as blacks, women, and the elderly often feel helpless (paragraph 13). What experiences do you think might teach them helplessness? What other groups of people might have the same feelings? Why?

3. Some people think that experimenting on animals is morally wrong, even when the result improves people's lives. How do you feel about the experiments on rats and dogs described in this selection?
4. This selection explains that helplessness is learned, but it doesn't discuss whether or not it can be unlearned. What are some ways people might learn to have more hope and therefore try harder?

Paragraph Assignments

1. Imagine that you are a college counselor. A student tells you he is about to drop out because of a serious problem, such as an overwhelming workload, homesickness, or bad grades. Write a paragraph explaining how you would help this student realize that it's not necessary to quit. Your topic sentence might be, "A student who recently came to my office was thinking of dropping out because_____, and I tried to help him see there was more help than he realized."

2. In paragraph 1, Rosenfeld writes, "We all have an intuitive knowledge . . . that our attitudes toward life are of critical importance to our enjoyment of it." Below is a list of quotations that express different attitudes to life.

   - When the going gets tough, the tough get going.
   - When the going gets tough, the tough go shopping.
   - Life is what happens while you're making other plans.
   - The new Golden Rule: those who have the gold make the rules.
   - Lord, grant me the courage to change the things I must change, the patience to bear what I must bear, and the wisdom to know the difference.
   - Life is much too important to be taken seriously.
   - If I don't care about myself, who will? And if I care only about myself, who am I?

   Choose the quotation you agree with most and use it as the topic sentence of a serious or humorous paragraph. Explain how having this attitude affects your approach to problems and new experiences.

Essay Assignments

1. Write an essay about yourself, someone you know, or someone you've heard about who has refused to give up. You might begin with an introductory paragraph that states what the problem was. Next describe the person's first, unsuccessful attempts to solve the problem; then describe the solution that finally worked. Finally, tell what the person's life was like after the problem was solved. Your thesis statement might be something like the following:

Although it was a struggle, my daughter Jessica finally learned how to swim.

Coping with caring for my elderly grandmother became easier once I found out where to go for help.

2. Rosenfeld tells us that it's better to be a fighter than a quitter. However, there are times when it makes more sense to quit than fight. Write about a time when you—or someone you know—decided, for a good reason, to give up. For example, you could write about dropping out of an activity or social group, changing a major, breaking off a relationship, or quitting a job. Explain what you gave up and why.

Don't Let Stereotypes Warp Your Judgments

Robert L. Heilbroner

Preview

Do you think it's possible to judge people by their names, looks, or nationalities? If your answer is "yes," you probably rely on stereotypes when judging others. Most of us, at one time or another, do look at the world through the prejudgments of stereotypes. Is there anything wrong with this kind of thinking? If so, what's the alternative? In this article, economist Robert L. Heilbroner suggests answers to these questions.

Words to Watch

delve (4): search deeply
yokels (8): awkward or unsophisticated country people
dinned (8): repeated forcefully
stock (8): typical
perpetuated (8): caused to continue
synchronized (9): occurring at the same time
semantics (11): the study of word meanings
preconceptions (11): judgments made ahead of time
impoverish (12): make poor
reactionaries (12): opponents of change
inimitable (12): not able to be copied
lapse (15): end
chastening (18): humbling
edifice (18): structure

Is a girl called Gloria apt to be better-looking than one called Bertha? Are criminals more likely to be dark than blond? Can you tell a good deal about someone's personality from hearing his voice briefly over the phone? Can a person's nationality be pretty accurately guessed from his photograph? Does the fact that someone wears glasses imply that he is intelligent?

The answer to all these questions is obviously, "No."

Yet from all the evidence at hand, most of us believe these things. Ask any college boy if he'd rather take his chances with a Gloria or a Bertha, or ask a college girl if she'd rather blind-date a Richard or a Cuthbert. In fact, you don't have to ask: college students in questionnaires have revealed that names conjure up the same images in their minds as they do in yours—and for as little reason.

Look into the favorite suspects of persons who report "suspicious characters" and you will find a large percentage of them to be "swarthy" or "dark and foreign-looking"—despite the testimony of criminologists that criminals do not tend to be dark, foreign or "wild-eyed." Delve into the main asset of a telephone stock swindler and you will find it to be a marvelously confidence-inspiring telephone "personality." And whereas we all think we know what an Italian or a Swede looks like, it is the sad fact that when a group of Nebraska students sought to match faces and nationalities of 15 European countries, they were scored wrong in 93 percent of their identifications. Finally, for all the fact that horn-rimmed glasses have now become the standard televison sign of an "intellectual," optometrists know that the main thing that distinguishes people with glasses is just bad eyes.

Stereotypes are a kind of gossip about the world, a gossip that makes us prejudge people before we ever lay eyes on them. Hence it is not surprising that stereotypes have something to do with the dark world of prejudice. Explore most prejudices (note that the word means prejudgment) and you will find a cruel stereotype at the core of each one.

For it is the extraordinary fact that once we have typecast the world, we tend to see people in terms of our standardized pictures. In another demonstration of the power of stereotypes to affect our vision, a number of Columbia and Barnard students were shown 30 photographs of pretty but unidentified girls, and asked to rate each in terms of "general liking," "intelligence," "beauty" and so on. Two months later, the same group were shown the same photographs, this time with fictitious Irish, Italian, Jewish and "American" names attached to the pictures. Right away the ratings changed. Faces which were now seen as representing a national group went down in looks and still farther down in likability, while the "American" girls suddenly looked decidedly prettier and nicer.

Why is it that we stereotype the world in such irrational and harmful fashion? In part, we begin to type-cast people in our childhood years. Early in life, as every parent whose child has watched a TV Western knows, we learn to spot the Good Guys from the Bad Guys. Some years ago, a social psychologist showed very clearly how powerful these stereotypes of childhood vision are. He secretly asked the most popular youngsters in an elementary school to make errors in their morning gym exercises. Afterwards, he asked the class if anyone had noticed any mistakes during gym period. Oh, yes, said the children. But it was the *unpopular* members of the class—the "bad guys"—they remembered as being out of step.

We not only grow up with standardized pictures forming inside of us, but as grown-ups we are constantly having them thrust upon us. Some of them, like the half-joking, half-serious stereotypes of mothers-in-law, or country yokels, or psychiatrists, are dinned into us by the stock jokes we hear and repeat. In fact, without such stereotypes, there would be a lot fewer jokes. Still other stereotypes are perpetuated by the advertisements we read, the movies we see, the books we read.

And finally, we tend to stereotype because it helps us make sense out of a highly confusing world, a world which William James once described as "one great, blooming, buzzing confusion." It is a curious fact that if we don't know what we're looking at, we are often quite literally unable to see what we're looking at. People who recover their sight after a lifetime of blindness actually cannot at first tell a triangle from a square. A visitor to a factory sees only noisy chaos where the superintendent sees a perfectly synchronized flow of work. As Walter Lippmann has said, "For the most part we do not first see, and then define; we define first, and then we see."

Stereotypes are one way in which we "define" the world in order to see it. They classify the infinite variety of human beings into a convenient handful of "types" towards whom we learn to act in stereotyped fashion. Life would be a wearing process if we had to start from scratch with each and every human contact. Stereotypes economize on our mental effort by covering up the blooming, buzzing confusion with big recognizable cut-outs. They save us the "trouble" of finding out what the world is like—they give it its accustomed look.

Thus the trouble is that stereotypes make us mentally lazy. As S. I. Hayakawa, the authority on semantics, has written: "The danger of stereotypes lies not in their existence, but in the fact that they become for all people some of the time, and for some people all the time, *substitutes for observation*." Worse yet, stereotypes get in the way of our judgment, even when we do observe the world. Someone who has formed rigid preconceptions of all Latins as "excitable," or all teenagers as "wild," doesn't alter his point of view when he meets a calm and deliberate Genoese, or a serious-minded high school student. He brushes them aside as "exceptions that prove the rule." And, of course, if he meets someone true to type, he stands triumphantly vindicated. "They're all like that," he proclaims, having encountered an excited Latin, an ill-behaved adolescent.

Hence, quite aside from the injustice which stereotypes do to others, they <u>impoverish</u> ourselves. A person who lumps the world into simple categories, who type-casts all labor leaders as "racketeers," all businessmen as "<u>reactionaries</u>," all Harvard men as "snobs," and all Frenchmen as "sexy," is in danger of becoming a stereotype himself. He loses his capacity to be himself—which is to say, to see the world in his own absolutely unique, <u>inimitable</u> and independent fashion.

Instead, he votes for the man who fits his standardized picture of what a candidate "should" look like or sound like, buys the goods that someone in his "situation" in life "should" own, lives the life that others define for him. The mark of the stereotype person is that he never surprises us, that we do indeed have him "typed." And no one fits this strait-jacket so perfectly as someone whose opinions about *other people* are fixed and inflexible.

Impoverishing as they are, stereotypes are not easy to get rid of. The world we type-cast may be no better than a Grade B movie, but at least we know what to expect of our stock characters. When we let them act for themselves in the strangely unpredictable way that people do act, who knows but that many of our fondest convictions will be proved wrong?

Nor do we suddenly drop our standardized pictures for a blinding vision of the Truth. Sharp swings of ideas about people often just substitute one stereotype for another. The true process of change is a slow one that adds bits and pieces of reality to the pictures in our heads, until gradually they take on some of the blurriness of life itself. Little by little, we learn not that Jews and Negroes and Catholics and Puerto Ricans are "just like everybody else"—for that, too, is a stereotype—but that each and every one of them is unique, special, different and individual. Often we do not even know that we have let a stereotype <u>lapse</u> until we hear someone saying, "All so-and-so's are like such-and-such," and we hear ourselves saying, "Well—maybe."

Can we speed the process along? Of course we can.

First, we can become *aware* of the standardized pictures in our heads, in other people's heads, in the world around us.

Second, we can become suspicious of all judgments that we allow exceptions to "prove." There is no more <u>chastening</u> thought than that in the vast intellectual adventure of science, it takes but one tiny exception to topple a whole <u>edifice</u> of ideas.

Third, we can learn to be chary of generalizations about people. As

F. Scott Fitzgerald once wrote: "Begin with an individual, and before you know it you have created a type; begin with a type, and you find you have created—nothing."

Most of the time, when we type-cast the world, we are not in fact generalizing about people at all. We are only revealing the embarrassing facts about the pictures that hang in the gallery of stereotypes in our own heads.

First Impressions

Freewrite for ten minutes on one of the following.

1. Did you enjoy reading this selection? Why or why not?
2. What do you think of when you picture each of the following?

   - someone named Mildred
   - a pro basketball player
   - a high school English teacher
   - a used car salesman
   - someone named Oswald
   - a librarian
   - a nurse
   - a detective

   Write about as many of these as you can in the time provided. Tell what they look like and how they speak and act. When you finish, look at what you have written. Does any of it contain the kind of stereotyped thinking Heilbroner describes in his article?
3. Have you ever been the victim of stereotyping? If so, explain what happened and how it felt. Did you do anything about it?

Vocabulary Check

Circle the letter of the word or phrase that best completes each of the following four sentences.

1. The words *conjure up* in "college students in questionnaires have revealed that names conjure up the same images in their minds as they do in yours" (paragraph 3) mean
   a. destroy.   c. shrink.
   b. produce.   d. reward.
2. The word *typecast* in "once we have typecast the world, we tend to see people in terms of our standardized pictures" (paragraph 6) means
   a. left.   c. forgiven.
   b. grown tired of.   d. judged ahead of time.
3. The word *vindicated* in "He brushes them [a calm Genoese or a serious-minded high school student] aside as 'exceptions that prove the rule.' And of course, if he meets someone true to type, he stands triumphantly vindicated" (paragraph 11) means
   a. amazed.   c. silly.
   b. world famous.   d. proved right.

4. The words *chary of* in "Can we speed the process [of getting rid of stereotypes] along? Of course we can. . . . we can learn to be chary of generalizations about people" (paragraphs 16 and 19) mean
   a. encouraging about.   c. optimistic about.
   b. cautious about.   d. proud of.

Circle the letter of the answer that best completes each of the following four items. Each sentence uses a word (or form of a word) from "Words to Watch."

5. The researchers *delved* into the question of family violence
   a. for a few minutes.
   b. for months.
6. Since my subscription to *Newsweek* has *lapsed*, I
   a. haven't gotten any copies.
   b. read it every week.
7. The mayor's *stock* response, "We'll form a committee to investigate that," was one we'd
   a. never heard before.
   b. heard over and over.
8. The *reactionaries* on our club's board of directors
   a. are constantly suggesting new activities.
   b. want to go back to the old ways of doing things.

Reading Check

Central Point and Main Ideas

1. Which sentence best expresses the central point of the selection?
   a. Stereotyping harms our thinking, but we can learn to avoid it.
   b. We stereotype in order to make sense of the world.
   c. There are several ways to get rid of stereotyped thinking.
   d. We can learn to stereotype better.
2. Which sentence best expresses the main idea of paragraph 8?
   a. Many jokes are based on stereotypes.
   b. Stereotypes make growing up difficult.
   c. As adults, we are surrounded by stereotypes.
   d. Advertisements, movies, and books use stereotypes.
3. Which sentence best expresses the main idea of paragraph 15?
   a. Minority groups are not "just like everybody else."
   b. We need to stop depending on stereotypes.
   c. Changes in our thinking about people often involve the substitution of one stereotype for another.
   d. Learning not to stereotype is a gradual process.

UNDERSTANDING OURSELVES

Key Supporting Details

4. According to the article, which of the following does *not* encourage stereotyping?
    a. childhood influences
    b. careful observation
    c. advertisements, movies, and books
    d. the urge to make sense of the world

5. _____ TRUE OR FALSE? One study showed that it's easy to guess people's nationalities by their looks.

6. According to the author, stereotyping
    a. is rare.
    b. is often accurate.
    c. makes us mentally lazy.
    d. broadens our view of the world.

Inferences

7. _____ TRUE OR FALSE? The author implies that prejudice is based on stereotypes.

8. From the experiment with Columbia and Barnard students (paragraph 6), we can infer that
    a. names have nothing to do with stereotypes.
    b. college students are good judges of beauty.
    c. the students tended to prefer nationalities different from their own.
    d. the students tended to prefer people who were not members of minority groups.

The Writer's Craft

9. The author begins this selection with a series of questions on familiar stereotypes because
    a. he doesn't know the answers.
    b. he thinks readers won't know the answers.
    c. he wants to show readers that they may be relying on stereotypes.
    d. he wants to show his dislike for foreign-looking people with strange names.

10. The word *thus* in "Thus the trouble is that stereotypes make us mentally lazy" (paragraph 11) signals
    a. a contrast.
    b. an illustration.
    c. an introduction.
    d. a conclusion.

Summarizing Activity

1. Circle the letter of the statement that summarizes the introduction of "Don't Let Stereotypes Warp Your Judgments" (paragraphs 1 through 6).

a. Some people assume that a person with a name like Bertha or Cuthbert is unattractive.
   b. Stereotypes are common but inaccurate.
   c. Even college students think in stereotyped terms.
2. Circle the letter of the statement that summarizes the supporting details in paragraphs 7 through 10.
   a. We begin to stereotype in childhood.
   b. We stereotype because we grow up with stereotypes, which help us make sense of the world.
   c. Stereotypes will always be part of our lives.
3. Circle the letter of the statement that summarizes the supporting details in paragraphs 11 through 13.
   a. Stereotypes are harmful to us and unjust to others.
   b. Stereotypes help us choose which candidate to vote for.
   c. Stereotypes are sometimes proved correct.
4. Circle the letter of the statement that summarizes the supporting details in paragraphs 14 through 20.
   a. It is impossible to get rid of stereotypes, no matter how hard we try.
   b. Ridding ourselves of stereotypes is easy because they are all around us.
   c. Ridding ourselves of stereotypes is a slow process, but there are ways to speed it up.

Discussion Questions

1. What are some of the stereotypes you have heard or seen in jokes, ads, movies, books, or television shows? Did you think they were stereotypes when you first encountered them?
2. What stereotyped attitudes towards men and women have you come across? Are these stereotypes harmful in any way?
3. What are some good ways to respond to people who reveal prejudiced or stereotyped attitudes?
4. What is the relationship between a stereotype and a prejudice? Do we have to get rid of stereotypes to get rid of prejudice?

Paragraph Assignments

1. Have you ever felt that someone was stereotyping you? Perhaps someone thought he or she knew all about you because of a stereotyped image of your race, nationality, sex, age, appearance, or job. Write a paragraph about what it was like to be stereotyped. Your topic sentence might be similar to this: "I was once the victim of stereotyping because of my _____."
2. Think of a name you would (or would *not*) name your child. Then explain why you would or would not choose this name for your son or daughter. Support your point by discussing what qualities, abilities, or characteristics

you and other people might associate with this name. You might want to mention:

- famous people who have the same name
- how "masculine" or "feminine" the name sounds
- the personal qualities that this name suggests
- what the name really means (for example, *Leo* means "lion")
- the fact that the name has been in your family for generations

Essay Assignments

1. Stereotypes frequently appear in TV programs, movies, and novels. Write an essay in which you show how TV programs, movies, or romance novels stereotype one or more groups of people. For instance, you might examine how single female executives or medical doctors are portrayed in daytime soaps. Or you might show how blacks or people from a particular region such as the South are stereotyped in TV dramas. Your thesis might be similar to one of these:

    In three daytime soaps, medical doctors are stereotyped as being _____.

    Recent science fiction movies contain stereotypes of helpless women, mad scientists, and unfriendly aliens.

2. Write an essay entitled "All _____ Aren't _____," in which you tell how you discovered that all members of a certain group are not what the stereotype says they are. For example, you might write about one or more redheads who turned out to be gentle and patient, not hot-headed or temperamental. Or you might write about a "jock" who is sensitive, likes classical music, or writes poetry. Or perhaps you know an eighty-year-old person who likes rock music. Your essay should tell about two or three incidents (either ones that you observed or ones that you heard or read about) which proved the stereotype wrong.

Social Issues

A Crime of Compassion

Barbara Huttmann

Preview

Should dying patients be kept alive as long as possible? This is the question Barbara Huttmann, a nurse and writer, had to answer. In the following article written for *Newsweek*'s "My Turn" column, she tells the story of Mac, a young man suffering from cancer. The problem she faced every day was, "Should Mac be allowed to die?"

Words to Watch

compassion (title): sympathy
i.v. (6): abbreviation for *intravenous*, given by an injection into a vein
irrigate (7): wash out
craters (7): hollows
feces (7): solid bodily waste
negligence (9): failure to do one's duty
lucid (10): clear-minded
infusing (10): filling
impotence (10): powerlessness
riddled (13): pierced
clutch (15): tight grip
pallor (15): paleness

"Murderer," a man shouted. "God help patients who get you for a nurse."

"What gives you the right to play God?" another one asked.

It was the Phil Donahue show where the guest is a fatted calf and the audience a 200-strong flock of vultures hungering to pick up the bones. I had told them about Mac, one of my favorite cancer patients. "We resuscitated him 52 times in just one month. I refused to resuscitate him again. I simply sat there and held his hand while he died."

There wasn't time to explain that Mac was a young, witty, macho cop who walked into the hospital with 32 pounds of attack equipment, looking as if he could single-handedly protect the whole city, if not the entire state. "Can't get rid of this cough," he said. Otherwise, he felt great.

Before the day was over, tests confirmed that he had lung cancer. And before the year was over, I loved him, his wife, Maura, and their three kids as if they were my own. All the nurses loved him. And we all battled his disease for six months without ever giving death a thought. Six months isn't such a long time in the whole scheme of things, but it was long enough to see him lose his youth, his wit, his macho, his hair, his bowel and bladder control, his sense of taste and smell, and his ability to do the slightest thing for himself. It was long enough to watch Maura's transformation from a young woman into a haggard, beaten old lady.

When Mac had wasted away to a 60-pound skeleton kept alive by liquid food we poured down a tube, i.v. solutions we dripped into his veins, and oxygen we piped to a mask on his face, he begged us: "Mercy . . . for God's sake, please just let me go."

Miracles: The first time he stopped breathing, the nurse pushed the button that calls a "code blue" throughout the hospital and sends a team rushing to resuscitate the patient. Each time he stopped breathing, sometimes two or three times in one day, the code team came again. The doctors and technicians worked their miracles and walked away. The nurses stayed to wipe the saliva that drooled from his mouth, irrigate the big craters of bedsores that covered his hips, suction the lung fluids that threatened to drown him, clean the feces that burned his skin like lye, pour the liquid food down the tube attached to his stomach, put pillows between his knees to ease the bone-on-bone pain, turn him every hour to keep the bedsores from getting worse, and change his gown and linen every two hours to keep him from being soaked in perspiration.

At night I went home and tried to scrub away the smell of decaying flesh that seemed woven into the fabric of my uniform. It was in my hair, the upholstery of my car—there was no washing it away. And every night I prayed that his agonized eyes would never again plead with me to let him die.

Every morning I asked the doctor for a "no code" order. Without that order, we had to resuscitate every patient who stopped breathing. His doctor was one of the several who believe we must extend life as long as we have the means and knowledge to do it. To not do it is to be liable for negligence, at least in the eyes of many people, including some nurses. I thought about what it would be like to stand before a judge, accused of murder, if Mac stopped breathing and I didn't call a code.

And after the 52nd code, when Mac was still lucid enough to beg for death again, and Maura was crumbled in my arms again, and when no amount of pain medication stilled his moaning and agony, I wondered about a spiritual judge. Was all this misery and suffering supposed to be building character or infusing us all with the sense of humility that comes from impotence?

Had we, the whole medical community, become so arrogant that we believed in the illusion of salvation through science? Had we become so self-righteous that we thought meddling in God's work was our duty, our moral imperative, and our legal obligation? Did we really believe that we had the right to force "life" on a suffering man who had begged for the right to die?

Such questions haunted me more than ever early one morning when Maura went home to change her clothes and I was bathing Mac. He had been still for so long, I thought he at last had the blessed relief of coma. Then he opened his eyes and moaned, "Pain . . . no more . . . Barbara . . . do something . . . God, let me go."

Death: The desperation in the eyes and voice riddled me with guilt. "I'll stop," I told him as I injected the pain medication.

I sat on the bed and held Mac's hands in mine. He pressed his bony fingers against my hand and muttered, "Thanks." Then there was the one soft sigh and I felt his hands go cold in mine. "Mac?" I whispered, as I waited for his chest to rise and fall again.

A clutch of panic banded my chest, drew my finger to the code button, urged me to do something, anything . . . but sit there alone with death. I kept one finger on the button, without pressing it, as a waxen pallor slowly transformed his face from person to empty shell. Nothing I've ever done in my 47 years has taken so much effort as it took not to press that code button.

Eventually, when I was as sure as I could be that the code team would fail to bring him back, I entered the legal twilight zone and pushed the button. The team tried. And while they were trying, Maura walked in the room and shrieked, "No . . . don't let them do this to him . . . for God's sake . . . please, no more."

Cradling her in my arms was like cradling myself, Mac, and all those patients and nurses who had been in this place before who do the best they can in a death-denying society.

So a TV audience accused me of murder. Perhaps I am guilty. If a doctor had written a no-code order, which is the only legal alternative, would he have felt any less guilty? Until there is legislation making it a criminal act to code a patient who has requested the right to die, we will all of us risk the same fate as Mac. For whatever reason, we developed the means to prolong life, and now we are forced to use it. We do not have the right to die.

First Impressions

Freewrite for ten minutes on one of the following.

1. Did you enjoy reading this selection? Why or why not?
2. Do you think that Huttmann did the right thing? Why or why not?
3. Whom do you feel sorriest for—Mac, his wife Maura, or Barbara Huttmann? Why?

Vocabulary Check

Circle the letter of the word or phrase that best completes each of the following four sentences.

1. The word *resuscitated* in "We resuscitated him 52 times in just one month. I refused to resuscitate him again. I simply sat there and held his hand while he died" (paragraph 3) means
    a. showed.
    b. gave a bath.
    c. brought back to life.
    d. ignored.
2. The word *confirmed* in "Before the day was over, tests confirmed that he had lung cancer" (paragraph 5) means
    a. asked.
    b. proved.
    c. confused.
    d. passed.
3. The word *haggard* in "Maura's transformation from a young woman into a haggard, beaten old lady" (paragraph 5) means
    a. worn out.
    b. smiling.
    c. singing.
    d. silly.
4. The word *imperative* in "Had we ... thought meddling in God's work was our duty, our moral imperative, and our legal obligation?" (paragraph 11) means
    a. sin.
    b. confusion.
    c. taste.
    d. requirement.

Insert each of the following words (or forms of words) from "Words to Watch" where it belongs in one of the four sentences below.

        clutch   negligence   pallor   riddled

5. The door of the saloon was _____ with bullet holes after the gunfight.
6. Just as I was about to slip off the cliff, I felt the firm _____ of my rescuer's hands.
7. Because of her pale bleached hair, her snowy white gown, and the sickly _____ of her face, Ruth resembled a ghost.

8. Due to Bill and Annie's _____, their children came to school every day without their lunches.

Reading Check

Central Point and Main Ideas

1. Which sentence best expresses the central point of the selection?
   a. Doctors feel that all patients should be kept alive as long as possible.
   b. Hopelessly ill patients should have the right to die when they choose.
   c. In less than a year, Mac died from lung cancer.
   d. Medical science has developed miraculous ways to prolong life.
2. Which sentence best expresses the main idea of paragraph 5?
   a. After hospital tests proved Mac had lung cancer, he gradually lost his ability to taste or smell food.
   b. Huttmann loved Mac, his wife Maura, and their three children.
   c. Cancer can kill people in six months.
   d. In spite of loving care, Mac and Maura suffered greatly in the six months after his cancer was diagnosed.
3. Which sentence best expresses the main idea of paragraph 15?
   a. Huttmann was afraid that Mac would die.
   b. Huttmann forced herself not to push the code button when Mac stopped breathing.
   c. Huttmann did not press the code button because she did not know that Mac had stopped breathing.
   d. Mac's face changed dramatically as he began to die.

Key Supporting Details

4. _____ TRUE OR FALSE? Mac was feeling weak and dizzy when he first came to the hospital.
5. After Mac had been revived more than fifty times, his wife, Maura,
   a. wanted Mac to live as long as possible.
   b. wanted Mac to be allowed to die.
   c. stopped visiting Mac.
   d. disliked Huttmann.

Inferences

6. Judging by paragraph 7, the phrase "code blue" probably means that
   a. the patient is covered by an insurance plan.
   b. the patient has been discharged and may leave the hospital.
   c. all treatment must be stopped because the patient has died.
   d. an emergency team must go to the patient's room at once.
7. _____ TRUE OR FALSE? The author implies that a law should be passed preventing teams from reviving those patients who wish to die.

A CRIME OF COMPASSION

The Writer's Craft

8. Huttmann begins this selection with
   a. a dramatic statement of her point of view.
   b. dramatic statements of her opponents' point of view.
   c. statistics.
   d. a series of questions.
9. The author supports her central point with
   a. statistics.
   b. several stories of dying patients.
   c. one story of a dying patient.
   d. research.
10. Huttmann's purpose in writing this selection was mainly to
    a. inform readers about the techniques used to extend the lives of dying patients.
    b. persuade readers that laws should be passed giving patients the right to die.
    c. entertain readers with a hospital drama.
    d. describe a typical day in a nurse's life.

Summarizing Activity

Complete the following summary of "A Crime of Compassion" by filling in each blank with one or more words.

When Barbara Huttmann appeared on the *Donahue* show, some of the people in the audience called her a (1) _____ because of what had happened to Mac, a young (2) _____. When Mac was admitted to the hospital where Huttmann worked as a nurse, he looked (3) _____, but tests showed that he had (4) _____. Within six months he was being kept alive by tubes, and he had lost the ability to do the slightest thing for himself. He stopped breathing (5) _____ times, and each time, (6) _____ _____.

He begged to be allowed to (7) _____, but his doctor insisted that (8) _____ _____.

Huttmann began to question why Mac should have to suffer so much. One day when Mac stopped breathing again, she refused to call for resuscitation until (9) _____ _____.

192   SOCIAL ISSUES

Huttmann feels cases like Mac's show that (10) _____
_____.

Discussion Questions

1. Huttmann titled her essay "A Crime of Compassion." Do you think Huttmann is guilty of a crime? If so, what crime?
2. Who should decide whether an incurably ill patient should be allowed to die—the patient, the doctor, or someone else? What should happen when patients are too ill to decide for themselves?
3. Judging by Huttmann's article, what are some of the disadvantages of being a nurse? Should nurses have more authority to make decisions about patients, as Huttmann suggests?
4. Some people suggest that the kind of suffering Mac and Maura endured builds character. Do you think suffering ever makes people stronger? If so, how?

Paragraph Assignments

1. Suppose you were a member of a jury trying Huttmann for murder. All the evidence has been given, and now you have to decide whether she is innocent or guilty. Write a paragraph that presents your reasons for either convicting or not convicting Huttmann of murder. Your topic sentence might be something like one of the following:

   I think Barbara Huttmann is guilty of murder for several reasons.
   Finding Barbara Huttmann guilty of murder would be a terrible injustice.

2. Write a paragraph about a time you or someone you know was hospitalized, visited someone else in a hospital, or went to a doctor or an emergency ward. How was the patient treated by physicians, hospital staff, family, and visitors? As Huttmann does, use explanations and descriptions to tell your story.

Essay Assignments

1. Huttmann begins her essay by describing how she was attacked by the audience on the *Donahue* show. Do you think talk shows like *Donahue* do a good job of informing the public about important issues, or are they merely entertaining? Write an essay discussing three issues you learned about through one radio or TV talk show or three talk shows. As an alternative, discuss several aspects of talk shows that you either like or dislike. Use a thesis similar to one of the following:

   I learned about _____, _____ and _____
   on the _____ *Show*.

TV talk shows appeal to people's desire to pry into other people's lives.

I dislike the way _____ attacks his guests, encourages his audience to make fools of themselves, and refuses to discuss issues seriously.

2. Write an essay about a compassionate act that you or someone else performed. Perhaps you treated an injured animal or performed an act of kindness for someone who was lost, hungry, injured, or ill. As an alternative, write about a commitment to helping others made by you or someone you know. Maybe you know a person who works with homeless people or who has volunteered as a fire fighter or member of a rescue squad. Let your readers see through vivid description how you or someone else took the trouble to do something kind.

How About Low-Cost Drugs for Addicts?
Louis Nizer

Preview

Drug addiction is a serious problem that seems to have no easy solution. And it has led to other problems, such as increased street crime and overworked police. Can anything be done? In this article, Louis Nizer, one of America's most brilliant and famous attorneys, offers a startling suggestion.

Words to Watch

nominal (2): very small
apparatus (3): equipment
interdict (3): forbid
stifle (3): hold back
caches (4): hidden supplies
domestic (6): within a country
pittance (6): very small amount
profound (7): far-reaching
exacted (8): demanded
compulsion (9): irresistible force
diminish (9): decrease
salutary (11): helpful
induced (13): caused
demoralization (15): loss of hope
illicit (17): illegal

We are losing the war against drug addiction. Our strategy is wrong. I propose a different approach.

The government should create clinics, manned by psychiatrists, that would provide drugs for <u>nominal</u> charges or even free to addicts under controlled regulations. It would cost the government only 20 cents for a heroin shot, for which the addicts must now pay the mob more than $100, and there are similar price discrepancies in cocaine, crack and other such substances.

Such a service, which would also include the staff support of psychiatrists and doctors, would cost a fraction of what the nation now spends to maintain the land, sea and air apparatus necessary to interdict illegal imports of drugs. There would also be a savings of hundreds of millions of dollars from the elimination of the prosecutorial procedures that stifle our courts and overcrowd our prisons.

We see in our newspapers the triumphant announcements by government agents that they have intercepted hugh caches of cocaine, the street prices of which are in the tens of millions of dollars. Should we be gratified? Will this achievement reduce the number of addicts by one? All it will do is increase the cost to the addict of his illegal supply.

Many addicts who are caught committing a crime admit that they have mugged or stolen as many as six or seven times a day to accumulate the $100 needed for a fix. Since many of them need two or three fixes a day, particularly for crack, one can understand the terror in our streets and homes. It is estimated that there are in New York City alone 200,000 addicts, and this is typical of cities across the nation. Even if we were to assume that only a modest percentage of a city's addicts engage in criminal conduct to obtain the money for the habit, requiring multiple muggings and thefts each day, we could nevertheless account for many of the tens of thousands of crimes each day in New York City alone.

Not long ago, a Justice Department division issued a report stating that more than half the perpetrators of murder and other serious crimes were under the influence of drugs. This symbolizes the new domestic terror in our nation. This is why our citizens are unsafe in broad daylight on the most traveled thoroughfares. This is why typewriters and television sets are stolen from offices and homes and sold for a pittance. This is why parks are closed to the public and why murders are committed. This is why homes need multiple locks, and burglary systems, and why store windows, even in the most fashionable areas, require iron gates.

The benefits of the new strategy to control this terrorism would be immediate and profound.

First, the mob would lose the main source of its income. It could not compete against a free supply for which previously it exacted tribute estimated to be hundreds of millions of dollars, perhaps billions, from hopeless victims.

Second, pushers would be put out of business. There would be no purpose in creating addicts who would be driven by desperate compulsion to steal and kill for the money necessary to maintain their habit. Children would not be enticed. The mob's macabre public-relations program is to tempt children with free drugs in order to create customers for the future. The wave of street crimes in broad daylight would <u>diminish</u> to a trickle. Homes and stores would not have to be fortresses. Our recreational areas could again be used. Neighborhoods would not be scandalized by sordid street centers where addicts gather to obtain their supply from slimy merchants.

Third, police and other law-enforcement authorities, domestic or foreign, would be freed to deal with traditional nondrug crimes.

There are several objections that might be raised against such a <u>salutary</u> solution.

First, it could be argued that by providing free drugs to the addict we would consign him to permanent addiction. The answer is that medical and psychiatric help at the source would be more effective in controlling the addict's descent than the extremely limited remedies available to the victim today. I am not arguing that the new strategy will cure everything. But I do not see many addicts being freed from their bonds under the present system.

In addition, as between the addict's predicament and the safety of our innocent citizens, which deserves our primary concern? Drug-<u>induced</u> crime has become so common that almost every citizen knows someone in his immediate family or among his friends who has been mugged. It is these citizens who should be our chief concern.

Another possible objection is that addicts will cheat the system by obtaining more than the allowable free shot. Without discounting the resourcefulness of the bedeviled addict, it should be possible to have government cards issued that would be punched so as to limit the free supply in accord with medical authorization.

Yet all objections become trivial when matched against the crisis itself. What we are witnessing is the <u>demoralization</u> of a great society: the ruination of its school children, athletes and executives, the corrosion of the workforce in general.

Many thoughtful sociologists consider the rapidly spreading drug use the greatest problem that our nation faces—greater and more real and urgent than nuclear bombs or economic reversal. In China, a similar crisis drove the authorities to apply capital punishment to those who trafficked in opium—an extreme solution that arose from the deepest reaches of frustration.

Free drugs will win the war against the domestic terrorism caused by <u>illicit</u> drugs. As a strategy, it is at once resourceful, sensible and simple. We are getting nowhere in our efforts to hold back the ocean of supply. The answer is to dry up demand.

HOW ABOUT LOW-COST DRUGS FOR ADDICTS? 197

First Impressions

Freewrite for ten minutes on one of the following.

1. Did you enjoy reading this selection? Why or why not?
2. Has anyone you know (including yourself) been affected by drugs or crime? If so, describe what happened.
3. Did your high school or community have an anti-drug program? If so, how well did it work?

Vocabulary Check

Circle the letter of the word or phrase that best completes each of the following four sentences.

1. The word *discrepancies* in "It would cost . . . only 20 cents for a heroin shot, for which the addicts must now pay . . . more than $100, and there are similar price discrepancies in cocaine, crack and other such substances" (paragraph 2) means
   a. excitements.　　　c. differences.
   b. similarities.　　　d. mistakes.
2. The word *enticed* in "Children would not be enticed. . . . with free drugs in order to create customers for the future" (paragraph 9) means
   a. attracted.　　　c. tired.
   b. punished.　　　d. ignored.
3. The word *sordid* in "Neighborhoods would not be scandalized by sordid street centers where addicts gather to obtain their supply from slimy merchants" (paragraph 9) means
   a. closed tightly.　　　c. dirty and shameful.
   b. pleasant and wholesome.　　d. well-lit.
4. The word *corrosion* in "What we are witnessing is the demoralization of a great society: the ruination of its school children, athletes and executives, the corrosion of the workforce in general" (paragraph 15) means
   a. promotion.　　　c. employment.
   b. improvement.　　d. weakening.

Insert four of the following words (or forms of words) from "Words to Watch" where they belong in the sentences below.

　　compulsion　　diminished　　illicit　　pittance　　stifled

5. Joanne _____ a yawn as she watched slides of her neighbor's vacation.

6. Putting a down payment on our house _____ our bank account to less than five hundred dollars.

7. Because Al Capone did not report his _____ income, he was jailed for not paying his taxes.
8. At the turn of the century, factory workers put in long hours, but they were usually paid a mere _____ .

Reading Check

Central Point and Main Ideas
1. Which sentence best expresses the central point of the selection?
    a. Drug addiction is the greatest problem the United States faces today.
    b. Providing low-cost drugs to addicts would win the war against drug-related crime.
    c. Addicts commit crimes to get money for drugs.
    d. Drug dealers should receive the death penalty.
2. Which sentence best expresses the main idea of paragraph 3?
    a. Psychiatrists should be on the staffs of government drug clinics.
    b. Our courts and prisons are overcrowded.
    c. The government would save huge amounts of money by providing low-cost drugs.
    d. We need more land, sea, and air equipment to stop the importing of illegal drugs.
3. Which sentence best expresses the main idea of paragraph 9?
    a. Low-cost drugs would put pushers out of business and make cities safe again.
    b. Drug addicts commit crimes to support their habits.
    c. Drugs must be kept out of the hands of children.
    d. Our homes and stores are not safe.

Key Supporting Details
4. According to Nizer, government seizures of huge drug shipments
    a. reduce the number of addicts.
    b. increase the cost of illegal drugs to the addict.
    c. decrease the cost of illegal drugs to the addict.
    d. result in less crime.

5. _____ TRUE OR FALSE? The author thinks we should be more concerned with the addict's problems than with the safety of innocent citizens.

6. Many sociologists believe that the increasing drug abuse in America
    a. cannot be avoided.
    b. is unlikely to continue.
    c. is not a cause for concern.
    d. is the greatest problem our nation faces.

HOW ABOUT LOW-COST DRUGS FOR ADDICTS? 199

Inferences

7. The author implies that if addicts can get low-cost drugs,
   a. they will naturally use more drugs.
   b. the crime rate will decrease dramatically.
   c. addicts will still avoid government clinics.
   d. the government will need to spend more on stopping illegal drug imports.

8. _____ TRUE OR FALSE? In paragraph 4, Nizer implies that government agents cannot put an end to drug addiction.

The Writer's Craft

9. In which paragraph does the author use repetition to emphasize his point?
   a. Paragraph 2
   b. Paragraph 5
   c. Paragraph 6
   d. Paragraph 8

10. The author's main purpose in writing this selection is to
    a. inform readers about the problem of drug-related crime.
    b. persuade readers to support his drug plan.
    c. persuade readers to demand severe penalties for drug sellers.
    d. entertain readers with the story of how he intercepted a huge drug shipment.

Outlining Activity

Complete the following outline of "How About Low-Cost Drugs for Addicts?" by filling in the missing items where they belong.

Central point: We can win the war against drug addiction by giving addicts free or low-cost drugs.

A. The plan: free or low-cost drugs for addicts

B. The situation today
   1. High cost of law enforcement
   2. High crime rate

C. Advantages of new approach

   1. _____

   2. _____

   3. _____

SOCIAL ISSUES

   D. Possible objections to new approach
      1. _____
      2. _____
   E. Conclusion: objections minor compared to plan's benefits

Discussion Questions

1. What do you think of Nizer's proposal? Do you think it would solve problems—or create new ones?
2. In addition to the approach Nizer suggests, what other ways might there be to cut down on drug abuse? Which of them do you think are worth trying? Why?
3. What do you think is the most harmful effect of drug abuse? Why?
4. Is drug abuse the most serious problem America faces today? If so, why? If not, what is?

Paragraph Assignments

1. Write a paragraph about some other things that you think the government should provide free or at low cost to its citizens. You might choose to write about one or more of the following or think of a topic of your own:

   - housing for the homeless
   - medical care
   - child care
   - higher education
   - food for the needy
   - public transportation

   In your paragraph, describe the services you think should be offered and explain why they should be provided at such low cost. Your topic sentence could be something like the following: "The government should come up with a plan to make low-cost housing available to the homeless."

2. Is your community doing a good job of combatting drugs and drug-related crime? Write a paragraph describing an approach your community uses. You might write about such methods as a neighborood watch, extra police patrols, crackdowns on locations where drugs are used, or education campaigns. Support your topic sentence with examples and details. As an alternative, write your paragraph on ways your community could make its war on drugs more successful.

Essay Assignments

1. Drug addiction is such a terrible problem because drugs can take complete control of a user's life. Other habits, however, are easier to break. Write

an essay explaining the reasons why you broke a habit. Or write about one or more habits you've overcome in your lifetime. Consider topics such as:

- being late
- smoking
- wasting time
- eating junk food
- spending more than you can afford
- chewing your fingernails

Use a thesis similar to one of the following:

I gave up smoking after I realized that it was endangering my health, upsetting my parents, and annoying my boyfriend.

_____, _____, and _____ are three habits I've overcome.

2. As Nizer suggests, drug addiction is responsible for many crimes. Even people who have not been victims of crime themselves have probably taken steps to protect themselves from crime. Write an essay in which you discuss some precautions people can take to help make their lives safer. Some topics you might want to discuss are:

- putting triple locks on doors and bars on windows
- getting a watchdog
- teaching children not to speak to strangers
- not carrying large amounts of money
- staying out of bad neighborhoods, especially at night
- going places in groups

Why We Throw Food Away
William Rathje

Preview

What would investigators find if they sorted through your garbage each week? According to this selection, they might find more wasted food than you suspect. As a member of the Garbage Project of the University of Arizona, the author unearthed surprising information about the tons of good food we toss out every year. He reported his findings in this magazine article, written for *The Atlantic*. Reading this selection may give you food for thought about your family's buying and eating habits.

Words to Watch

dutifully (1): obediently
ultimately (1): eventually
tract (2): persuasive pamphlet
dynamics (2): pattern of forces
embedded (5): firmly placed
axioms (5): basic truths
replenished (6): resupplied
counterintuitive (8): opposite to what people would assume
postulate (8): principle
hedge (8): protection
inevitably (9): unavoidably
capital (10): punishable by death
plight (10): desperate situation
comestibles (10): food
longevity (10): long life

Most of the 400,000 residents of Tucson, Arizona, are unaware that they waste a lot of food, but every year the Tucson Sanitation Division dutifully hauls 9,500 tons of edible or once-edible food to landfills. One third of this amount consists of plate scrapings, but the remainder consists of items like spoiled heads of lettuce, apples with one bite gone, wedges of rancid cheese, and soggy clumps of macaroni. The people of Tucson ultimately discard about 15 percent of the food they buy. If this pattern is representative of patterns nationwide—and studies conducted in Milwaukee and Marin County, California, suggest that it is—then the United States throws away enough food every year to feed all of Canada, including the lumberjacks.

I know about Tucson's food waste because I work with a crew that has been studying the city's garbage for more than a decade—sorting it, weighing it, keeping track of the relative volumes of this and that. (By the way, we don't count peels, tops, rinds, bones, or fat as waste, and we do correct for garbage disposals.) What follows is not a righteous tract about the immorality of wasting food in a world where millions starve. To be sure, people shouldn't waste food—at the very least, it costs money to buy and to cart to the dump—and people shouldn't starve, but these two social ills are not, in most cases, causally linked. The dynamics of food distribution and hunger work otherwise. I believe that Hubert Humphrey once suggested that America could feed its needy if only the "haves" would give up one hamburger a month. The suggestion was noble. As a prescription for public policy, however, it was hardly workable.

One reason why Americans waste so much food is that we doubt (and rightly so) that the bits and pieces we might actually save at home would ever find their way into the mouths of the hungry masses. We also waste a lot because we have a lot to waste. We waste food because it is often cheaper to save time than to save food. We waste food because we do not know whether something is still safe to eat, or because we do not know how to use "spoiled" items like stale bread or clabbered milk in recipes. (If you'd like to learn, see Lois Willand's *Use-It-Up Cookbook*.) We waste food for many reasons, but perhaps the most important reason of all is simply that we don't realize how much food is being wasted.

Studies consistently bear this out. When participants in surveys are asked to write down every edible item they waste, the amounts recorded decline day after day as people become aware of how much food they normally consign to the trash. Most people, however, do not keep track of day-to-day food wastage and thus have no idea how much they discard. Americans are reasonably good about recycling aluminum cans and newspapers, because when they allow these things to accumulate, they can see how quickly the piles grow. They never allow discarded food to accumulate, however—at least not at home. Instead, it is whisked away and buried in landfills (or what archaeologists call middens).

Researchers in recent years have shown a growing interest in contemporary human refuse for what it implies about contemporary human behavior. Garbage is very revealing. Halloween garbage includes candy wrappers but no candy; Valentine's Day garbage contains both wrappers and candy. Embedded in these data is telling information about the character of each holiday. (On Halloween what's important is the candy; on Valentine's Day what's important is the gesture.) Such information is the goal of the thirteen-year-old Garbage Project of the University of Arizona, where I teach. In recent years it has branched out to Milwaukee and Marin County. Other studies have been conducted by Occidental College, in Los Angeles, and by Barnard College, in New York. Though largely confined to reports in academic journals, a literature now exists on the matter of refuse. As far as food, specifically, is concerned, a handful of axioms has been reaped.

The more repetitious a family's diet, the less food the family discards. This is the First Principle of Edible Food Loss, and it helps to explain why sorters tend to find less wasted food in the garbage of Mexican-Americans than in the garbage of Americans generally. Mexican cuisine includes a wide variety of dishes—tamales, tacos, burritos, tostadas, chimichangas—but all of them are made with the same dozen or so ingredients. Those ingredients are always being used and replenished; they do not sit on a shelf and spoil. Moreover, leftovers can readily be incorporated into the next meal.

Similarly, there is not much wastage of commercial white bread. Households tend to go through standard loaves continually and methodically. More exotic breads are another story. Hamburger rolls, for example, usually come in packages of eight. How often is the number of hamburgers consumed at a cookout a multiple of eight? In my experience at least three hamburger rolls always go unused—are toasted unnecessarily and then thrown away, or are left in the refrigerator to grow moldy behind a jar of pickles. Judging from Tucson's garbage, between 40 and 50 percent (by weight) of all specialty breads—rolls and muffins, buns and biscuits—finds its way into garbage cans, versus about 10 percent of standard bread loaves.

The wastage of a foodstuff increases when people believe it to be in short supply. This proposition seems at first glance counterintuitive, like a postulate in non-Euclidean geometry, but consider the case of the "beef shortage" of 1973. There wasn't a beef shortage in the sense that beef could not be bought, but less beef was available than had been previously, and the result was that red meat became expensive. Suddenly the amount of beef waste in Tucson's garbage tripled. Careful studies revealed that the elevated waste level was due to the disruption of familiar buying habits. Some people bought cheaper and unfamiliar cuts of beef, failed to prepare them satisfactorily, and threw out the results. Others, as a <u>hedge</u> against future price increases, resorted to panic buying and stockpiled larger quantities of meat than they normally would have—without knowing how to store them properly in the freezer. It seems clear that at the household level, stockpiling usually means spoilage.

Living on processed food doesn't help matters any. The problem here is not that people don't finish their Lean Cuisine fettucine or their Stouffer's spinach souffles. They do. The problem is what they don't eat instead. The people who buy products like these usually heat them up so that they won't have to spend time preparing the fresh food in their refrigerators, not because they have carefully charted a week's menu of frozen food. And, of course, fresh food, especially produce, tends <u>inevitably</u> toward rot. Households whose garbage contains the highest proportion of processed-food artifacts—the tripartite TV-dinner tray, the plastic broccoli-hollandaise pouch—also have the highest produce-wastage rates.

Wasting food is not a <u>capital</u> crime, and America's shortcomings at the dinner table are not responsible for the <u>plight</u> of Ethiopia. If anything, our record is considerably better than it once was. During the Second World War the War Food Administration estimated that the average household threw away between a quarter and a third of all solid <u>comestibles</u> acquired. That proportion has since been halved. As with our lengthening life-spans, however, improvement has come not by virtue of individual effort but through broad institutional progress—vaccination and better sanitation in the case of <u>longevity</u>, refrigeration and better transportation, processing, and packaging in the case of food. Further reduction in food waste depends on what takes place in 85 million American kitchens. Now you've got a few tips. Don't just throw them away.

First Impressions

Freewrite for ten minutes on one of the following.
1. Did you enjoy reading this selection? Why or why not?
2. How would you feel if you found out that someone had been going through your garbage? What do you think a garbage researcher might learn about you?
3. How much food would you say you waste? What kinds do you waste most often?

Vocabulary Check

Circle the letter of the word or phrase that best completes each of the following four sentences.

1. The word *rancid* in "items like spoiled heads of lettuce, apples with one bite gone, wedges of rancid cheese, and soggy clumps of macaroni" (paragraph 1) means
   a. ready to eat.
   b. appealing and delicious.
   c. imported from Switzerland.
   d. smelly and bad tasting.
2. The words *consign to* in "When participants in surveys are asked to write down every edible item they waste, the amounts recorded decline day after day as people become aware of how much food they normally consign to the trash" (paragraph 4) mean
   a. send to.
   b. take from.
   c. follow to.
   d. don't lose in.
3. The word *refuse* in "Researchers in recent years have shown a growing interest in contemporary human refuse. . . . Garbage is very revealing" (paragraph 5) means
   a. misbehavior.
   b. trash.
   c. laughter.
   d. speech.
4. The word *stockpiled* in "Others . . . resorted to panic buying and stockpiled larger quantities of meat than they normally would have" (paragraph 8) means
   a. stored.
   b. sold.
   c. burned up.
   d. avoided.

Circle the letter of the answer that best completes each of the following four items. Each sentence uses a word (or form of a word) from "Words to Watch."

5. As a boy I usually went *dutifully* to bed
   a. whenever I felt like it.
   b. as soon as my parents told me to.
6. The food supply in the cabin had been *replenished*, so
   a. the cupboard was bare.
   b. the shelves were full.
7. Cindy told me about her *plight*. She just
   a. lost her job.
   b. won $1,000 in a lottery.
8. My family is well known for its *longevity*; all my grandparents
   a. lived past 90.
   b. died young.

Reading Check

Central Point and Main Ideas

1. Which sentence best expresses the central point of the selection?
   a. Americans waste a lot of food without realizing it.

b. America's excess food could feed many starving nations.
   c. Families that regularly eat the same meals discard less food.
   d. Studying garbage can be very interesting.
2. Which sentence best expresses the main idea of paragraph 5?
   a. Garbage reveals a great deal about people.
   b. Americans are very wasteful.
   c. Valentine's Day is more important than Halloween.
   d. The University of Arizona Garbage Project is 13 years old.

Key Supporting Details

3. _____ TRUE OR FALSE? Most food waste consists of plate scrapings.
4. According to the article, when people become aware of how much food they waste, they
   a. are angry.
   b. eat less processed food.
   c. donate more food to the hungry.
   d. waste less.
5. People with repetitious diets waste less food because they
   a. buy smaller amounts.
   b. are less hungry.
   c. never have any leftovers.
   d. use up ingredients before they can spoil.

Inferences

6. From the article we can conclude that one way to avoid wasting food is to
   a. eat more frozen dinners.
   b. eat a lot of hamburgers.
   c. avoid buying unusually large amounts of food.
   d. avoid eating Mexican food.
7. _____ TRUE OR FALSE? From the article we can conclude that garbage research is a growing field.

The Writer's Craft

8. In paragraph 7, the author supports his point by
   a. telling a story.
   b. using dialogue.
   c. asking a series of questions.
   d. making a comparison.
9. The tone of the article is
   a. factual.
   b. bitter.
   c. light-hearted.
   d. excited.

10. The type of support Rathje uses most often in the selection is
    a. interviews with government officials.
    b. summaries of research findings.
    c. comments by ordinary consumers.
    d. jokes that illustrate his central point.

Summarizing Activity

1. Circle the letter of the statement that summarizes the introduction of "Why We Throw Food Away" (paragraphs 1 through 3).
    a. Americans should not waste food in a world where so many people are starving.
    b. The people of Tucson, Arizona, throw out 15 percent of the food they buy.
    c. Garbage research indicates that Americans throw away a great deal of food for a variety of reasons.
2. Circle the letter of the statement that summarizes the supporting details in paragraph 4.
    a. Survey participants were asked to write down what food they wasted.
    b. Studies prove Americans are unaware of how much food they're wasting.
    c. Americans are good at recycling aluminum cans and newspapers.
3. Circle the letter of the statement that summarizes the supporting details in paragraphs 5 through 9.
    a. Garbage reveals a great deal about contemporary human behavior.
    b. Specialty and stockpiled foods are the foods most often discarded.
    c. Repetitious diets minimize waste, but people who stockpile food or buy prepared meals waste more food than others do.
4. Circle the letter of the statement that summarizes the conclusion of this selection (paragraph 10).
    a. Americans waste less food today than they did during World War II.
    b. Although some progress has been made in cutting food waste, further progress depends on individuals.
    c. Government and industry have helped eliminate food waste.

Discussion Questions

1. Do you waste food at home? At school? Why or why not?
2. Do you think children should be urged to finish all the food on their plates even though they are no longer hungry? Why or why not?
3. In this article, the author focuses on what garbage research tells us about food waste. What else do you think might be learned about us from garbage research?
4. In your opinion, is it ever all right to waste food—or anything else? If so, when and why?

Paragraph Assignments

1. In general, are you a wasteful person or not? Write a paragraph describing some of the ways you are or are not wasteful. Your topic sentence could be similar to one of the following:

   I try never to waste anything if I can help it.
   I am not as careful about money as I should be.

2. Write a paragraph on specific ways to avoid food waste. You could make recommendations to one of more of the following:

   - your family
   - your friends
   - restaurant owners
   - food companies
   - supermarkets and convenience stores
   - the general public

   For example, you might suggest that restaurants serve smaller portions or supermarkets not throw away edible produce just because it looks wilted. Explain each suggestion in detail, and tell what would be gained by following it.

Essay Assignments

1. Americans have a reputation for being very wasteful people. Besides food, they waste time, money, water, electricity, gas, and other resources. In an essay, describe one or more ways Americans are wasteful, and tell how they might cut down on some of that waste. Your thesis statement could be something like this one: "Americans should try harder not to waste _____, _____, and _____."

2. Although people throw away food they could have put to good use, they also save things which have little practical value—magazines, old clothing, dishes, children's art work, even string. Write an essay about the things people in your household refuse to throw out. Describe what they save and why they save it. You could organize your essay by describing several kinds of things your family saves. As an alternative, you could focus on different members of your family and tell what each one saves.

24

Escape Valve
Gregg Easterbrook

Preview

Would you stay in a romance if you knew it would end at a certain point? Some people do. In fact, many people prefer short-term commitments at work as well as in relationships. The result is a throwaway approach to love and work. In this article, originally published in *The New York Times*, Gregg Easterbrook tells why the trend towards the temporary has gone so far.

Words to Watch

unique (3): one of a kind
phenomenon (3): unusual event
stable (3): lasting
beneficiaries of (5): people who profit from
truism (5): obvious truth
mania (6): madness
hierarchies (6): ranks
integrity (7): high standards
disrepute (8): disgrace
perpetuate (9): cause to continue
disrepair (9): neglected condition
exempt (9): free

A man and woman I know moved in together recently. It was, as such occasions are, a moment of sentiment and celebration. It was also a limited engagement. Before moving in, they had already set a fixed date when they would break up. 1

They explained their reasons to one and all. In a year, the woman planned to change jobs and cities; the man did not plan to follow. An eventual split is unfortunate, they said, but also inevitable, so why not 2 plan on it? Yet, far from being a sad twist of fate, my woman friend's scheduled departure, I fear, was a liberating force, making possible whatever short-term romance the couple will enjoy. Without the escape clause of a pre-set termination of their affair, they might never have lived together at all.

This situation is not unique. More and more, people are ordering their lives along a principle I call the "automatic-out." In love, friendship, work, and the community, people increasingly prefer arrangements that automatically end at some pre-set date. Automatic-out is not a phenomenon confined to my still-unsettled generation (the late 20's), with its flair for "flexible" styles of life. It is a force in society as a whole, as more of us hunger for lives that appear stable and deep-rooted but lack the complications of commitment.

Automatic-out may have its foundations in the pre-set cycles of academic life. In recent decades, an ever-higher percentage of the population has been able to attend college and postgraduate schools. That's a good thing for the cause of education but perhaps not so good for society's spirit. Longtime students learn to view institutions as places where people briefly come to rest, and from which they will be automatically removed on a date known years in advance. They also tend to see institutions as a means by which to take things for themselves, instead of adding things for others.

So it may be no surprise that professionals—usually the beneficiaries of advanced schooling—seem increasingly uninterested in staying put. Or, if they remain with one organization, lean toward fellowships, temporary assignments, and other stints with automatic-outs. For some time, this has been a troubling truism of Washington. A Brookings Institution study shows that government-agency managers immediately below the rank of Presidential appointees turn over, on average, every 21 months. Now it is becoming true of private enterprise as well. According to the Conference Board, a business research organization, top corporate executives now switch jobs every 4.5 years on average—an all-time high.

The job-switching mania, it is sometimes suggested, stems from a combination of boredom and expectations of promotion. But most switches among government agencies and corporate hierarchies do not involve dramatic changes of life; they are changes from one job to another fairly similar to it, in a fairly similar organization. The number of top-level positions available doesn't increase just because the switching rate is increasing.

The switch mania is, I think, motivated by the desire for automatic-outs. When you know in advance that you will soon be changing jobs, you are relieved of concern for the overall integrity of your institution—

whether the quality of its products, the fairness of its service, the odds of its survival. You have a built-in excuse for selfishness ("I'll be leaving in a year anyway") and can concentrate on advancing yourself, secure in the knowledge that if you fail to improve your organization—or, as in the case of so many business and government managers, actively damage it—you personally won't suffer. You'll be one step ahead of the crumbling walls.

It seems to be the same way in love. If a romance operates under some pre-set restriction, neither partner feels obliged to sacrifice his interests for joint interests. Why sacrifice for something not expected to last anyway? Thus, the short-term benefits of marriage and living together (companionship, warmth, convenience) remain popular. But long-term obligation to the institution of marriage has fallen into <u>disrepute</u> among many young people. Children and family life are especially in disrepute today, for whenever children are present there is no easy out, emotionally or legally. The weekend romance is especially desirable today, not because "people move around more now" but because distance guarantees an automatic-out. Just step back on the plane Sunday night.

Many troublesome aspects of life <u>perpetuate</u> themselves through downward-drawing spirals. As corporate and public institutions fall deeper into <u>disrepair</u>, as men and women are becoming increasingly small-minded and cool to the touch, there seems all the more reason to opt for automatic-outs. Who wants to be committed to the kinds of people and organizations at loose in the world today? This, of course, helps only to accelerate the decay. Many people capable of helping right what's wrong with society seek instead mainly to <u>exempt</u> themselves from responsibility for its condition. Why should I care? I'll be leaving in a year anyway.

First Impressions

Freewrite for ten minutes on one of the following.

1. Did you enjoy reading this selection? Why or why not?
2. Have you ever been in a job or relationship that you knew would end at a certain time? If so, how did you feel about it?
3. Is there anything in your life now that you would like to escape from? At home? At school? At work? If so, describe it and tell why you would like to escape.

Vocabulary Check

Circle the letter of the word or phrase that best completes each of the following four sentences.

1. The word *inevitable* in "An eventual split is unfortunate . . . but also inevitable, so why not plan on it?" (paragraph 2) means
   a. angry.
   b. far away.
   c. sure to happen.
   d. unlikely.
2. The word *termination* in "my woman friend's scheduled departure . . . was a liberating force. . . . Without the escape clause of a pre-set termination of their affair, they might never have lived together at all" (paragraph 2) means
   a. beginning.
   b. end.
   c. dislike.
   d. continuing.
3. The word *stints* in "fellowships, temporary assignments, and other stints with automatic-outs" (paragraph 5) means
   a. short-term activities.
   b. jokes.
   c. months.
   d. long-term involvements.
4. The words *opt for* in "As . . . institutions fall deeper into disrepair . . . there seems all the more reason to opt for automatic-outs" (paragraph 9) mean
   a. avoid.
   b. choose.
   c. ignore.
   d. flatter.

Circle the letter of the word (or form of the word) from "Words to Watch" that best completes each of the following four sentences.

5. The museum was the _____ the old man's will; it received his art collection as well as all his money.
   a. beneficiary of
   b. truism in
   c. exemption from
   d. hierarchy of
6. Because Gerald had a _____ for fresh air, he kept all the windows open, no matter what the weather was like.
   a. disrepair
   b. mania
   c. phenomenon
   d. truism
7. Any student who gets an A on the mid-term exam will be _____ from the final.
   a. in disrepair
   b. in disrepute
   c. exempted
   d. perpetuated
8. The house hadn't been lived in for years and was in great _____.
   a. hierarchy
   b. disrepair
   c. mania
   d. perpetuation

Reading Check

Central Point and Main Ideas

1. Which sentence best expresses the central point of the selection?
   a. Professionals change jobs more often than those in other types of work.

SOCIAL ISSUES

b. Unfortunately, more and more people are unwilling to make permanent commitments to jobs and relationships.
c. Weekend romances are examples of people wanting an "automatic-out."
d. "Automatic-out" is a good idea because it allows people to have more interesting careers.

2. Which sentence best expresses the main idea of paragraph 4?
   a. In recent times, more people than ever before have been able to attend college.
   b. Long-time students do not expect to graduate.
   c. Because college life is temporary, it might have started the desire for "automatic-out."
   d. Increased enrollment in colleges is good for education.

3. Which sentence best expresses the main idea of paragraph 8?
   a. Romance is another area in which the "automatic-out" has become popular.
   b. One reason the weekend romance is desirable is that people move around a lot.
   c. There is no "automatic-out" where children are concerned.
   d. Weekend romances are immoral.

Key Supporting Details

4. "Automatic-out," according to Easterbrook, is
   a. confined to people under thirty.
   b. especially common in Washington.
   c. a good thing for society in general.
   d. found only in romantic relationships.

5. Research has shown that government and corporate executives
   a. are deeply committed to their jobs.
   b. are uneducated.
   c. are fired frequently.
   d. switch jobs frequently.

6. Most job switches in government and business
   a. involve moving to higher positions.
   b. have a good effect on the organizations involved.
   c. are from one job to another similar one.
   d. increase the number of top-level jobs available.

Inferences

7. The author implies that
   a. more people are getting married today.
   b. companies force people to leave their jobs early.
   c. more and more people enjoy working in the same place for many years.
   d. people don't want to get involved in permanent relationships.

8. _____ TRUE OR FALSE? The author implies that people wanting an "automatic-out" are selfish.

The Writer's Craft

9. The introduction to this article (paragraphs 1 and 2)
   a. tells an anecdote to illustrate "automatic-out."
   b. states the problem of "automatic-out."
   c. asks interesting questions.
   d. presents a list of statistics.
10. The tone of the last two sentences of the selection can be described as
    a. objective.
    b. formal.
    c. optimistic.
    d. sarcastic.

Outlining Activity

Complete the following outline of "Escape Valve" by filling in the missing items where they belong.

Central point: More and more people are choosing "automatic-outs" to avoid commitment, which results in fewer people and organizations worth being committed to.

A. Introductory anecdote
B. Definition and explanation of "automatic-out"

C. _____
   1. High turnover
   2. Movement to similar jobs
D. "Automatic-out" in relationships
   1. Less commitment to marriage and children
   2. _____
E. Conclusion

Discussion Questions

1. Do you feel, right now, that some things in your life are temporary? If so, what are they? Do you wish any of them could be permanent?
2. In your experience, are "automatic-out" attitudes becoming more common? Or are the people you know looking for involvement and commitment?
3. In paragraph 8, Easterbrook suggests that long-term relationships and children require some sacrifices. What might these sacrifices be? What benefits do you think are gained in return?
4. Are there any things in life that you think *should* last forever? If so, what are they?

Paragraph Assignments

1. Write a paragraph in which you argue that a temporary job (for example, seasonal labor or work for an office temporary agency) is more desirable— or less desirable—than a permanent position. Some factors you may wish to discuss are salary, benefits, seniority, job security, self-improvement, and variety. Your topic sentence could be something like this: "Working at temporary jobs lets me investigate different companies and fields before choosing a career."
2. Have you ever been in a situation you could have gotten out of, but, instead, chose to stay in and make things work? In a paragraph, write about such a situation—for example, a job, a class, a friendship or relationship, or an exercise or weight-control program. Describe the situation and explain why you decided not to escape.

Essay Assignments

1. Easterbrook implies that long-term relationships are going out of style. But should they be? Write an essay defending long-term commitments in romance or business. Think of several reasons to support your position, and devote a separate paragraph to each. Use a thesis statement such as one of the following:

   There are three benefits to building a lasting marriage.
   There is great personal satisfaction in spending an entire career
      with the same company.

2. What suggestions can you give for making a long-term commitment last? In an essay, discuss some successful strategies for one of the following topics:

   - staying in college
   - continuing a friendship
   - performing well in a full-time job
   - staying married
   - raising children

   Write a separate paragraph of your essay on each suggestion. Be sure to give examples to support your main ideas.

25

What We Can Learn from Japan's Prisons
James Webb

Preview

Many aspects of Japanese prisons might horrify you. The cells are unheated, prisoners are forbidden to look out the windows, and the diet consists of seaweed, fish and rice. Still, after reading the following article from *Parade* written by lawyer and novelist James Webb, you may decide that if you *had* to go to jail, you'd prefer one in Japan.

Words to Watch

dank (1):   damp
recidivism (6):   returning to crime
raises . . . hackles (7):   angers
litigation (8):   legal action
aboveboard (11):   honestly
rehabilitative (12):   returning to a useful life
juncture (13):   place where two things are joined
vaults (15):   jumps over
standardization (18):   sameness
austere (19):   severely simple
oppressors (20):   tyrants
unimpeachable (20):   above suspicion
mandatory (21):   required
incarceration (23):   imprisonment
accreditation (24):   official approval

Fuchu Prison, near Tokyo, is home to 2500 of Japan's most hardened criminals. Ed Arnett is an alumnus who thinks of Fuchu daily. The <u>dank</u>, unheated buildings, the harshness of the guards' reports to their superiors, the high stone walls—these are as near to him as the scars on his legs, from the frostbite he picked up in his Fuchu cell.

"I didn't know I could still cry until I went to prison in Japan," says Arnett, convicted in 1979 for possession of two kilograms of marijuana. "I wouldn't put that experience on anybody."

Arrested on Okinawa, Arnett was kept in pretrial confinement for a month. He endured days of intense interrogation without an attorney and signed a confession—written in Japanese—that he could not read. He met his lawyer for the first time at his trial. The trial took 30 minutes. He was not allowed a jury.

At Fuchu, Arnett lived in a 9-by-5-foot cell furnished with a hard, narrow bed, a sink that also was his desk and a toilet that he could flush only when permitted by the guards. His mail was censored, and he was not allowed writing materials. The books he read were the few approved by his guards. Gifts from home were kept from him until his release. Despite his diabetes, Arnett's diet was dominated by seaweed, fish and rice. He lost 55 pounds in 18 months. Fourteen of those months were spent in solitary, in a room where a television camera recorded his every move. His scalp was shaved every two weeks. He was forbidden to look out the window or to communicate with other inmates. He worked eight hours a day, even in solitary, making paper bags in his cell. He could not touch his bunk during the day, but when the lights went out at night, if he was not lying down, he was punished. On his release, due to improper treatment of his diabetes, an American doctor called him "a walking dead man."

Arnett's experiences were not unusual for Japanese prison inmates, about 100 of whom at any time are Americans serving sentences for crimes ranging from minor drug offenses to murder. But, surprisingly, Arnett, home in Omaha, Nebraska, says he prefers Japan's legal system to ours. Why? "Because it's fair," he says. "The Japanese never tried to trick me, even in interrogation. They were always trustworthy. I could have got five years, and they gave me two. The Americans who were helping them wanted me to get 20. The guards at Fuchu were hard, but they never messed with you unless there was a reason. You didn't have to worry about the other prisoners coming after you, either. And the laws of Japan are for everybody. That's the main thing. The laws in this country depend on how much you can pay. I'd rather live under a hard system that's fair."

In 1981, Japan, with about half our population, had only 922 homicides; we had 1832 in New York City alone. An American is 12 times more likely to be murdered than a Japanese, 14 times more likely to be raped and 20 times more likely to be the victim of a property crime.

Although recidivism rates are similar—50 percent in Japan, 64 percent here—our problem with criminal repeaters is actually nine times greater than Japan's because our crime rate is so much higher.

A defendant's lack of counsel during interrogation and the absence of a jury trial, a U.S. Constitutional right, raises no hackles. "There are scholars who criticize this, but they have no social or political support," notes Kotaro Ohno of Japan's Ministry of Justice, who studied law at Harvard. "A Japanese believes the judge is more knowledgeable about his situation than a collection of citizens." Ohno defends Japan's very narrow use of the exclusionary rule and says the U.S. "goes too far" in excluding illegally obtained evidence.

Japan has a low crime rate without either a police state or excessive litigation. Only 50,000 prisoners, including pretrial detention inmates, are presently confined in Japan, and fewer than 4 percent of the prisoners are sentenced for longer than three years. In the U.S., there are 580,000 adult inmates, and 80 percent of those in state institutions have been sentenced for longer than five years.

Observes Yoshio Suzuki, until recently director general of the Correction Bureau in Japan's Ministry of Justice: "The law in Japan is severe in the attitude toward offenders as a whole. This allows it to be lenient in the punishment of an individual. We involve the victim in the criminal process. If the accused has shown proper penance to the victim through repayment or an expression of grief, and the victim tells this to the court, it will go much easier on the accused."

Japan brings 70 percent of its crimes to conviction. The U.S. brings only 19.8 percent of its crimes to arrest. But the contrast in prisons themselves is most startling. Americans familiar with the horrors of Attica and New Mexico and the routine tales of brutality and homosexual rape would find the orderly corridors of a Japanese prison mind-boggling.

"They don't coddle them, but they don't abuse them, either," says U.S. Navy Capt. Everette Stumbaugh, a lawyer for the commander of U.S. forces in Japan. "Japan plays it aboveboard all the way."

There never has been a hostage crisis in a Japanese prison. There has been only one "prison disturbance"—30 years ago. There never has been a reported case of homosexual rape, or of prisoner gang wars. No guard ever has been killed by inmates: there has been only one inmate death in the last 10 years at the hands of another. There have been only 35 escapes from Japanese prisons in the last seven years (the U.S. average is more than 8000 escapes a year). Almost 94 percent of Japan's prisoners perform labor that is geared to their aptitude and rehabilitative potential, rather than based on the crime committed. Guards typically are unarmed. There are 58 major prisons in Japan. In addition to Fuchu, I toured prisons in Yokosuka and Okinawa. Only Fuchu had armed guards. There, fewer than 10 percent carry weapons—police sticks.

"What about the guard in the tower?" I asked Kaoru Kayaba, Yokosuka's warden, as I stared at the juncture of two walls on the far side of a large athletic field. "Doesn't he carry a rifle?"

Kayaba smiled. "We don't keep a guard in the tower. Except when the prisoners play softball."

"In case a prisoner vaults the wall?"

"In case a ball goes over the wall."

Much of the success of Japan's prisons is due to a classification system that analyzes and separates hardened criminals ("Category B") from those not likely to become repeat offenders ("Category A"). Yokosuka and Okinawa house "A" prisoners. The A's often earn certificates in trades such as plastering and auto repair. The B's—many of whom are members of the *Yakuza*, Japan's Mafia—might do such mundane tasks as maintenance work or making toys.

Prison officials are highly trained. Last year, though two-thirds of those who passed the national qualifying test for prison guards were university graduates, only one-fourth were hired. Successful applicants must spend two weeks as observers in a prison and then complete eight months of intense training before they may begin work. Guards are transferred every few years to promote standardization within the system.

All Japanese wardens began as guards. Their experiences have given them both "hands on" time with prisoners and philosophical depth. Yokosuka's Warden Kayaba affirms the good of man. "All human beings are 98 percent good and 2 percent bad," he says. "The men who end up in prison are not more evil than others in our society. They are weaker. With the proper education, we can make even the worst offenders as calm as the others." Guards do this not through force, but through intense counseling and psychical denial. A difficult prisoner is removed from the collective environment and placed in an even more austere "punishment cell," where counseling continues. "We make them think," says Kayaba. "We talk to them again and again about why they were sent to prison, until gradually they understand."

"We are their caretakers, not their oppressors," says Fuchu's present warden, Kiyoshi Taru, of Japan's most hardened criminals. An aircraft gunner during World War II, Taru saw the corrections field as a way to continue serving his country after Japan's military was disbanded. "Criminals have violated the well-being of others in order to satisfy their greed," says Taru. "We teach them how to control their desires and still satisfy themselves. You cannot do this unless you are unimpeachable yourself. We use our example as the instrument for their rehabilitation."

Taru says all guards are martial arts experts but adds, "If a guard unfairly strikes a prisoner, he will himself be imprisoned for a mandatory seven-year sentence."

Okinawa's warden, Yoshitaka Myojin, followed his father into the field. He says the key to prison stability lies in the workshop: "The guard who runs the workshop performs three functions—instructor, disciplinarian and counselor—so the prisoner does not direct his anger toward the guard purely as an authority figure. The guard is part of the overall unit, the father figure." Noting with irony that many fundamentals of the Japanese system were adapted from the U.S. system, Myojin wonders, "What has happened in America?"

His question is echoed by many here. If the U.S. incarceration rate is one of the highest in the free world, so is its crime rate. Overcrowding—our prison population has expanded by 30 percent in the last three years—contributes to abuse and acts of violence. So does idleness. Few prisoners work in U.S. jails because of trade-union pressure and "state use" laws that forbid their making competitive products. Only about 10 percent of the inmates in our state systems are allowed to work.

Our guards are often unskilled and untrained. Robert Fosen, director of the Commission on Accreditation for Corrections, indicates that the "recommended levels of training" that his group recently set for U.S. prisons consist of a mere 40 hours of "orientation training," followed during the guard's first year by 120 hours of further training in supervision and the use of force. He notes that standards had to rise "in well over half the states" to meet these new requirements.

Could we adopt parts of the Japanese system? I asked three Americans of markedly differing political views and responsibilities: Norman Carlson, director of the Federal Bureau of Prisons since 1970, who inspected the Japanese system in 1971; Fosen, who was a New York prison official during the Attica riots; and Edward Koren, an attorney for the American Civil Liberties Union's National Prison Project.

All three support more inmates working, and Carlson and Fosen favor a decrease in the length of sentences for nonviolent, nondangerous offenders but longer sentences for others.

Carlson notes that all federal wardens begin as line officers. Fosen argues that our varied institutions require a wider range of training. Koren agrees.

Their greatest resistance to the Japanese system concerns individual treatment. Says Koren: "No heat in a prisoner's cell is outrageous. That would be a clear violation of the Constitution's prohibition against cruel and unusual punishment. The other living conditions are quite extreme. The denial of reading materials without clearly showing they are a threat to prison order, the withholding of writing materials from inmates and the censorship of correspondence all violate the First Amendment." He suggests many of Japan's methods would end in U.S. lawsuits.

Koren says of Japanese trial procedures: "The exclusionary rule is our way of enforcing Constitutional rights. Involving the victim *before* a person is convicted should be done only at a defendant's initiative. Eliminating plea bargaining would be impractical."

But is the present U.S. way fair?

"American jails are filled with hate," says Arnett. "If their walls fell down today, do you think the prisoners would run past you without stopping? An American prisoner might kill you, just because you're the first person he sees. If the walls of the Japanese prisons fell down, the Japanese prisoners would just go on home."

I told this to Toyofumi Yoshinaga, a legal assistant at the Corrections Bureau in Tokyo who had spent several hours providing me with statistics. His eyes lit up. Said Yoshinaga: "During the great Kanto earthquake of 1923, the walls of one of our prisons *did* fall down." He smiled. "No one escaped."

First Impressions

Freewrite for ten minutes on one of the following.

1. Did you enjoy reading this selection? Why or why not?
2. What do you picture when you hear the word *prison*? Where did you get your ideas about what prisons are like?
3. If you were a judge and could sentence a criminal to either an American or a Japanese prison, which would you choose? Explain your decision.

Vocabulary Check

Circle the letter of the word or phrase that best completes each of the following four sentences.

1. The word *penance* in "If the accused has shown proper penance to the victim through repayment or an expression of grief" (paragraph 9) means
   a. attempt to make up for wrongdoing.
   b. ignorance of the consequences.
   c. anger at injustice.
   d. disrespect for the law.
2. The word *coddle* in "They don't coddle them, but they don't abuse them, either" (paragraph 11) means
   a. hurt.   c. promote.
   b. treat gently.   d. compare to others.
3. The word *mundane* in "The A's often earn certificates in trades such as

plastering and auto repair. The B's . . . might do such mundane tasks as maintenance work" (paragraph 17) means
   a. routine.
   b. exciting.
   c. clean.
   d. unnatural.
4. The word *affirms* in "Warden Kayaba affirms the good of man. 'All human beings are 98 percent good and 2 percent bad,' he says" (paragraph 19) means
   a. laughs at.
   b. refuses to support.
   c. declares positively.
   d. ignores completely.

Circle the letter of the answer that best completes each of the following four items. Each sentence uses a word (or form of a word) from "Words to Watch."

5. Helen learned about her promotion from a (an) _____ source: the president of the company.
   a. austere
   b. dank
   c. incarcerated
   d. unimpeachable
6. Although other students decorated their dorm rooms with posters, I like the _____ look of bare concrete walls.
   a. dank
   b. accredited
   c. austere
   d. mandatory
7. After the _____ of the testing program, all the accounting teachers gave the same test.
   a. incarceration
   b. recidivism
   c. standardization
   d. juncture
8. Our basement is so _____ that all the boxes down there smell of mildew.
   a. dank
   b. rehabilitative
   c. austere
   d. unimpeachable

Reading Check

Central Point and Main Ideas

1. Which sentence best expresses the central point of the selection?
   a. Arnett would rather be in a Japanese prison than in an American one.
   b. In spite of their harshness, Japanese prisons are more fair and effective than American prisons.
   c. Conditions in Japanese prisons are terrible.
   d. Japanese prisoners are safe, are treated equally, and rarely try to escape.
2. Which sentence best expresses the main idea of paragraph 18?
   a. Many Japanese prison guards are former prisoners.
   b. Many applicants for jobs as prison guards in Japan are university graduates.

SOCIAL ISSUES

    c. Japanese prison guards are transferred every few years.
    d. Japanese prison officials are well qualified and carefully trained.
3. Which sentence best expresses the main idea of paragraph 28?
    a. American legal experts agree that Japanese prison conditions would violate American inmates' rights.
    b. Japanese prisons are unheated.
    c. Denying prisoners reading materials violates their rights.
    d. The U.S. government should force the Japanese to improve their prisons.

Key Supporting Details

4. While he was in a Japanese prison, Ed Arnett
    a. received special treatment because he was American.
    b. spent most of his time in solitary confinement.
    c. was cured of his diabetes.
    d. was given no work to do.
5. Prisoners in Japan
    a. often riot.
    b. do not get jury trials.
    c. are often abused by other prisoners.
    d. frequently attack their guards.

Inferences

6. _____ TRUE OR FALSE? The author implies that most American prison guards are not well enough qualified for their jobs.
7. We can conclude from paragraphs 12 through 16 that Japanese prison guards
    a. expect prisoners to be cooperative.
    b. expect prisoners to be violent.
    c. are underpaid.
    d. don't play softball.

The Writer's Craft

8. _____ TRUE OR FALSE? The author begins his essay with Ed Arnett's story (paragraphs 1 through 5) in order to introduce his central point.
9. The main pattern of organization in paragraph 6 is
    a. space order.
    b. time order.
    c. cause and effect.
    d. contrast.
10. In paragraph 12, Webb supports his point of view with
    a. anecdotes.
    b. statistics.
    c. definitions.
    d. predictions.

Summarizing Activity

Complete the following summary of "What We Can Learn From Japan's Prisons" by filling in each blank with one or more words.

While in a Japanese prison, Ed Arnett endured harsh conditions and was permitted few individual rights. But he still prefers (1) _____'s criminal justice system to (2) _____'s system because it is safer and more (3) _____. In Japan, the crime rate is (4) _____, the conviction rate is (5) _____, and prisons are not violent places. The success of Japanese prisons seems to be due largely to a system that (6) _____ hardened criminals from the others and provides useful work for both. Also, Japanese prison officials are highly (7) _____ and use counseling techniques instead of force. In contrast, the United States has a very high crime rate, crowded and violent (8) _____, few opportunities for prisoners to work, and many poorly trained (9) _____. Some American experts agree with a few of the Japanese methods, but they also think (10) _____ _____.

Discussion Questions

1. Do you think Ed Arnett was treated fairly? Why or why not?
2. Which features of Japanese prisons do you think the U.S. might adopt? Which do you think it should not adopt? Why?
3. What do you think the purpose of a prison term should be? What rights should prisoners have?
4. What do you think the differences between American and Japanese prisons reveal about the differences between the two countries?

Paragraph Assignments

1. Write a paragraph about a time you were punished. Describe what happened and tell why you think the punishment was or was not a good one. Was it hard but fair, as Arnett describes his Japanese jail sentence? Or was it too easy or unfair? Your topic sentence might be similar to one of the following:

    Grounding me for a week when I came in only fifteen minutes late was unfair.

Serving a month's detention convinced me never to be late to school again.

2. Write a one-paragraph letter to the governor of your state in which you suggest that your state's prison system adopt one of the features of Japanese prisons. Select one aspect of Japanese prisons that you think is a good idea. Describe how it would work, and explain the benefits which would result if it were put into practice in the United States.

Essay Assignments

1. In his article, Webb contrasts the United States' justice system to Japan's. Write an essay in which, like Webb, you contrast two ways of doing something in order to prove that one is better. Choose a topic such as two approaches to disciplining children, two ways people study, the teaching methods of two of your teachers, two methods of getting household chores done, or two ways families treat elderly parents and grandparents. Then compare several aspects of the two methods you have chosen. Your thesis statement could be similar to "I believe my way of disciplining my children is superior to the way my sister disciplines hers for three reasons."

2. In paragraph 22, Webb quotes a Japanese prison warden who calls the workshop guard a "father figure" who performs "three functions—instructor, disciplinarian, and counselor." This description might also be used to characterize a parent, educator, or member of the clergy. Write about someone you know who is an instructor, disciplinarian, and counselor all rolled into one. Use examples to show how he or she performs each of these functions.

26

Turning On Turned-Off Workers
Michael LeBoeuf

Preview

Do workers have the right to ask more from a job than just a paycheck? Should they expect a sense of satisfaction from their work as well? In this article from *Japan: The Productivity Challenge*, Michael LeBoeuf explains that these days, job satisfaction *does* matter. He argues that today's managers can succeed—but not by using yesterday's methods.

Words to Watch

productivity (5): worker output
host (5): great number
counterproductive (5): interfering with the output of goods or services
incentives (8): motivating forces
disenchanted (8): disillusioned
diluted (9): watered down
virtually (9): nearly
automated (16): done by machine
oriented (16): directed
inherent (19): built in
atrocities (20): shockingly cruel acts
actuarial (21): referring to statistics on how long people live
symptomatic of (25): a sign of
capitalize on (28): take advantage of
autonomous (29): independent

"Take this job and shove it!" 1
"Try to imagine how little I care." 2
"Why should I worry about going to hell? I already work there five days a week." 3

Does that sound like you? If you work for a living, you may see yourself in those statements, because today's American worker is becoming more and more frustrated with his job. In fact, the situation has deteriorated to such an extent that fewer than half of all Americans report being very satisfied with their jobs and 60 percent would prefer to have a different job.

At first glance, all this discontent seems confusing. Today's workers are very well paid and have more benefits than at any time in American history. Yet survey after survey reveals increasing worker discontent. And almost everyone agrees that worker attitudes play an important factor in declining U.S. productivity. While it's true that satisfied workers aren't necessarily productive, it's also true that worker discontent can lead to absenteeism, high turnover, unnecessary conflicts, and a host of other counterproductive problems. Perhaps the impact of turned-off workers was best illustrated by the boss who was asked, "How many people do you have working here?" His reply: "About half."

The problem isn't that people are apathetic or that the work ethic is dead. In fact, while today's worker is dissatisfied, it's also true that his job is more important to him than ever. The decline of close family ties, church membership, and small communities has resulted in work becoming a more important place to satisfy needs that used to be satisfied off the job, such as status, self-fulfillment, and friendship. And it's the demand to satisfy these needs through work that's causing a lot of worker frustration.

To define the problem as lazy young people or social misfits is a grave mistake. And the number of turned-off workers has become so large that it would be economic suicide to fire or ignore them. It's another crucial problem that all of us are going to have to work together to solve.

Old Incentives Don't Work As They Used To

Years ago, motivating people to work was much simpler, and management had a number of basic tools that could be readily applied. But the workforce has become so diverse and values have changed so much that the traditional motivational incentives have lost some or all of their effectiveness. Young people today come to work with very different expectations and motivations; it's the failure to recognize this fact that is creating so many disenchanted younger and older workers. Here are some of the basic motivational tools management has traditionally relied on:

The Big Stick

Fear, traditionally the big stick of management, is very simple in concept. The manager doesn't have to play amateur psychologist but simply demands that workers perform or else. In leaner times fear was an effective but distasteful motivator. But today fear has lost practically all its clout for the following reasons:

1. The fear of being fired has been diluted by the two-income family. If one wage-earner gets fired, there is another income.
2. Social programs and unemployment benefits virtually guarantee that no one is going to starve if he loses his job. In fact, 20 percent of all households have no wage-earners but live on pensions and welfare programs.
3. The plentifulness of skilled and high-technology jobs in the labor market is such that many young workers have other options. Getting fired is no longer always an economic disaster. What many young workers fear more than dismissal is meaningless work that leaves them feeling empty.
4. The new breed perceives job security as a right rather than a privilege. This attitude is completely alien to traditional workers, who were grateful just to have a job. Younger workers feel that the company owes them job security. And this is simply a natural byproduct of a generation reared during prosperous times. Nevertheless, it's difficult to motivate someone to work by promising job security when he feels it should be given rather than earned. All workers think job security is important, but it's more of a demand than an incentive.
5. Fear has always been a rather expensive way to motivate people. The worker has to believe that he will be caught and punished if he doesn't do the job. And this in turn means that elaborate and costly control systems have to be formed to keep a close check on workers.

One of the classic modern examples of fear motivation was practiced by the W. T. Grant Co. on its store managers. The Steak and Beans program, as it was called, attempted to motivate store managers with a host of negative incentives. Store managers who failed to meet their credit quotas were hit in the face with custard pies, had their ties cut in half, were forced to run around their stores backward and to push peanuts with their noses. There was even one unconfirmed report of a district manager being required to walk around a hotel lobby dressed in nothing but a diaper! The W. T. Grant Co. went bankrupt in 1977.

Money

Money is still very important to people and always will be, and many of our traditional incentives are tied to money in one form or another. Everybody wants more and most people will tell you that they don't have enough.

For most of us money is still a very effective incentive. However, for a growing percentage of younger workers, money has little effect on motivating them to work harder. Their attitude is: "Work until you have enough money to pay the bills and then opt for leisure time." All of this is very puzzling to those who hold traditional values.

One example is the young machinist who wanted to take three days' vacation to go deer hunting. His supervisor refused his request because the department was very pressed and being forced to work overtime and on Saturdays. The machinist, who had a record of tardiness, came to work thirty minutes late and the harassed supervisor told him, "If you are tardy one more time this month, you'll be suspended for three days without pay." You can guess who was late the next morning. The machinist perceived the monetary "threat" as his chance to go deer hunting and showed up tardy. The machinist was suspended, went deer hunting, and got what he asked for. And management applied the "proper" disciplinary policy. But the work didn't get done.

Another reason money has lost some of its clout is that most jobs don't have monetary incentives directly linked to productivity. Seven out of ten jobs in the U.S. have no direct relationship between money and performance. And study after study has concluded that simply paying someone a higher salary or increasing fringe benefits has no effect on motivation to work.

In many jobs today, money causes people to hold back efforts rather than work harder. When each of us goes to work, we make an unwritten psychological contract with our employers in which we agree to give time and effort in return for certain rewards such as money, meaningful work, security, status, acceptance, and the like. We also demand that we be rewarded fairly, as we perceive it, relative to our peers. Whenever we feel someone is being paid more for doing what we perceive as the same or less work, motivation can only suffer and we tend to hold back our efforts and do the minimum. Worse yet, in many salaried jobs the most highly paid people are the most recently hired ones. All of this can have a disastrous effect on company loyalty and the motivation to work.

Reliance on Technology and Structure

Another traditional management technique to ensure productivity has been to create a work situation where individual motivation really isn't important. Work has been automated or workers organized into assembly lines where they have little control over their jobs and are forced to do repetitious, boring tasks. While this may have been effective in a manufacturing-oriented economy, most of us no longer work in manufacturing. Over 70 percent of us are in government and service-oriented jobs where productivity isn't as easily and directly measurable. In a service job, productivity is much more than simply output per manhour. It's the overall picture of how well things get done. And service organizations and jobs depend much more on such human factors as employee dedication, motivation, and a willingness to give without holding back. As more of us assume white-collar service jobs, structure and technology will become less important and human motivation and incentives will become more important.

The Belief That Hard Work Pays Off

At one time management could simply assume that most workers came to the job believing that hard work and sacrifice paid off. This was a correct assumption. However, a decreasing percentage of younger workers believe in the value of hard work. While they are willing to work hard under the right conditions, they're too smart to believe that sweat and elbow grease automatically guarantee success. Younger workers are much more likely to be dedicated to self-fulfillment and leisure pursuits than company loyalty and hard work for its own sake. And if they don't like the job or the way they're being treated, you can count on them to leave—or, worse yet, retire psychologically and continue to draw a paycheck.

What Everybody Wants

Motivating anyone is a very complicated business. And the job has been further complicated by the fact that the workforce today is more diverse than ever. Yet for all the differences in race, sex, education, and age, almost all of us would like to satisfy several very strong needs through our work if given the opportunity. Here are four.

To Feel Free and in Charge of Our Own Life

Everyone likes to be the captain of his own ship and to feel that he has control over his present and future. And work is one way we try to exercise control over our lives. Traditional values hold that work is an unpleasant necessity and most people are lazy and will avoid it if they can. But is this really true? One research study found just the opposite and suggests that we have an inherent need to work. In the study, small children were given the opportunity to obtain an equal number of marbles with or without working for them. The results revealed that the majority of children wanted to work for their marbles rather than have them given to them. Researcher Devendra Singh concluded: "The important thing appears not to be that human beings get food, water and shelter, but that they get these things in ways that convey to the individual that he is important, that he does control what happens to him." It's when people feel controlled, rather than in control, that they are likely to lose the motivation to work.

To Do Something That's Meaningful to Us

According to Viktor Frankl, the greatest drive in life is meaning. Frankl came to this conclusion while being held prisoner in a Nazi concentration camp. He observed that many fellow inmates when subjected to atrocities and inhumane conditions died unprotesting while others clung to their lives with an almost unreal tenacity. He concluded that those who felt that their lives had meaning, worth, and a purpose to be served were far more likely to survive.

You don't have to observe anything as drastic as concentration-camp victims to reach the same conclusions. Look at the actuarial statistics on death and retirement, and you'll find high rates of illness and death occurring shortly after retirement. On the other hand, those who never retire and remain active and productive all their lives tend to live much longer. Creative professionals such as Arthur Fiedler, Grandma Moses, George Bernard Shaw, and others are only a few examples. They live longer, healthier lives because their work has meaning and it isn't taken from them like persons forced into retirement.

All of us can't be great artists or composers, but everyone likes to feel that he is doing something that's important and useful as he sees it. Look at the people at work around you and talk to the people you feel are the most motivated. More often than not, they are driven because they feel what they are doing has meaning and importance.

If you examine your own feelings about your job, you will likely find that you like doing things about the job that give it meaning and make a contribution. On the other hand, the things that turn you off will very likely be those tasks that you perceive as time-wasting and meaningless. Everyone likes to feel that what he does counts for something.

To Be Appreciated, Accepted, and Valued As an Individual

One turned-off worker I know has a cartoon drawing of the Peanuts character Linus hanging on his office wall. In the picture Linus says, "Doing a good job around here is like wetting your pants in a dark suit—it gives you a warm feeling but nobody notices." In addition to being an economic-technical system, every organization is a social system, and most of us have a very strong need to feel appreciated and accepted as one of the group. In addition, we have a strong need to feel that our efforts don't go unrecognized by the people we work for. Nobody likes to be taken for granted. And the boss who takes people's efforts for granted is in for hard times.

Very often strikes, grievances, work slowdowns, and conflicts appear on the surface to be over issues such as salary, working conditions, and benefits. But many of these areas of conflict are really caused by people who feel that their efforts aren't being recognized and appreciated. It isn't socially acceptable for an adult to say, "You hurt my feelings by not recognizing the loyalty and effort I've given you." But it is socially acceptable to complain, be apathetic, strike, grieve, or resign over an issue that is symptomatic of the problem. With the loosening of family and community ties in our society, the worker's need to be appreciated, recognized, and accepted on the job is greater than ever.

To Feel Good About Ourselves

This is the most important need of all. Each of us carries around in our brain an image of who we are, and this image is the single greatest factor in deciding how we behave. In short, how you see yourself determines who you are. Believe you are a healthy, worthwhile, valuable, responsible person and you will tend to become that person. Unfortunately, however, a negative self-image determines behavior just as much as a positive one.

Obviously everyone's self-image is a mixed bag of positive and negative beliefs. But it's the negative beliefs that cause problems. The more I read, observe, and research human behavior, the more I'm convinced that many of the world's people problems are caused by those who feel unworthy, inadequate, and unsure of themselves. The insecure boss is most likely to be a tyrant and the insecure worker is most likely to be a poor performer. People who feel comfortable with themselves and their work usually perform well under the right conditions.

A smart boss can capitalize on a worker's need to feel good about himself because achieving meaningful goals is one key to improving anyone's self-image. "My basic job as a manager is to convince every worker that he is better than he believes he is," said one very successful executive. "And I prove it to him by giving him challenging tasks that cause him to stretch and grow. As he achieves his goals, I point out his progress and encourage him to climb bigger mountains. And every succeeding mountain he climbs makes him feel better about himself."

There is a whole lot more to building a positive self-image than achieving goals. Self-image depends on many factors, including how autonomous we are, how other people react to us, and whether we feel our work is meaningful. These are all factors a boss can have some control over in motivating people to work smarter.

First Impressions

Freewrite for ten minutes on one of the following.

1. Did you enjoy reading this selection? Why or why not?
2. Have you ever felt "turned off" by school, work, or something similar? If so, what made you feel this way?
3. Describe your ideal job, either one you have had or one you would like to have. What kinds of rewards or extras would the job provide?

Vocabulary Check

Circle the letter of the word or phrase that best completes each of the following four sentences.

1. The word *clout* in "In leaner times fear was an effective . . . motivator. But today fear has lost practically all its clout" (paragraph 9) means
   a. color.   c. weakness.
   b. pleasure.   d. power.
2. The word *alien* in "The new breed perceives job security as a right rather than a privilege. This attitude is completely alien to traditional workers, who were grateful just to have a job" (paragraph 9) means
   a. strange.   c. correct.
   b. sensible.   d. expensive.
3. The word *diverse* in "the workforce today is more diverse than ever. Yet for all the differences in race, sex, education and age . . . ." (paragraph 18) means
   a. hard-working.   c. well-behaved.
   b. untrained.   d. made up of different kinds.
4. The word *tenacity* in "He observed that many fellow inmates . . . died unprotesting while others clung to their lives with an almost unreal tenacity" (paragraph 20) means
   a. softness.   c. determination.
   b. defeat.   d. lack of purpose.

Circle the letter of the word (or form of the word) from "Words to Watch" that best completes each of the following four sentences.

5. I don't think pass-fail courses are a good idea; without _____ such as high grades, students won't feel like doing the work.
   a. atrocities   c. incentives
   b. hosts   d. productions

6 I'd wanted to be a cocktail waitress for a long time, but I became _____ after finding out how exhausting the job was.
   a. inherent   c. automated
   b. disenchanted   d. virtual

7. Edgar's chain smoking and nervous knuckle-cracking are _____ the stress he is feeling.
   a. counterproductive of   c. capitalized on
   b. diluted by   d. symptomatic of

8. Our English instructor said he would _____ the three-day weekend by catching up on our essays.
   a. dilute   c. disenchant
   b. capitalize on d. automate

Reading Check

Central Point and Main Ideas

1. Which sentence best expresses the central point of the selection?
   a. Most American workers would prefer different jobs.
   b. Turned-off workers are either lazy or social misfits.
   c. To motivate today's employees, managers must help them feel more satisfied with themselves and their work.
   d. Worker dissatisfaction is causing absenteeism, high turnover, conflicts, and other problems.

2. Which sentence best expresses the main idea of paragraph 15?
   a. Unfair salaries can have a harmful effect on workers' motivation.
   b. Salaries are never determined fairly.
   c. Employers always give equal pay for equal work.
   d. The best-paid employees are often the newest ones.

3. Which sentence best expresses the main idea of paragraph 17?
   a. Hard work and sacrifice pay off.
   b. Today's workers have more free time than ever before.
   c. Today's younger workers are more interested in themselves than in their jobs.
   d. Young workers would rather quit than stay in jobs they dislike.

Key Supporting Details

4. _____ TRUE OR FALSE? One study mentioned in this selection suggests that people prefer working to getting something for nothing.

5. Viktor Frankl realized that the concentration camp inmates who survived were the ones who
   a. had been treated most brutally.
   b. had been treated least brutally.
   c. were the healthiest.
   d. believed their lives had a purpose.

SOCIAL ISSUES

Inferences

6. The author implies that workers
   a. can never be satisfied.
   b. are no different now than in the past.
   c. will always choose money over other incentives.
   d. can be motivated by good managers.
7. From the W. T. Grant example (paragraph 10), we can infer that
   a. big companies have more problems than small companies.
   b. fear is not a good way to motivate people.
   c. store managers are lazy.
   d. store managers have no sense of humor.
8. From paragraph 21, we might conclude that
   a. no one should retire.
   b. retirement always results in illness and early death.
   c. people who retire should plan to stay active.
   d. the healthiest people become artists.

The Writer's Craft

9. Paragraph 9 consists of
   a. descriptions of different kinds of workers.
   b. opinions about which jobs are harder than others.
   c. anecdotes about workers who have quit their jobs.
   d. reasons why fear no longer motivates workers.
10. In paragraphs 10, 13, and 21, the author supports his central point with
    a. opinions of experts.
    b. examples.
    c. definitions.
    d. statistics.

Outlining Activity

Complete the following outline of "Turning On Turned-Off Workers" by filling in the missing items where they belong.

Central point: To do their jobs well, today's workers need new incentives that build their self-images.

   A. Introduction

   B. _____
   1. Fear
   2. _____
   3. Technology and structure
   4. _____

C. What today's workers want
   1. To feel free and in charge of their own lives
   2. To do something that's meaningful to them

   3. _____

   4. _____

Discussion Questions

1. What was the worst job you ever had? What made it so bad?
2. LeBoeuf says that many of today's workers no longer believe in the value of hard work. Do you think hard work is worth the effort? Why or why not?
3. Which do you think is a supervisor's job—to help workers do their jobs better, watch them to make sure that they keep working, or simply leave them alone? Which type of supervisor would you prefer to work for, and why?
4. Other than money, what would motivate you to work hard on the job or at school?

Paragraph Assignments

1. Assume you are the president of a company whose workers have been having morale problems. Write a paragraph giving the managers in your company some suggestions based on LeBoeuf's article. You could begin your paragraph by writing something like this: "According to Michael LeBoeuf, all workers need _____. Therefore, when dealing with your employees, be sure to. . . ."

2. Have you ever had a job that you definitely would *not* recommend to someone else? Maybe you've worked in a hot, busy fast-food restaurant or baled hay in the sweltering summer or tried to sell unwilling customers merchandise by telephone. Write a paragraph in which you use reasons and examples to show why you would not recommend this job.

Essay Assignments

1. Which boss, coach, or teacher have you most enjoyed (or least enjoyed) working for? Why? In an essay, write about several reasons why your experience with this person was enjoyable (or unenjoyable). You might discuss whether he or she made you feel important or accepted, gave you meaningful work to do, and helped you feel good about yourself. Your thesis statement might be something like this:

   My high school football coach never let me call my own plays, kept me on the bench too much, and insulted me in front of the rest of the squad.

_____ was the best boss I ever had for several reasons.

2. What qualities in a job are most valuable to you? For instance, how important do you consider each of the following?

- flexible working hours
- plenty of vacation time
- medical benefits
- control over your duties
- meaningful work
- chance for promotion
- a boss that shows appreciation for you and your work
- feeling competent enough to do an excellent job

Are there other factors you would consider? Write an essay in which you discuss the most important qualities you want in a job. In your essay, arrange these qualities from least important to most important. Your thesis might be similar to this: "In whatever job I take, I will look for _____, _____, and, most importantly, _____."

Survival Skills

The Smart Way to Buy a New Car
Luella Fern Sanders

Preview

Have you ever been a victim of sticker shock? Are you convinced that a car salesperson is likely to "take you for a ride"—but not in a demonstration model? If so, you need to read the following selection by Luella Fern Sanders. It explains the pitfalls of automobile buying and the steps you can take to make sure you get your money's worth.

Words to Watch

forlorn (2): very unhappy
reverie (4): daydream
initial (5): first
negotiated (5): bargained for
intensified (7): made stronger
pliant (8): flexible
vital (9): very important
subsidized (18): helped with payment
unscrupulous (19): lacking morals
verbal (19): spoken
hamper (20): interfere with

"I'm really sorry," said the saleswoman to Rick, who was glancing at a big, beautiful red car. "Joe over there just told me this car is spoken for."

Seeing Rick's <u>forlorn</u> expression, she went on. "Look, we're holding it for a woman who said she might not be able to raise the down payment. Let me go check with the manager and see what the situation is."

As she walked off towards the office, Rick gazed at the luxurious upholstery and the space-age dashboard of his dream car. His old clunker had been stalling at stoplights for the past six months, and the last repairs had cost as much as the car was worth. He knew he needed a new car, but he hadn't known until he had taken this shiny beauty for a ten-minute test drive that he could no longer be happy without this particular car. He realized it was a bigger car than he needed and got fewer miles to the gallon than he wanted, but still. . . .

"You're in luck." The saleswoman interrupted his reverie. "My boss says we can't hold it any longer. It's all yours—let's sit down and do the paperwork."

The paperwork, it turned out, needed some doing. When Rick balked at the initial price, objecting that it was far higher than he could afford, the saleswoman said, "You give me a price. What do you think is a good price?" Rick said, "I'd just like a fair shake. The sticker price posted on the car is $12,300. I bet if I shopped around I could get a lower price." The saleswoman said, "Let me try something. Let me go back and see if I can persuade my boss to give you an extra $150 for your trade-in. Would that clinch it?" Rick said, "Make it $200 and you have a deal." The saleswoman disappeared for ten minutes, and when she reappeared, she was smiling. "He agreed," she said. "You drive a hard bargain." Rick then signed the sales agreement, feeling pleased that he had negotiated a good deal.

Rick, however, had been taken for a ride, just as many new car buyers are taken every day by salespeople who sell cars for many hundreds, even thousands, of dollars more than they are worth. Rick had violated rules one, two, three, and four for buying new cars: he held onto his old car too long before shopping for a new one, fell in love with a new model, did no homework before visiting a car dealer, and combined negotiating for a new car with trading in his old one.

Rick had waited to shop for a new car until he was unprepared to continue driving the one he already owned. His car was ready to expire, so he hardly had the time it might take to go about making a wise purchase on a new one. Also, he was psychologically unable to deal any longer with the troubles of his old clunker; he desperately wanted it out of his life, at any cost. As a result, he felt a sense of longing as soon as he entered the showroom—a feeling intensified by his spin around the block in the new, smooth-riding model. Consider, though, that his brief test drive told Rick almost nothing except how pleasant it would be to drive away from the dealership behind the wheel of a new car.

Clearly, Rick hadn't given much thought to what he really wanted. He bought on impulse, falling in love with one of the first cars he saw. Once his emotions overcame his judgment, he lost the only source of leverage a customer has in such negotiations—a willingness to walk away from the deal. Car salespeople often become amazingly pliant when they see a potential customer leaving the showroom. Unfortunately, Americans are conditioned to fall in love with cars. Many believe what the ads tell them—that a particular car will make them seem more attractive, richer, and sexier. They forget that the main reason for getting a car is transportation. As a result, many car buyers do not control their emotions enough to walk away from the "dream" car sitting in front of them. But customers who lose their hearts to a car may also lose many of their hard-earned dollars.

To decide what kind of car he really wanted and how much it was actually worth, Rick should have done some homework. Instead of evaluating his needs in the privacy of his home, he trusted that chance would guide him to the right make and model. As a result, he bought a car better suited to an upper-middle-class family of five than to a single person on a tight budget. Rick also had no idea how the car would perform, what kind of repair record it had, if it would stand up in a crash, and other vital information.

To find out, he should have consulted one of two sources before visiting any auto showroom: the latest April issue of the monthly magazine *Consumer Reports*, or *The Car Book*, an annual publication by Jack Gillis available at any local bookstore. If the April issue of *Consumer Reports* is not in a nearby library, one can obtain it by sending $4 to the Back Issue Department, Consumer Reports, P.O. Box 2485, Boulder, Colorado 80322. The April issue is almost entirely devoted to cars and is particularly valuable, since it provides detailed information on such matters as cost, performance, comfort, safety, reliability, and options.

After finding out what cars appealed to him, Rick should then have visited some auto showrooms for more information-gathering. When a salesperson approached, he should have said, "Hi, you have a Ford Taurus GL that I'd like to test drive." At the same time, Rick should make it crystal clear that while he seriously intends to buy a car, he is not ready to commit to a deal. Rick might say, for example, "It's my policy never to decide anything right away. This is a major purchase, and I intend to sleep on it for several days before doing anything." There is a high probability that Rick will get some pressure from the salesperson, who is likely to ask something like, "What can I do to sell you this car today?" Rick should make it clear there is *nothing* the salesperson or the manager can do; he will not agree to even a supposedly fabulous, cannot-be-repeated, once-in-a-lifetime offer.

After learning what model he wanted, Rick could then have found out the dealer's cost. *Discovering what the dealer paid for a car is extremely useful, even invaluable in negotiating the lowest price, and this information is easy and inexpensive to get.* There are at least two good sources for this information. First, available for about $4 at local bookstores is *Edmund's New Car Prices*, with separate booklets for domestic and foreign cars.

Second, for $11, *Consumer Reports* will provide a complete computer printout with information on any car model. Information on two cars costs $20 and on three cars costs $27. Printouts for each additional car cost $7. A copy of the following order form can be used:

```
Consumer Reports Auto Price Service          Please send me a Consumer Reports price and
Please print                                 options printout for each model listed below.
Name_____                    Make        Model          Style
Address_____       Example    BUICK   CENTURY LIMITED   SEDAN 4-DOOR
                        1st car   _____
City_____       2nd car   _____
State_____Zip___       3rd car   _____
Mail with payment to:
Consumer Reports, Box 8005         PRICES: $11 for 1 car. $20 for 2 cars. $27 for 3 cars.
Novi, Michigan 48050                       $7 for each additional printout after 3.       JG
```

Each printout gives detailed information on standard and optional equipment as well as the dealer's cost and list price for the basic model and all available options. Having this information means one can go to a dealer well equipped to negotiate. Here, for example, is the basic price information for a Ford Taurus GL 4-door given in a recent edition of *Consumer Reports*:

	Dealer cost	Sticker price (on the side window of the car)
Basic car	$9,981	$11,622

At this point, Rick is ready to negotiate, and he should do this *without even going to a showroom*. He should check the telephone yellow pages and get the numbers of five or so car dealers in his area that carry the car he wants to buy. He should then call and ask for a salesperson and say, "Hi, I'm going to buy a Taurus GL and want to get a good price. I know from a *Consumer Reports* printout that your cost for the car is $9,981. What is the lowest price you can quote me above that cost?" In most cases, the salesperson will want to call Rick back. Rick should make clear he is shopping around, but that he will be waiting for the salesperson's call. In this situation, Rick is clearly in the driver's seat. Because he knows the dealer's cost, all the power in the situation belongs to him, the customer.

While some salespeople may be irritated by a customer who is not interested in paying for a huge markup, others will take the opportunity to make a legitimate profit of about $200 to $400. A profit of $200 on the above Ford Taurus, for instance, would mean a savings of $1,581 off sticker price for the consumer. That's a fair markup for the dealership too, considering that all a salesperson must then do is write up the sale, a matter of about fifteen minutes' work. As the dealer will also receive a "holdback," about 3 percent of the car's invoice price given by the manufacturer, he will make enough on the sale to cover his advertising costs and other overhead and make a decent profit as well.

After Rick gets the best price, he should visit the dealer to get the dealer's price on his trade-in. If the price does not seem good enough, Rick should take his car to the dealer with the next lowest price for the new car. When he gets the lowest combination of new car price plus credit for his trade-in, he is ready to do one final bit of homework: getting the lowest interest rate on a new-car loan.

Car loans are expensive, and a knowledgeable consumer will shop around, trying to find the best deal. The price of borrowing money may vary, but whatever the cost of the loan, the price of the car itself should remain the same. While factory-subsidized loans are often among the best deals, low-interest dealer-subsidized loans may be tied to a higher price for the car. A wise shopper keeps the two items separate.

With the trade-in price and the loan interest rate taken care of, Rick is ready to sit down with the dealer he has chosen and get everything in writing. Some unscrupulous dealers will try to add on costs, such as a dealer's preparation fee, even *after* you've agreed on a price. Dealers will also try to sell service contracts, which generally make sense only for high-risk cars—ones likely to have a number of mechanical problems as predicted by ratings in the April issue of *Consumer Reports*. Except, of course, for such legitimate charges as sales tax, initial gas and oil charges, and title and inspection fees, a buyer should respond to any additions to the price by saying, "That's not acceptable. I am buying the car on the basis of our original verbal agreement."

In paying too much for a hastily chosen car, Rick was not alone. Because they fail to do any homework and allow their emotions to hamper their judgment, most people are poor car buyers. This situation is unfortunate because, next to a home, a car is the most expensive purchase for most people. The consumers who do a little research are likely to be well rewarded for the time they spend. They will also have the satisfaction of knowing that they have acted wisely and aggressively. Instead of being a car dealer's victims, they will have taken the steps needed to put themselves in the driver's seat.

First Impressions

Freewrite for ten minutes on one of the following.

1. Did you enjoy reading this selection? Why or why not?
2. Have you ever bought a car? If so, what made you choose that car?
3. In general, do you believe what you see in ads? Why or why not? Explain.

Vocabulary Check

Circle the letter of the word or phrase that best completes each of the following four sentences.

1. The words *balked at* in "When Rick balked at the initial price, objecting that it was far higher than he could afford, the saleswoman said, 'You give me a price'"(paragraph 5) mean
   a. accepted.   c. named.
   b. refused.   d. forgot.
2. The word *expire* in "His car was ready to expire, so he hardly had the time it might take to go about making a wise purchase" (paragraph 7) means
   a. drive.   c. die.
   b. last.   d. jump.
3. The word *leverage* in "he lost the only source of leverage a customer has in such negotiations—a willingness to walk away from the deal" (paragraph 8) means
   a. distress.   c. weakness.
   b. light.   d. power.
4. The word *invaluable* in "Discovering what the dealer paid for the car is extremely useful, even invaluable in negotiating the lowest price" (paragraph 12) means
   a. dangerous.   c. essential.
   b. worthless.   d. boring.

Circle the letter of the answer that best completes each of the following four items. Each sentence uses a word (or form of a word) from "Words to Watch."

5. I just took out a three-year home improvement loan, and my *initial* payment is due
   a. next month.
   b. in three years.
6. That instructor is amazingly *pliant*—she
   a. never listens to anyone else's ideas.
   b. is always willing to change an exam date if a student asks her to.
7. My college education is *subsidized*, so I
   a. don't have to pay for it all myself.
   b. have to work at McDonald's to pay my tuition.

8. My cousin Nick is so *unscrupulous* that he
   a. sold my pet poodle to a lab.
   b. returned the wallet he found on a bus to its owner.

Reading Check

Central Point and Main Ideas

1. Which sentence best expresses the central point of the selection?
   a. Car dealers often treat buyers unfairly.
   b. With some research and know-how, you can get a fair deal on a new car.
   c. Because he had not planned well, Rick bought the wrong car.
   d. New cars are more expensive than people think.
2. Which sentence best expresses the main idea of paragraph 8?
   a. People shouldn't be emotional when buying a car.
   b. Americans spend too much money on their cars.
   c. Americans believe what car ads tell them.
   d. Rick didn't really know what kind of car he wanted.
3. Which sentence best expresses the main idea of paragraph 19?
   a. Rick was ready to get everything in writing.
   b. Some car dealers are dishonest.
   c. The April issue of *Consumer Reports* predicts how many mechanical problems a car will have.
   d. Buyers should not permit dealers to change their original verbal agreements.

Key Supporting Details

4. _____ TRUE OR FALSE? It is impossible for the consumer to learn the dealer's actual cost for a car.
5. According to the article, the time to establish a trade-in price for your old car is
   a. before doing anything else.
   b. when you test drive a new car.
   c. after you have learned the dealer's cost.
   d. after you have agreed upon a price for the new car.
6. _____ TRUE OR FALSE? Buyers of new cars should generally buy service contracts only for high-risk cars.

Inferences

7. The author implies that many car salespeople
   a. help their customers find the best buy.
   b. do not hesitate to take advantage of their customers.
   c. prefer not to pressure their customers.
   d. make more money from knowledgeable customers than from uninformed ones.

THE SMART WAY TO BUY A NEW CAR   **247**

8. _____ TRUE OR FALSE? In paragraph 18, the author implies that the cost of a car loan can add a great deal to the price of a car.

The Writer's Craft

9. To interest the reader, the author begins this article with
   a. an anecdote.
   b. convincing statistics.
   c. a quotation from *Consumer Reports*.
   d. definitions.
10. The author organizes the steps of buying a car
    a. in the order they should be performed.
    b. from least important to most important.
    c. from most important to least important.
    d. in no particular order.

Outlining Activity

Complete the following outline of "The Smart Way to Buy a New Car" by filling in the missing items where they belong.

Central point: _____

_____

A. Keep your emotions under control.
   1. Don't buy just because you're disgusted with your own car.
   2. _____

   _____

B. _____

   _____

   1. Learn about cars from reliable publications.
   2. Visit auto showrooms to get more information.
   3. Find out the dealer's cost from *Edmund's New Car Prices* and *Consumer Reports*.
C. Negotiate for the best deal you can get.

   1. _____

   _____

   2. Go to the dealers with the best prices to get trade-in offers.
   3. Choose the dealer with the best new-car and trade-in package.

   4. _____

   _____

D. Sign the contract.
      1. Make sure it is the same as the dealer's verbal agreement.
      2. Beware of the dealer's additions to the contract.

Discussion Questions

1. Have you ever bought a new car (or a used one)? What was the experience like? Who was "in the driver's seat"—you or the salesperson?
2. Do you think you will follow any of the suggestions in the article if you decide to buy a new car? Why or why not?
3. In paragraph 8, Sanders writes: "Unfortunately, Americans are conditioned to fall in love with cars. Many believe what the ads tell them—that a particular car will make them seem more attractive, richer, and sexier." What messages are current car ads communicating? How?
4. In addition to cars, what other purchases or decisions do people often make for the wrong reasons or without enough information? How could they avoid making these mistakes?

Paragraph Assignments

1. Have you ever made a purchase that you later regretted? If so, write a paragraph describing what you bought, telling why you bought it, and explaining how you realized that you should not have bought it. Your topic sentence could be something like this: "After I bought _____, I realized I had made a mistake."
2. If you could buy your dream car (or dream house, or the best possible furnishings for your own room or apartment), what would you choose? Describe your ideal car, house, or decorating scheme in detail so that the reader can appreciate it as much as you would.

Essay Assignments

1. Write an essay titled "The Smart Way to Buy _____." Like Sanders, divide the process you are writing about into several clear steps, and explain each step in detail. Your thesis might be similar to this: "Following a few simple steps can make buying a dirt bike easier and less expensive." Here are some other purchases you might want to consider:

   - a used car
   - a kitchen appliance
   - children's clothing
   - a pet
   - stereo equipment
   - sports equipment
   - a TV set or VCR
   - a computer

2. According to this selection, automobile ads often appeal to our desires to feel "attractive, richer, and sexier." Ads for other products in newspapers, in magazines, and on radio or television also try to get us to make

purchases for reasons that have little or nothing to do with the products themselves. Write an essay about several of these ads. Devote a separate paragraph to each ad, explaining what it promises and why the ad has little to do with the product. Or, as an alternative, write about ads for several different types of purchases. You might wish to consider ads for the following products:

- cosmetics
- toothpaste
- perfumes
- cigarettes
- soft drinks
- beer
- clothing
- frozen and convenience foods
- cleaning supplies
- personal care products

Classroom Note-Taking
Clarissa White

Preview
Many students find note-taking difficult—for good reasons. They don't know what to write, and if they do get something written, by the time they look at their notes again, the scribbles have turned into a foreign language. But help is on the way. Author and educator Clarissa White, herself a veteran of many hours in lecture halls, offers practical techniques for mastering this essential study skill.

Words to Watch

equivalent (1): equal
showmanship (5): dramatic skill
vividly (5): very strongly
supplementary (9): additional
convey (14): communicate
verbatim (15): word for word
enumeration (18): list
reconstruct (20): recreate
transitional (24): connecting

How would you feel if you were forced to spend 1800 hours—the equivalent of 45 days in a row—sitting in a hard-backed chair, eyes wide open, listening to the sound of someone else's voice? You wouldn't be allowed to sleep, eat, or smoke. You couldn't leave the room. To make matters worse, you'd be expected to remember every important point the speaker made, and you'd be punished for forgetting. And, to top it off, you'd have to pay thousands of dollars for the experience.

Sound like the torture scene from the latest spy thriller? Actually, it's nothing of the kind. It's what all college students do who take a full load of five courses for four years. Those 1800 hours are the time they'll spend in the lecture room.

Unfortunately, many students do regard these hours as torture, and they do all sorts of things to deaden the pain. Some of them sit through class with glazed eyes, minds wandering to the athletic field or the movie theater. Others hide in the back of the room, sneaking glances at the newspaper or the book they're being tested on in their next class. Still others reduce the pain to zero: they simply don't come to class. These students do not realize that they're missing out on one of the most important aspects of their education.

Why Take Lecture Notes?

Colleges are not known for wasting money. If all they wanted you to do was read textbooks and take exams, they could save a fortune on faculty salaries. However, your college has gathered a group of experts and is paying them to lecture to you on a regular basis. There must be a reason.

Lecturers, in fact, accomplish several things that mere textbook reading cannot. They combine the material and approaches of many texts, saving you the trouble of researching an entire field. They keep up to date with their subjects and can include the latest studies or discoveries in their presentations; they needn't wait for the next edition of the book to come out. They can provide additional examples or simplify difficult concepts, making it easier for you to master tricky material. Finally, the best of them combine knowledge with expert showmanship. Both informative and entertaining speakers, they can make any subject from ancient civilizations to computers leap vividly to life.

True, you say, but isn't it good enough just to listen to these wonderful people without writing down what they say? Actually, it isn't. Studies have shown that after two weeks, you'll forget 80% of it. And you didn't come to the lecture room just to be entertained. You came to learn. The only way to keep the material in your head is to get some of it down in permanent form . . . in the form of lecture notes.

Taking lecture notes offers several advantages besides allowing you to keep a permanent record of what the lecturer says. You'll know which parts of the material the instructor thinks are the most important. Also, since you'll be looking and writing as well as listening, you'll be more alert, using three senses instead of just one. Learning will be easier, since you'll be organizing the lecture material and picking out the main points as you write. In addition, the mere act of writing something down helps you to remember it longer. Best of all, if you listen carefully, you might even get a sneak preview of the final exam into your notes. At any rate, you'll be busy writing and thinking instead of daydreaming or doodling, and the busier you are, the less bored you'll be.

How to Take Lecture Notes

There are three steps to mastering the art of taking good lecture notes: the preparation, the note-taking process itself, and the post-lecture review.

Preparation

First, mentally prepare yourself to take good notes. Examine your attitude. Remember, you're not going to the lecture room to be bored, tortured, or entertained; you're going there to learn. Also, examine the material the lecture will cover. Read the textbook chapter in advance. If your instructor's lecture usually follows the organization of the textbook, you'll be familiar with the material and won't have to spend half the lecture wondering what it's about or how to spell a key term. If, however, your instructor merely uses the textbook as a launching pad and devotes most of the lecture to <u>supplementary</u> material, at least you'll have the background to follow what is being said.

Second, prepare yourself physically. Get a good night's sleep, and get to class—on time. Even better, get to class early, so you can get a good seat near the front of the room. You'll hear better there and be less tempted to let your mind wander. You'll also have time to open your notebook to a new page, find your pen, and write the date, course, and topic of the lecture at the top. This way, you won't still be groping under your chair or flipping through pages when the instructor begins to speak.

Process

When you take class notes, always use 8 1/2 x 11" paper, preferably in a looseleaf notebook so you can insert handouts. Write on only one side of the paper; later, you might want to spread all your notes out in front of you. Before class, draw two vertical lines on your paper, one two inches from the left edge and the other an inch or so from the right edge. The space on the left will be reserved for the key words you'll write after class, while the one-inch strip on the right will contain your own thoughts and reactions to the lecture. The large middle section, of course, is for the lecture notes themselves. And you'll be writing in ink, preferably with a felt-tipped pen for speed. Remember, you'll want to keep these notes for a while.

Of course, your instructor will have a great deal to say during the class period. Obviously, you won't have time to write down every pearl of wisdom in your notes. How much is enough? The answer lies in *active listening* and *organization*. Before you write anything, listen and be sure you understand the point being made. Then, write down only the main points, secondary points, and as many examples as you need to make the points clear. Your instructor may have given you a head start by writing an outline for the lecture on the board. Copy it at the beginning of your notes and use it for main points. Organize your notes by starting main points at the first vertical line, indenting secondary points under main points, and indenting examples even further. Skip lines between main sections. Wherever possible, number the points; they'll be easier to learn if you know how many there are.

Here are some other hints for taking good classroom notes:

1. Don't try to write in complete, grammatical sentences or get down everything the instructor says. However, do write complete phrases that convey the gist of the lecturer's information. Isolated words won't mean much at exam time.

2. Use your own words or the instructor's, whichever are quicker and easier for you. Be sure, though, to take down definitions, formulas, or technical language verbatim.

3. If you miss something, don't panic. Leave space for it in your notes and keep going. Later, get the missing information from a classmate or your textbook.

4. As you take notes, think about what you are hearing. If you have a question about or an objection to something the lecturer says, make a note of it in the right-hand margin of your page.

5. Be alert for signals that something is an important point ("A major cause of anxiety is. . . ."), a new topic ("Another problem of urban living is. . . ."), the beginning of an enumeration ("There are seven warning signals. . . ."), or a summary ("In conclusion. . . ."). These signals will help you organize your note-taking. If your instructor says, "The point I am trying to make is. . . ," be sure you *get* the point—in your notes.

6. Finally, don't ignore the very beginning and end of class. Often, instructors devote the first five minutes of their lectures to a review of material already covered or a preview of the day's lecture. The last five minutes of a lecture can contain a clear summary of the class—or ten more major points the instructor simply *has* to make before the bell rings. Don't spend the first five minutes of class getting your materials out and the last five minutes putting them away. If you do, you'll probably miss something important.

Post-Lecture Review

Taking good notes lets you bring the lecture home with you. However, the real learning takes place after class. As soon as you have time, sit down and reread your notes. Fill in anything unclear or missing while it's still fresh in your mind. Then, in the left-hand column of each page, write a few key words and phrases that summarize the points of the lecture. Cover your notes, and, using only these key words, try to <u>reconstruct</u> as much of the lecture as you can. This review will cement the major points in your memory—and will save significant time when you study for the exam.

Some Questions and Answers About Note-Taking

"What if I already know what's being explained? Do I have to write it down?"—Yes, because you'll know it's important to the instructor . . . and may be on the exam.

"How can I tell when something's important?"—Your instructor may say so. Or there will be a strong hint: a dramatic pause, a slightly raised voice, something written on the board, a repetition. Hint: If you hear it more than once, be sure to write it down.

"My instructor talks too fast. Shouldn't I use shorthand or a tape recorder?"—No. Shorthand notes need to be transcribed in order to be read; tape recordings have to be played back in their entirety. Both processes are time-consuming. In addition, they'll keep you from listening actively and organizing what you are hearing—and thus hinder the learning process.

"Is it OK to abbreviate?"—Certainly. Abbreviations are a great time-saver. Just don't overdo it, or your notes will look as though they're in Martian. You can use initials for major concepts or names, such as TM for *transcendental meditation.* Or you can shorten words by writing just the first syllable, omitting vowels, reducing the last syllable to one letter, or using an apostrophe, as in *gov't.* You can even use symbols for common <u>transitional</u> words: + for *and,* w/ for *with,* vs. for *against,* ∴ for *therefore,* ~ for *like.* Feel free to make up your own code. To paraphrase an old advertising slogan: if you cn wrt ~ ths, you cn tk gd notes.

First Impressions

Freewrite for ten minutes on one of the following.

1. Did you enjoy reading this selection? Why or why not?
2. Does your mind ever wander during class? If so, what happens?

3. Which study skill (such as listening, note-taking, underlining or highlighting textbooks, budgeting your time, and reviewing for tests) is easiest for you? Which is hardest? Why?

Vocabulary Check

Circle the letter of the word or phrase that best completes each of the following four sentences.

1. The word *groping* in "This way, you won't still be groping under your chair [for your notebook] . . . when the instructor begins to speak" (paragraph 10) means
   a. fast asleep.
   b. sitting quietly.
   c. leaving quickly.
   d. searching blindly.
2. The word *gist* in "Don't try to write in complete, grammatical sentences or get down everything the instructor says. However, do write complete phrases that convey the gist of the lecturer's information" (paragraph 14) means
   a. real weakness.
   b. most important part.
   c. title.
   d. original source.
3. The word *transcribed* in " 'Shouldn't I use shorthand or a tape recorder?'— No. Shorthand notes need to be transcribed in order to be read; tape recordings have to be played back in their entirety. Both processes are time-consuming" (paragraph 23) means
   a. memorized.
   b. written out fully.
   c. thrown away.
   d. tape recorded.
4. The word *hinder* in "Both processes are time-consuming. In addition, they'll keep you from listening actively and organizing what you are hearing—and thus hinder the learning process" (paragraph 23) means
   a. compare.
   b. speed up.
   c. explain.
   d. block.

Insert four of the following words (or forms of words) from "Words to Watch" where they belong in the sentences below.

conveyed   equivalent   transitional   verbatim   vivid

5. The dream was so _____ that for a few minutes I wondered if it had really happened.

6. Junior high school is a _____ period between grade school and high school.

7. Taking one of Mr. Furst's classes is the _____ of a three-month sentence to hard labor.

8. After hearing *The Cat in the Hat* so many times, my daughter knows it _____ .

Reading Check

Central Point and Main Ideas

1. Which sentence best expresses the central point of the selection?
    a. Students should pay close attention in lecture classes.
    b. Taking notes in lecture classes is an important skill which involves three main steps.
    c. Lecture classes are usually more valuable to students than textbooks are.
    d. Students do many things to make attending lecture classes easier.
2. Which sentence best expresses the main idea of paragraph 5?
    a. College lecturers deserve better salaries.
    b. Lecturers keep up with the latest developments in their fields.
    c. Lecturers have certain advantages over textbooks.
    d. Lecturers have to be entertaining speakers.
3. Which sentence best expresses the main idea of paragraph 19?
    a. Students should take notes during the beginning and end of class.
    b. Many instructors review old material or give previews of new material during the first five minutes of a class.
    c. Often something important is said at the end of class.
    d. Too many instructors keep talking even after the period is over.

Key Supporting Details

4. _____ TRUE OR FALSE? If you take careful lecture notes in a class, there's no need to read the textbook.
5. According to the article, real learning of lecture material takes place
    a. at the beginning of class when the instructor gives a preview.
    b. in the last five minutes of class when the lecture is summarized.
    c. after class when students review their notes.
    d. just before the exam.
6. _____ TRUE OR FALSE? Lecture notes should always be written in the student's own words.

Inferences

7. The author implies that people who take good lecture notes will
    a. get A's in all their courses.
    b. write their notes in shorthand.
    c. know everything their instructors know.
    d. learn more from their classes.
8. _____ TRUE OR FALSE? The author implies that students can invent their own systems for abbreviating in their lecture notes.

The Writer's Craft
9. The introduction to White's article (paragraphs 1 and 2) includes
   a. quotations from experts.
   b. a startling statistic about college life.
   c. an anecdote about a student who never takes notes.
   d. a list of note-taking hints.
10. The material on how to take notes in paragraphs 8 through 12 is presented in
    a. order of importance.
    b. time order.
    c. the form of a comparison.
    d. the form of an anecdote.

Outlining Activity

Complete the following outline of "Classroom Note-Taking" by filling in the missing items where they belong.

A. Reasons to take lecture notes

B. _____

    1. _____

       a. Mentally

       b. _____

    2. _____

    3. _____

C. Questions and answers about note-taking

Discussion Questions

1. Have you ever had trouble taking lecture notes? If so, what happened? Which of the suggestions in this article might have helped?
2. Which would you rather do in class, talk or listen? Why? How does it change your approach to a class if you know you'll be expected to ask and answer questions?
3. Besides knowing how to take good notes on lectures, what must students know how to do to be successful in college? What suggestions could you give a beginning student who wants to survive in college?
4. How much of the responsibility for the success of any class is the instructor's? How much of the responsibility is the student's?

Paragraph Assignments

1. Have you ever had a teacher who could "make any subject . . . leap vividly to life"? Or have you had a teacher who puts students to sleep? In a

paragraph, describe one of your best teachers or one of your worst. Use specific, vivid examples of your teacher's words and actions to show why he or she was effective or ineffective. Your topic sentence might be similar to one of these:

> Ms. Timmons was my best professor so far because she made her subject come alive.
>
> Mr. Atkins was one of the worst teachers I ever had because he was so disorganized.

2. Aside from note-taking, what other study skills are essential to a student's success in college? Choose a valuable skill such as reviewing for a test, budgeting study time, planning a daily or weekly schedule, organizing a study group, taking notes on assigned reading, or underlining in a textbook. Write a paragraph giving step-by-step instructions on how to perform the skill.

Essay Assignments

1. Like White, many people believe that lectures can add a great deal to a student's education. But some believe that the lecture system does more harm than good. What do you think? Write an essay either supporting or attacking the system of teaching by lecture. Here are two possible central points for this assignment:

   > The lecture system of teaching has three advantages.
   >
   > The lecture system of teaching should be done away with for several reasons.

   Be sure to support your thesis with interesting and convincing examples.

2. Write a humorous essay titled "Surefire Ways to Flunk Out of College." In the paper, use humor to show how college students can be sure of failing. Like White, you could organize your essay in steps with specific examples to illustrate each step. Here are some ideas you might want to suggest:

   - Take advantage of the library's quiet atmosphere to catch up on your sleep.
   - Skip class again. It'll be just as boring today as it was yesterday when you weren't there.
   - Don't skip a party. You only live once.
   - Leave those term papers for the last minute—if you finish them early, you'll just lose them anyway.

Owning a Pet Can Have Therapeutic Value
Jane Brody

Preview

Have you ever known anyone who treated a pet dog, cat, parakeet, or even a boa constrictor as if it were a person? To those who don't own animals, pet lovers who lavish affection and money on their furry, feathery, or scaly friends may seem a little odd. But now well-known health expert Jane Brody shows that pet lovers may have better arguments in their favor than they suspected. In this selection from *The New York Times*, she tells how pets can benefit people in unexpected ways.

Words to Watch

boon (2): benefit
transmissible (2): spreadable
gerontology (3): study of old people
unconditional (3): unlimited
enhance (6): increase
alleviate (6): relieve
adverse (6): harmful
dissipate (7): get rid of
nurturing (9): caring
empathy (9): sharing another's thoughts and feelings
reclusive (13): withdrawn from the world
facilitated (14): helped
catatonic schizophrenia (17): a mental illness in which the patient cannot move or speak
autistic (21): having a mental illness whose symptoms are withdrawal and uncontrolled behavior
organic (26): physical

Given the opportunity, most pet owners will rave about the joys of sharing their homes with an animal, be it a collie or a chameleon. But they may not realize that, beyond pleasure, their nonhuman companions could help to improve their mental and physical health and even extend their lives.

To be sure, pets are not always a blessing. They can be costly, demanding of time, care and energy, and can even become a source of family conflict, such as when Father ends up having to walk the dog his child had agreed to care for. Urban dwellers may find large pets to be more a bother than a boon, and in some cases pets can be a source of ailments transmissible to their owners. Still, many benefits of owning a pet have been noted in various recent studies.

Benefits to young and old

According to Gerald Jay Westbrook of the Andrus Gerontology Center at the University of Southern California, pets, and especially pet dogs, can offer protection, companionship and unconditional love.

Pets are, he said, "nonthreatening, nonjudgmental, open, welcoming, accepting and attentive." Unlike spouses or parents, they don't talk back, criticize or issue commands. They give people something to care and worry about and be responsible for and make them feel needed and wanted. They also provide a socially acceptable outlet for the need for physical contact. Men have been observed to touch their pets as often and as lovingly as women do.

Pets help to combat loneliness and have been shown to increase their owners' chances of meeting other people. A study in London's Hyde Park showed that when accompanied by their dogs, pet owners spoke to more people and had longer conversations than when they walked alone. In Sweden, 63 percent of dog owners surveyed said their pets had added to their opportunities to talk to people, and 57 percent said their dogs had "got them friends."

Pets also help to organize a person's day (a dog used to being walked and fed at 7 A.M. is not likely to let you loll in bed until 9). They provide sense of purpose, help to enhance self-esteem and self-control and generally alleviate the adverse effects of stress.

Pets can also be a source of solace (a teddy bear for all ages) and help to dissipate negative emotions like anger, disappointment and grief. Virtually all people talk to their pets and sometimes use them to work through conflicts or problems. Some couples have been observed to talk to each other through their pets.

A study at the University of Maryland suggested that pets help to bring families closer together, reducing conflict and tension and increasing play among family members. Dr. Erika Friedman, a health scientist at

Brooklyn College, says that people who are "depressed by the loss of a relative or friend can learn to love others again through first learning to love and care for a pet."

For children, pets help to teach responsibility, nurturing, compassion, loyalty and empathy. Unlike adults in their interaction with children, pets are uncritical, consistently loving and don't give orders. In this age when both parents are often at work when children come home from school, pets offer children a dependable "welcome home" and a feeling of security.

Pets are becoming popular visitors to nursing homes and old-age homes, and in some cases, residents themselves.

A University of Minnesota study of 774 long-term health care facilities disclosed that about half were using pets to help their residents. Pets were said to provide nursing-home residents with entertainment and enjoyment, to serve as an outlet for the expression of feelings, rekindle pleasant memories and create a more homelike atmosphere.

Dramatic improvements in outlook and ability have been noted among nursing-home residents as a result of pet programs. Previously uncommunicative and bedridden patients have started talking to the staff and other residents about their pets, and some have even got up and gone out to walk their pets.

Dr. Daniel Lago's program at Pennsylvania State University has given pets to 65 rural elderly people, nearly half of whom live alone. For some, he reports, the pets have sparked "dramatic transformations," enabling severely disabled people to rise above their disability and helping depressed, reclusive people become more socially active. His preliminary observations suggest that closeness to a pet is the key to its benefits, showing an association with higher morale, greater social activity and better physical health.

Treating the emotionally disturbed

Pet-facilitated therapy has brought sometimes remarkable improvement in patients with otherwise intractable mental illnesses.

According to psychotherapists at the Ohio State University College of Medicine, Sonny was a 19-year-old psychotic who spent nearly all his time lying in his hospital bed. Nothing seemed to interest or reach him, his answers to questions were limited to "yes," "no" and "I don't know," and he did not respond to traditional therapies. But when a wire-haired fox terrier was brought to his bed, Sonny showed an immediate interest, smiled broadly and was soon out of bed frolicking with the dog. He then asked his first question, "Where can I keep him?"

For Sonny, his psychiatrist said, the terrier was the turning point of therapy, providing the needed wedge in Sonny's emotionally locked door. He began to take an interest in his surroundings and to request and respond to therapy, and he was soon discharged as recovered.

In another instance, 25-year-old Marsha, diagnosed as suffering from catatonic schizophrenia, showed no improvement after drug and electro-shock therapy. In fact, her condition worsened and she became totally withdrawn, frozen and almost mute.

Then a dog was brought to her and she began to follow it about, walk it, stroke it and talk about it to the other patients. Within six days of receiving the dog, Marsha had improved markedly, and shortly afterward she was discharged from the hospital.

The Ohio therapists, Samuel A. Corson, Elizabeth O'Leary Corson and Peter H. Gwynne, stumbled upon the value of pets in treatment. They had established a dog ward at the hospital to study animal behavior. Hearing the dogs bark, several patients, some of whom had been uncommunicative throughout their hospital stay, broke their self-imposed silence and asked if they could play with or help care for the animals.

Impressed with the apparent benefits of the interaction between patients and dogs, the therapists began a more systematic study, discovering in the process that pets have been used occasionally in psychotherapy as far back as the 18th century and that modern pet-oriented psychotherapy had been described in detail by Boris M. Levinson in 1969. However, its effectiveness has received little systematic study to date.

Autistic children have shown some improvement in a special program in Florida involving dolphins. Pets have also helped to calm hyperactive and overly aggressive children. In an institution for the criminally insane, inmates were given pet birds, fish, hamsters, guinea pigs and gerbils. Some of the men became very nurturing and assumed full responsibility for the care of their pets. The animals helped to establish trust and a communications link between inmates and staff.

Many questions remain to be answered about pet-facilitated therapy. Who is likely to be helped by it, for example, how should the pet be matched to the patient, and when in treatment should a pet be introduced?

Aiding the sick and handicapped

Seeing Eye dogs for the blind are universally known, but few realize that now there are also "hearing-ear" dogs for the deaf. Dogs can also be trained to retrieve and carry things for people confined to wheelchair or bed.

In addition, a pet can provide the impetus for improvement in a physical disability. Dr. Lago at Penn State tells of a woman disabled by a broken hip who was given a dog for protection. One day the dog ran upstairs and, not knowing why, the woman followed, discovering for the first time that she could navigate the stairs.

Learning to ride a horse can help to put a handicapped child on a more equal basis with normal children. Therapists have noted an improvement in muscle tone, self-confidence and spirits of handicapped children as a result of horseback riding.

The value of pets to people with various <u>organic</u> ailments is just beginning to be explored. In a pioneering study, Dr. Friedman of Brooklyn College and her former colleagues at the University of Pennsylvania's Center for the Interaction of Animals and Society showed that among 92 victims of heart disease, significantly more pet owners survived for at least one year than did those without pets. 28 percent of those without a pet were dead in a year, whereas only 6 percent of those with pets had died.

Dr. Friedman and Alan Beck of the University of Pennsylvania report that watching fish in a tank lowers blood pressure, promotes relaxation and counters the adverse physiological effects of stress. Dr. Aaron H. Katcher, a psychiatrist who heads the university's people-animal center, says his group is studying the importance of touching animals as a source of comfort that might not be available from other people.

First Impressions

Freewrite for ten minutes on one of the following.

1. Did you enjoy reading this selection? Why or why not?
2. Have you ever had a pet? If so, what pleasures or comforts did it provide?
3. What are some reasons why pets are such good companions for people?

Vocabulary Check

Circle the letter of the word or phrase that best completes each of the following four sentences.

1. The words *loll in* in "a dog used to being walked and fed at 7 A.M. is not likely to let you loll in bed until 9" (paragraph 6) mean
   a. clean up in.
   b. walk.
   c. relax lazily in.
   d. get out of.
2. The word *solace* in "Pets can also be a source of solace (a teddy bear for all ages)" (paragraph 7) means
   a. comfort.
   b. food.
   c. worry.
   d. pain.

3. The word *intractable* in "Pet-facilitated therapy has brought sometimes remarkable improvement in patients with otherwise intractable mental illnesses" (paragraph 14) means
   a. interesting.
   b. brief.
   c. difficult to cure.
   d. easily manage.
4. The word *impetus* in "a pet can provide the impetus for improvement in a physical disability. . . . One day the dog ran upstairs and, not knowing why, the woman [with a broken hip] followed, discovering for the first time that she could navigate the stairs" (paragraph 24) means
   a. discouragement.
   b. motivation.
   c. interference.
   d. transportation.

Insert each of the following words (or forms of words) from "Words to Watch" where it belongs in one of the four sentences below.

          dissipate   empathy   facilitated   reclusive

5. When Violet lost her job, her friend Marcia was the only person to show any _____ with her.
6. My boss's suggestions _____ the successful completion of the project.
7. The old man's suspicion that everyone wanted to take advantage of him made him more _____ than ever.
8. Bright sunlight will quickly _____ fog.

Reading Check

Central Point and Main Ideas

1. Which sentence best expresses the central point of the selection?
   a. Studies show that pets do more for people than doctors do.
   b. Pets help the elderly take a renewed interest in life.
   c. Recent studies show that pets can improve their owners' mental and physical health.
   d. Every family should own a pet.
2. Which sentence best expresses the main idea of paragraph 9?
   a. Pets help children learn responsibility.
   b. Pets are less threatening to children than to adults.
   c. Pets keep children whose parents work from returning to an empty home after school.
   d. Pets help children in several ways.
3. Which sentence best expresses the main idea of paragraph 21?
   a. Dolphins have helped autistic children.
   b. Pets can calm children.

c. Various pets have been helpful at an institution for the criminally insane.
d. Pets have helped both mentally disturbed children and criminally insane adults.

Key Supporting Details

4. According to the article, elderly residents of nursing homes who are given pets
   a. become more talkative and active.
   b. treat the pets like children.
   c. end up disliking the pets.
   d. cannot care for the pets on a full-time basis.
5. _____ TRUE OR FALSE? Watching fish in a tank can lower a person's blood pressure.
6. According to the article, dog owners
   a. rarely speak to their pets.
   b. do not live as long as cat owners.
   c. are more likely to make friends than are people who don't own dogs.
   d. are more likely to be depressed than people who do not own pets.

Inferences

7. In paragraph 4, Brody implies that
   a. spouses and parents tend to be critical.
   b. people without pets have nothing to care about.
   c. men are more loving than women.
   d. pets require a great deal of time and trouble.
8. _____ TRUE OR FALSE? From the article we can conclude that people have a basic need for affection.

The Writer's Craft

9. The title of this selection
   a. contains a joke.
   b. is a quotation.
   c. offers the reader a choice.
   d. states the article's central point.
10. The tone of this article is mainly
    a. humorous.
    b. sarcastic.
    c. objective.
    d. questioning.

Summarizing Activity

Complete the following summary of "Owning a Pet Can Have Therapeutic Value" by filling in each blank with one or more words.

Although pets are not always a blessing, they can be good for people both mentally and physically. One important advantage of owning pets is that they don't criticize their owners. Instead, they (1) _____

_____.

Pets bring families together and teach children (2) _____

_____.

The elderly also benefit from owning pets. Nursing home residents (3) ___

_____.

Severely disturbed people, including a psychotic patient and a schizophrenic, were transformed by pet ownership. Recent studies note that pet ownership brings improvement to both (4) _____

_____.

Dogs have been trained to help deaf and disabled people, and riding horses has improved muscle tone in handicapped children. Heart patients with pets (5) _____

_____,

and even watching fish in a tank reduces stress.

Discussion Questions

1. Many pet owners regard their pets not as animals, but as members of the family. If you've ever had a pet, did you treat it as an animal—or as a person?
2. Gerald Jay Westbrook is quoted in the article as saying that "pets, especially pet dogs, can offer protection, companionship and unconditional love." Do you agree? Which do you think make better pets, cats or dogs? Why?
3. What might be some disadvantages of giving a pet to a sick or elderly person?
4. What basic needs do pets meet for their owners? Can people fulfill the same needs for each other? If so, how?

Paragraph Assignments

1. Write a paragraph describing how a pet has made you feel better. You could focus, for instance, on how having the responsibility for an animal made you feel more grown up when you were a child. Or you could describe how your pet cheered you when you needed a totally accepting friend. Use specific incidents so your reader can understand the feelings you're writing about. Here are some possible topic sentences for this paragraph:

For me, owning a dog has had therapeutic value.
Living alone in an apartment would be lonely for me if it weren't for my cat.
As a child, I learned a lot about responsibility from a pair of gerbils.

Or, as an alternative, write a similar paragraph about someone you know or have read about who has benefited from owning or caring for a pet.

2. In paragraph 2, Brody writes, "To be sure, pets are not always a blessing." Write a paragraph about a time an animal was a nuisance—or worse. You could write about a problem Brody mentions in paragraph 2 or any other type of trouble, including a time a pet was sick, got loose, or perhaps even bit someone. In your paragraph tell about what happened in detail and describe what happened afterwards. Or, as an alternative, write about a time a pet was a blessing or did something wonderful for you or someone you know.

Essay Assignments

1. Write an essay about an animal that was considered not just a pet but a valuable member of the family. In your supporting paragraphs, you could discuss topics such as the following:

   - how the family got this pet
   - how the family adjusted to the pet
   - how the pet is part of family life

   Another way of organizing this essay is to write about the relationship of each member of the family with the pet. Your thesis might be similar to one of these:

   From the day our dog Sparky showed up in ribbons and bows as my sister's birthday present, he has been a full-fledged part of our family.
   Members of my family react to my pet bird Alvin in very different ways.

2. Owning pets is only one of many activities that can have therapeutic value. Think of other relationships, activities, or objects that help you feel better physically or emotionally, or both. These might include the following:

   - music
   - a hobby
   - a book
   - housecleaning
   - volunteer work
   - an exercise program
   - a favorite souvenir
   - household repair work
   - a close friend or relative
   - work on a car

   Write an essay about the ways one or more of these forms of "therapy" strengthen you. For each one, give specific examples that show how the activity or relationship helps you.

Face Up to Your Fears
Lois B. Morris

Preview

"Everybody's afraid of something," Lois Morris points out—such as flying, public speaking, water, or final exams. But there's no need to spend a lifetime avoiding what frightens us. In this article from *Glamour*, Morris urges us to face our fears—and gives us useful strategies for doing just that.

Words to Watch

clammy (1): unpleasantly damp
phobias (8): abnormal terrors
confront (8): face
emerged (12): came out
obstacle to (13): something that is in the way of
bouts (14): attacks
venture (15): risky undertaking
podium (16): speaker's platform
desensitized (17): weakened the effect of
ensuing (22): following
discharge (22): get rid of
paradoxical (24): apparently contradictory
involuntary (24): automatic
tedious (28): boring

"I thought I was going to die," Christie Rhodes says. "I felt cold and clammy, and couldn't seem to draw a breath. I was clutching the side of the boat and my hand felt suddenly numb." 1

Everybody's afraid of something. Christie's (names have been changed) deepest fear was being out on the water. Yet there she was, 2 sailing on Lake Michigan on her first date with Paul Fried, trying to hide her panic.

Christie is a bold and adventurous woman, a super risk-taker. She's confident and accomplished and no one realizes she has fears like anybody else. No one knew how, after she gave up teaching high school to go to medical school, she had to struggle against her fear of competing in a "man's field."

Our fears can cripple us in many ways, especially if they're an excuse to protect ourselves against taking risks, says psychiatrist Arthur B. Hardy, M.D., of Menlo Park, California. "If you don't take risks you won't have much fear," says Dr. Hardy. "Of course you won't have much of anything else either."

Christie's fear of the water began at age four, when a rowboat she and her uncle were in capsized. Though her uncle grabbed on to her immediately and she was never in danger, the dread remained. Christie consistently avoided boating until that day, twenty-three years later, when Paul invited her to go sailing.

"Even thinking about it panicked me," she recalls. "I was all ready to suggest tennis instead, when suddenly I got angry at myself. If I wanted to go sailing with this man, why couldn't I? I hate it when something gets in my way, and here I was allowing a silly fear to stop me."

Although Christie sensed that if she could endure her terror long enough the feeling would begin to subside, it was a full year before she was truly comfortable on a boat. Now, four years later, Christie Rhodes, M.D., can't think of any activity she's more fond of than sailing with Paul, who's now her husband.

The technique that Christie used to overcome her fear is called "flooding" by psychotherapists who specialize in the treatment of phobias and fears. It is the quickest, but most difficult, method. "You jump in, confront the discomfort without any excuses and without trying to build up to it," says psychologist William Golden, Ph.D., director of the Stress and Pain Control Clinic of the Long Island Consultation Center in New York and director of stress management at the Institute for Rational Emotive Therapy in New York City. "You say to yourself, 'This is what I want to achieve and I'm going to go through it. I know it's going to feel uncomfortable, but it's worth it.'"

Determining whether it is worth it is the first step. Are all fears really worth eliminating?

Dr. Hardy and most mental health professionals believe that a fear is worth confronting if it immobilizes, restricts or otherwise prevents you from leading a full, active life and you're making personal and professional sacrifices to avoid it. It is not worth confronting if you use the fear to benefit your life. Dr. Golden calls the latter kind of avoidance "adaptive." The very common fear of public speaking, for example, is adaptive if it leads you to rehearse and master your material. It is MALadaptive if it causes you to turn down speaking engagements that could advance your career.

Julia Bernstein, for example, is in her forties and an outspoken activist for women's causes. She has always loved politics but was so afraid of public speaking that, while in her twenties, she decided against a political career and went into merchandising instead. "I would tell myself that I wasn't strong enough or smart enough to be in politics," she explains today. "And after I married, every time I was tempted to hop onto somebody's bandwagon, I'd tell myself that my husband wouldn't like it." Yet it was he who suggested that Julia run for a seat on the local board of education.

Julia agreed—and quickly found herself suffering from constant anxiety. She consulted a therapist. The reasons behind her fear soon emerged. "In my case, it had to do with my fear of competing with my older sister," she says. "Symbolically, public speaking meant standing up and speaking for myself, asserting my own identity—and that was a terrible conflict for me."

To chart the extent of your fears, Dr. Golden recommends that you make a list of the things that frighten you. You are probably already aware of any phobias you may have, since such intense fears are marked by panic attacks and alarm reactions. But inhale deeply and be very frank with yourself. You'll soon be able to understand the damage you may be doing by giving in to your fears if you measure your list against your personal and professional goals—both short- and long-term. Then ask yourself: What should I be doing that I'm not doing now? If you have a fear of flying, and yet you want to be manager for Midwest division sales in five years, you'd better start dealing with this obstacle to your advancement now. If you enjoy swimming, but even in a pool you worry about shark attacks, the price for not standing up to that fear will depend on your priorities: Just how important is swimming to you?

Dealing with fear really means coping with anxiety. In her book *Women and Anxiety*, psychiatrist Helen A. De Rosis, M.D., writes, "Anxiety is a feeling of dread, a nameless fear that distracts the minds and hearts of people of all ages." But, she also says, "Most bouts of anxiety are manageable, as well as self-limited." No matter how bad it is, anxiety always passes—and that's the key to toughing out your fears.

"Any new venture should have some anxiety," says Dr. Hardy. "It's unfamiliar territory and you don't have your confidence up yet. Once you do, your anxiety decreases." If you can endure a feared situation long enough to gain some confidence—as in giving a speech, performing before an audience, writing a company memo or asking an important favor—the self-assurance itself becomes convincing.

Once you have that confidence, you can choose the method of confronting your fear that's best suited to you. Christie Rhodes's sink-or-swim sailing technique was her way of coping. Julia Bernstein, the future politician, needed a more gradual approach to accustom herself to stepping up to a <u>podium</u>.

At her therapist's suggestion, Julia first practiced speaking into a tape recorder, then into a mirror. Next, she delivered the speech before her husband, and another time, in front of his parents and their neighbors. By pushing herself further and further into her fear, Julia "<u>desensitized</u>" it. It was a difficult process, requiring serious motivation. Today she's still a little nervous before giving a speech, but feels it's almost a kind of energy she can harness for a good, vibrant delivery. More and more, she even enjoys herself.

The gradual approach is especially useful in overcoming fears of a sexual nature. Adds Dr. Golden, "Instead of having sex with someone right away—the flooding approach—you do it the old-fashioned one-step-at-a-time way, gradually building up to it by kissing and hugging, another time petting clothed, then unclothed. You don't go on until you feel more comfortable with the easier step. That's the difference between the gradual approach and flooding."

If, by using either approach, you still can't face your fears, you may have to dig deeper, and move to traditional psychotherapy.

"It's much easier to overcome a fear if you know its basis," says Samuel V. Dunkell, M.D., assistant clinical professor of psychiatry at New York Hospital/Cornell Medical Center. For example, a fear of water could represent an early traumatic experience involving water, but in other cases the fear may be a metaphor. "The fear of water may be a response to something unstructured, and therefore, to some people, overwhelming," he says.

"Many of the uncomfortable feelings associated with fear—from muscle tension to the dead certainty you're having a heart attack—are caused by adrenaline and other hormones being released into the bloodstream," says Dr. DeRosis.

In a true danger situation these hormones fuel the <u>ensuing</u> fight or flight. But in anxiety attacks, no forceful action is taken, and they become, in her words, "body bound." The tension builds and must be released before you can begin to think and act appropriately. "Being actively competitive or aggressive are some of the ways you can <u>discharge</u> the effects of adrenaline in the body," she says. "Find some kind of game, sport or exercise that would help in activating your muscles or in confronting your anxiety more directly."

But what if exercise is not always appropriate? If you're trying to deal with a sexual hangup, you can't jog around the park every time your lover wants sex—so the solution is to try relaxation techniques. Dr. Golden recommends this one: Take long, slow, deep breaths, and each time you exhale, release the tension from a different part of your body. If you tense up after lovemaking has begun, for example, imagine yourself sitting on a cliff overlooking the ocean. "Use all your senses to conjure up the scene," he suggests. "See the waves, hear the sound of the ocean, feel the warmth of the sun, taste the salt air." Then, once you're more relaxed, you can get back to what's going on in bed.

You might even try humor in confronting your fears. Dr. Dunkell mentions a method called "paradoxical intentions," in which you make fun of your fear by challenging yourself to have exactly the reaction that you fear—but in a ridiculous way. Are you afraid that when you're on an airplane you'll lose control and scream? At the very moment the fear begins, laugh at yourself and imagine yourself taking the stewardess' microphone and announcing to the other passengers, "Please make sure your seat belts are securely fastened, because in just one moment you're going to hear the world's loudest scream." It works, says Dr. Dunkell, because "the minute you try to do something voluntary, the involuntary reaction of anxiety disappears."

A friend can also provide support, if only to "applaud" when you accomplish each step, or to help you set a schedule and keep to it. But don't depend on the friend's presence, Dr. Golden cautions. If someone accompanies you to the top of a tall building to help you overcome your fear of heights, go by yourself the next time. The same principle applies, he says, if you use a tranquilizer: Use it the first time, go without it the next. (If your doctor prescribes tranquilizers or antidepressant medication in conjunction with phobia therapy, you should, of course, follow orders.)

Maybe the only thing you'll need, however, is a change in attitude, something that experts call a "counterphobic" attitude—the desire to stand up, even if shaking and quaking, to what we fear. "Everybody's frightened. Everybody's anxious. Everybody's worried. In fact, the people who seem least so, like heroes, are often more frightened than anyone else," says New York psychoanalyst Lee Minoff. "The soldier might have so great a fear of dying that the only way he can deal with it is to rush right into combat in a counterphobic way. And he becomes the hero."

There are other, unexpected payoffs as well when you conquer your fears. More than one fear may topple by attacking only one. In the same way that unconfronted fears mushroom, says Dr. Golden, success also multiplies—he calls it the "ripple effect."

Secondly, being able to do something you've long avoided causes a lifelong "high." Says Dr. Dunkell, "Once the fear is overcome, people take an exaggerated pleasure in their former terror. My wife used to have a little phobia about flying. Now while to most people flying is a perhaps <u>tedious</u> necessity of modern life, for her each time is a real adventure."

Go up in that plane and walk onto that stage and set sail in that boat and *love* it?

Go ahead and try. You have nothing to fear.

First Impressions

Freewrite for ten minutes on one of the following.

1. Did you enjoy reading this selection? Why or why not?
2. What are some of the things you're afraid of? What effects (if any) do these fears have on your life?
3. Do you think of yourself as a risk-taker? Why or why not?

Vocabulary Check

Circle the letter of the word or phrase that best completes each of the following four sentences.

1. The word *subside* in "Although Christie sensed that if she could endure her terror long enough the feeling would begin to subside, it was a full year before she was truly comfortable on a boat" (paragraph 7) means
   a. be exciting.   c. show.
   b. decrease.   d. grow stronger.
2. The word *immobilizes* in "a fear is worth confronting if it immobilizes, restricts or otherwise prevents you from leading a full, active life" (paragraph 10) means
   a. encourages.   c. prevents movement.
   b. frees from.   d. embarrasses.
3. The word *vibrant* in "Today she's still a little nervous before giving a speech, but feels it's almost a kind of energy she can harness for a good, vibrant delivery" (paragraph 17) means
   a. dull.   c. expensive.
   b. lively.   d. shaky.
4. The word *mushroom* in "In the same way that unconfronted fears mushroom, . . . success also multiplies" (paragraph 27) means
   a. are buried.   c. disappear.
   b. grow quickly.   d. remain unchanged.

Insert four of the following words (or forms of words) from "Words to Watch" where they belong in the sentences below.

confront   emerge   obstacle   phobia   tedious

5. Jeff's refusal to get to work on time is a definite _____ to his career.
6. Although she knew that her son had forged the note to his teacher, Gloria hesitated to _____ him with the evidence.
7. The lesson was _____, so half the class fell asleep before it was over.
8. Our puppy was too frightened to _____ from its hiding place until we turned off the vacuum cleaner.

Reading Check

Central Point and Main Ideas

1. Which sentence best expresses the central point of the selection?
    a. All people have fears.
    b. Some fears are worse than others.
    c. Everyone's fears are different.
    d. We can overcome our fears.
2. Which sentence best expresses the main idea of paragraph 10?
    a. A fear should be confronted only if it keeps a person from leading a full life, but not if it is beneficial.
    b. Some fears are actually helpful because they make people more careful.
    c. Everyone is afraid of public speaking.
    d. There are two kinds of fears.
3. Which sentence best expresses the main idea of paragraph 25?
    a. Any tranquilizer should be used only once.
    b. Depending on help from another person makes overcoming fears too difficult.
    c. A friend's support is important to someone who is trying to overcome a fear.
    d. A friend or medication can help someone overcome fears, but neither should be depended upon too much.

Key Supporting Details

4. _____ TRUE OR FALSE? There's more than one way to confront a fear.
5. Christie Rhodes's fear of water
    a. prevented her from completing medical school.
    b. made her turn down a sailing date with Paul Fried.

        c. took a full year to overcome after she went sailing.
        d. lasted all her life.
    6. _____ TRUE OR FALSE? Participating in active sports can help a person deal with anxiety.

Inferences

    7. We can conclude from the article that anxiety
        a. can never be controlled.
        b. is a natural response to a new situation.
        c. must be treated by a therapist.
        d. affects more women than men.
    8. _____ TRUE OR FALSE? From the article, we can conclude that fears rarely begin in childhood.

The Writer's Craft

    9. Morris usually supports her main ideas by
        a. supplying anecdotes and quotations from experts.
        b. using statistics and reports on research.
        c. providing information on how she overcame her own fears.
        d. comparing people who face fears to people who do not.
    10. In the conclusion of her article (paragraphs 29 and 30), Morris
        a. encourages readers to take her advice.
        b. gives a final example of someone who overcame a fear.
        c. quotes an expert.
        d. summarizes methods people can use to overcome fears.

Summarizing Activity

Complete the following summary of "Face Up to Your Fears" by filling in each blank with one or more words.

As one woman, Christie Rhodes, learned, fear can be overcome by confronting it directly with a technique known as flooding. However, experts suggest that fears should be faced only when (1) _____. If people are honest with themselves, they'll find that their fears may be hurting them personally and professionally. Some fears should be overcome gradually, as Julia, a woman who feared public speaking, discovered. Anxiety, which is (2) _____

_____,
can also be overcome gradually. One key to overcoming fears gradually is psychotherapy. Because of the body's physical responses to fear, another good approach is (3) _____. Five additional ways to overcome fear

are (4) _____
_____.

The benefits of overcoming fears in these ways are (5) _____
_____
_____.

Discussion Questions

1. Have you or someone you know ever taken steps to combat a fear? If so, what was done? How successful was it?
2. Are you afraid to speak in public? If not, why not? If so, what do you think you could do to reduce your fears?
3. What kinds of fears should we try to conquer? What are some fears that might actually be good for us?
4. What are some fears that college students have? What have you found that works to combat these fears?

Paragraph Assignments

1. Write a paragraph about how you, or someone you know, overcame a fear. Begin by telling what the fear was and how long you (or the other person) had it. Then write about how the fear was finally conquered and how you or the other person felt afterwards. Use a topic sentence such as one of the following:

   I finally overcame my fear of heights when I got a job on the top
     floor of an office building.
   My sister's fear of crowds disappeared the day her boyfriend took her
     to a Bruce Springsteen concert.

2. In her article, Morris quotes Dr. Arthur B. Hardy, who suggests, "If you don't take risks you won't have much fear . . . Of course you won't have much of anything else either." Think of a time when you dared to take a risk. Write a paragraph telling what happened: what the risk was, why you took it, and what you gained or lost by it.

Essay Assignments

1. Many of our fears, like Christie Rhodes's fear of the water, come from childhood experiences. Think of an incident from your childhood that left you with a fear of something, perhaps a fear you still have. Then write an essay about that fear. Begin by telling exactly what happened, and then describe the effect this experience had on you. Your thesis could be similar to "I've been afraid of the dark ever since the time that my brother locked me in a closet."

2. Besides our fears, what other kinds of things should we "face up to"? Write an essay urging readers to stop avoiding situations such as one or more of the following:

- studying
- letter writing
- bill paying
- dieting
- housework
- doctor's or dentist's appointment
- car maintenance
- exercising

Make some clear suggestions, as Morris does, for ways that people could stop avoiding these situations.

31

Specific Details
David Skwire and Frances Chitwood

Preview

Making vague, general statements is easy—sometimes too easy. Having said something like "College registration is a nightmare," students are often unwilling to back up their generalization with specific details. In this selection, David Skwire and Frances Chitwood attack writing that is too general and show how almost every kind of writing—from job application letters to students' essays—can be made livelier and more interesting.

Words to Watch

vague (1): unclear
generalizations (1): broad statements
reflection (1): indication
slapstick humor (2): rowdy comedy
materialism (2): greed
technically (3): by the rules
vital (5): very important
conviction (7): believability
relevant (8): on the topic
trivial (8): unimportant

Abstract writing is writing that lacks specific details and is filled with vague, indefinite words and broad, general statements. Every piece of writing needs generalizations, of course, and vague words such as *nice* and *interesting* can be useful. But writing that is dominated by such words is abstract writing, and abstract writing is the main cause of bored readers. It is often a reflection of lazy or careless thinking. It can interfere with full communication of meaning. It prevents many students from developing their themes adequately. ("I've already said all I have to say. How am I supposed to get 300 more words on this subject?")

Abstract writing occurs when someone writes:

Too much poverty exists in this country.
instead of
I see one-third of a nation ill-housed, ill-clad, ill-nourished.

Mr. Jones is a tough grader.
instead of
Mr. Jones flunked 75% of his class and gave no higher than a C to the students who passed.

Don't fire until they're extremely close.
instead of
Don't fire until you see the whites of their eyes.

The story is quite amusing in places, but basically is very serious.
instead of
Underneath the slapstick humor, the story presents a bitter attack on materialism and snobbishness.

Religious faith is important, but practical considerations are also important.
instead of
Trust in God, and keep your powder dry.

Nothing is technically wrong with the above examples of abstract writing, but we need only compare them to the rewritten concrete versions to see their basic inadequacy. They convey less information. They are less interesting. They have less impact. There is nothing wrong with them except they are no good.

The use of specific details is the most direct way to avoid abstract writing. We tend to get irritated with a politician—or college dean—who, when confronted by a crucial issue, releases a press statement declaring, "We will give this matter our careful consideration." We get irritated not because the matter doesn't require careful consideration, but because the abstractness of the statement makes us suspect that we have just received a strong whiff of hot air. That suspicion will probably decrease significantly if the statement goes on to tell us the names of the people who will confer on this issue next Monday under orders to present recommendations within two weeks, those recommendations to be acted on inside of forty-eight hours. In this case, the specific details have served to support the generalization, have given us a clear notion of what the generalization means, and have helped create an impression of seriousness and sincerity.

Politicians and college deans are not the only people who sometimes seem too fond of hot air. Much of the material we read every day is abstract: flabby, dull, vague, and essentially meaningless. Like hot air, it lacks real body, real substance. The sports columnist writes, "The team should do better this year," and leaves it at that, instead of adding, "It should finish in third or fourth place and even has a fighting chance for the pennant." The teacher writes an angry letter saying, "This school ignores all vital needs of the faculty," and sounds like just another crank unless the letter goes on and points to *specific* needs that have in fact been ignored.

Student writing, from essay exams to themes in composition courses, could be vastly improved if more attention were paid to eliminating excessive abstraction and adding specific details. The more specific details, the less chance of hot air. Students should not tolerate the same things in their own writing that antagonize them in someone else's. Our use of language, not to mention our level of thought, would probably improve a hundredfold if we established an informal rule *never* to make an unsupported general statement, a general statement not backed up by specific details.

This rule sounds easy enough, but it means what it says. It means a writer should never try to get by with sentences such as, "The day was too hot"; "The hero of the story was very ambitious"; "The establishment is corrupt"; "The Industrial Revolution brought about many changes." These sentences are neither ungrammatical nor necessarily incorrect, but if they are not backed up by specific details they are worthless. "The day was too hot" is uninteresting and unpersuasive. *Back it up.* The reader should know that the temperature was 93 degrees, that Bill's sweaty glasses kept slipping off his nose, that even the little kids who usually filled the street were inside trying to keep cool, that a cocker spaniel who had managed to find a spot of shade was too exhausted and miserable to bother brushing away the flies. Whatever the piece of writing—a letter of application for a job, an analysis of a short story, a final exam in history—specific details give the writing life and conviction that abstractions alone can never achieve.

One more point about specific details: within reason, *the more specific the better*. As long as the detail is relevant—as long, that is, as it backs up the generalization and is not instantly obvious as too trivial for consideration—the writer is unlikely to go wrong by being too specific. On a history exam, a student may generalize, "In the Revolutionary War, the Americans had many difficulties." As specific support for that statement, the student may go on to write, "The number of Tories was quite large." But better in all respects would be, "Tories numbered as much as 30% of the population." The more specific the better, and one can almost always be more specific. Eventually, it is true, one can defeat one's purpose; it would be a mistake to give the reader the names and addresses of all the Tories during the Revolutionary War. The writing would then become so overwhelmed by specifics that the major point would be lost. Elementary common sense is usually the best guide in preventing that kind of mistake, and in actual practice few student writers run up against the problem of being too specific.

To summarize: support all your generalizations with relevant specific details. Remember that, within reason, the more specific the details, the better the writing.

Abstract (weak)

> The telephone is a great scientific achievement, but it can also be a great inconvenience. Who could begin to count the number of times that phone calls have come from unwelcome people or on unwelcome occasions? Telephones make me nervous.

More Specific (better)

> The telephone is a great scientific achievement, but it can also be a great pain. I get calls from bill collectors, hurt relatives, salespeople, charities and angry neighbors. The calls always seem to come at the worst times too. They've interrupted my meals, my baths, my parties, my sleep. I couldn't get along without telephones, but sometimes they make me a nervous wreck.

Still More Specific (much better)

> The telephone is a great scientific achievement, but it can also be a great big headache. More often than not, that cheery ringing in my ears brings messages from the Ace Bill Collecting Agency, my mother (who is feeling snubbed for the fourth time that week), salesmen of encyclopedias and magazines, solicitors for the Policemen's Ball and Disease of the Month Foundation, and neighbors complaining about my dog. That's not to mention frequent wrong numbers—usually for someone named "Arnie." The calls always seem to come at the worst times, too. They've interrupted steak dinners, hot tubs, Friday night parties, and Saturday morning sleep-ins. There's no escape. Sometimes I wonder if there are any telephones in padded cells.

First Impressions

Freewrite for ten minutes on one of the following.

1. Did you enjoy reading this selection? Why or why not?
2. Describe your hand, the pen or pencil you are writing with, some other object you have with you, or the chair or room you are in. Use as many specific details as you can.

3. Besides "Use specific details," what other advice about good writing have you heard? Was the advice helpful?

Vocabulary Check

Circle the letter of the word or phrase that best completes each of the following four sentences.

1. The word *concrete* in "Nothing is technically wrong with the above examples of abstract writing, but we need only compare them to the rewritten concrete versions to see their basic inadequacy" (paragraph 3) means
    a. general.   c. unusual.
    b. specific.   d. lying.
2. The word *convey* in "the above examples of abstract writing . . . . convey less information. They are less interesting" (paragraph 3) means
    a. lift.   c. seek.
    b. communicate.   d. deny.
3. The word *vastly* in "Student writing . . . could be vastly improved if more attention were paid to . . . adding specific details. The more specific details, the less chance of hot air" (paragraph 6) means
    a. ridiculously.   c. dangerously.
    b. sadly.   d. greatly.
4. The word *antagonize* in "Students should not tolerate the same things in their own writing that antagonize them in someone else's" (paragraph 6) means
    a. interrupt.   c. offend.
    b. please.   d. bury.

Insert four of the following words (or forms of words) from "Words to Watch" where they belong in the sentences below.

conviction   materialism   reflection   relevant   trivial

5. "We only have five minutes left, class," said the instructor. "So please limit your questions to those that are _____ to tomorrow's assignment."

6. A person's posture is often a _____ of his or her self-confidence.

7. My manager spends so much time worrying about _____ problems that he rarely gets around to the really important jobs.

8. Nina performed her role with such _____ that many people in the audience cried when the character she was playing died.

Reading Check

Central Point and Main Ideas

1. Which sentence best expresses the central point of the selection?
    a. Abstract writing is untruthful writing.
    b. A good writer uses specific details to support generalizations.
    c. Students must eliminate all abstractions from their writing.
    d. Writing that is too detailed can be overwhelming.
2. Which sentence best expresses the main idea of paragraph 5?
    a. Sports columnists cannot write well.
    b. Politicians and college deans are full of hot air.
    c. Much writing is ineffective because it is too abstract.
    d. Teachers must improve their writing skills.
3. Which sentence best expresses the main idea of paragraph 6?
    a. Students would think better if they learned to write better.
    b. Student writers need informal rules.
    c. Students should be less open-minded if they want to write forcefully.
    d. Fewer generalizations and more specific details would improve students' writing.

Key Supporting Details

4. _____ TRUE OR FALSE? Skwire and Chitwood think that student writers often use too many specific details.
5. According to the authors, abstract writing is often the result of
    a. lazy or careless thinking.
    b. careful rewriting.
    c. poor grammar.
    d. specific details.
6. Using specific details in writing adds
    a. broad, general statements.
    b. information and interest.
    c. clear organization.
    d. difficult words.

Inferences

7. _____ TRUE OR FALSE? From the essay we can conclude that statistics can be good supporting details.
8. From paragraphs 4 and 5 we can conclude that politicians, college deans, sports columnists, and teachers
    a. give all matters careful consideration.
    b. often make hasty decisions.
    c. like to write angry letters.
    d. sometimes avoid supporting their general statements.

The Writer's Craft

9. To focus the reader's attention, the authors begin this essay with
   a. a quotation.
   b. a definition.
   c. statistics.
   d. an anecdote.
10. To support their central point, the authors use many
    a. generalizations.
    b. famous quotations.
    c. examples.
    d. questions.

Summarizing Activity

Complete the following summary of "Specific Details" by filling in each blank with one or more words.

Abstract writing is filled with (1) _____

_____.

Unfortunately, without specific details, writing becomes (2) _____

_____.

In contrast, specific details (3) _____

_____.

Empty generalizations are common with everyone from politicians to college deans. However, writers are less likely to produce hot air when (4) _____

_____.

Usually, the more specific the details are, the better writing is, except when (5) _____

_____.

Discussion Questions

1. Which of the three paragraphs on telephones do you like best? Why? Which of them do you think is most like your own writing?
2. Why do you think so many students do not use specific details in their writing?
3. What is "hot air"? What examples of "hot air" have you read or heard? Why do you think it is so common?
4. Where else—other than in English assignments—are specific details important?

Paragraph Assignments

1. Pick the selection you've liked best from the book so far, and choose the specific details from it that made the greatest impression on you. Then write a paragraph explaining why the details impressed you. In your paragraph, quote at least three details from the selection. (Use quotation marks around the words you borrow from the selection.) Your paragraph could begin like this:

   The most unforgettable details in "What We Can Learn from Japan's Prisons" are the ones that describe Ed Arnett's jail sentence. For example, according to the selection, all Arnett had to eat was "seaweed, fish and rice." This detail impressed me because . . . .

2. Prove that specific details make writing more interesting and lively by writing two paragraphs on the same topic. Your first paragraph should contain only vague generalizations about the topic. The second paragraph, though, should contain many specific details to back up your generalizations. Choose a subject you know a great deal about, such as one of the following:

   - music you like
   - someone you admire
   - something you're proud of
   - a meal you enjoyed
   - an accident you had
   - an embarrassing experience
   - a job interview
   - someone who has influenced you

Essay Assignments

1. The authors state that all types of writing, including job application letters, benefit from the addition of specific details. Write a letter of application in which you list your educational and work background. Include carefully selected details to illustrate your abilities and accomplishments. Use a central point such as "Two years' experience as a sales manager, college courses in business and English, and a willingness to work hard make me the ideal candidate for the position you advertised in the January 17th edition of *The Daily Planet*."
2. Choose an essay you have already written, and improve it by supporting its central idea and topic sentences with interesting specific details. You may want to make other revisions as well in order to make the essay as good as possible.

Problems and Pain
M. Scott Peck

Preview

If you've ever had an entirely easy day at school or work, chances are you didn't accomplish very much. Doing anything worthwhile is difficult, as psychiatrist M. Scott Peck points out in this excerpt from his best-selling book *The Road Less Traveled*. Strange as it sounds, this may actually be good news. If Peck is right, we should welcome our problems rather than complain about them.

Words to Watch

transcend (2): rise above
incessantly (3): without stopping
subtly (3): faintly
affliction (3): suffering
visited upon (3): forced on
cutting edge (7): severe test
resolving (7): working out

Life is difficult.

This is a great truth, one of the greatest truths. It is a great truth because once we truly see this truth, we <u>transcend</u> it. Once we truly know that life is difficult—once we truly understand and accept it—then life is no longer difficult. Because once it is accepted, the fact that life is difficult no longer matters.

Most do not fully see this truth that life is difficult. Instead they moan more or less <u>incessantly</u>, noisily or <u>subtly</u>, about the enormity of their problems, their burdens, and their difficulties as if they were generally easy, as if life should be easy. They voice their belief, noisily or subtly, that their difficulties represent a unique kind of <u>affliction</u> that should not be and that has somehow been especially <u>visited upon</u> them, or else upon their families, their tribe, their class, their nation, their race or even their species, and not upon others. I know about this moaning because I have done my share.

Life is a series of problems. Do we want to moan about them or solve them? Do we want to teach our children to solve them? 4

Discipline is the basic set of tools we require to solve life's problems. Without discipline we can solve nothing. With only some discipline we can solve only some problems. With total discipline we can solve all problems. 5

What makes life difficult is that the process of confronting and solving problems is a painful one. Problems, depending upon their nature, evoke in us frustration or grief or sadness or loneliness or guilt or regret or anger or fear or anxiety or anguish or despair. These are uncomfortable feelings, often very uncomfortable, often as painful as any kind of physical pain, sometimes equaling the very worst kind of physical pain. Indeed, it is because of the pain that events or conflicts engender in us that we call them problems. And since life poses an endless series of problems, life is always difficult and is full of pain as well as joy. 6

Yet it is in this whole process of meeting and solving problems that life has its meaning. Problems are the cutting edge that distinguishes between success and failure. Problems call forth our courage and our wisdom; indeed, they create our courage and our wisdom. It is only because of problems that we grow mentally and spiritually. When we desire to encourage the growth of the human spirit, we challenge and encourage the human capacity to solve problems, just as in school we deliberately set problems for our children to solve. It is through the pain of confronting and resolving problems that we learn. As Benjamin Franklin said, "Those things that hurt, instruct." It is for this reason that wise people learn not to dread but actually to welcome problems and actually to welcome the pain of problems. 7

First Impressions

Freewrite for ten minutes on one of the following.

1. Did you enjoy reading this selection? Why or why not?
2. Describe a problem that has been on your mind, and suggest ways you could use discipline to help solve it.
3. Describe a problem you've heard someone complain about. What did you say (or what could you have said) to help?

Vocabulary Check

Circle the letter of the word or phrase that best completes each of the following four sentences.

SURVIVAL SKILLS

1. The word *enormity* in "they moan . . . about the enormity of their problems, their burdens, and their difficulties" (paragraph 3) means
   a. stillness.
   b. happiness.
   c. restfulness.
   d. great size.
2. The word *evoke* in "Problems, depending upon their nature, evoke in us frustration or grief or sadness" (paragraph 6) means
   a. discourage.
   b. produce.
   c. prevent.
   d. delight.
3. The word *engender* in "it is *because* of the pain that events or conflicts engender in us that we call them problems" (paragraph 6) means
   a. assist.
   b. disappear.
   c. destroy.
   d. cause.
4. The word *capacity* in "we challenge and encourage the human capacity to solve problems" (paragraph 7) means
   a. ability.
   b. lack of ability.
   c. confusion.
   d. lack of need.

Insert four of the following words (or forms of words) from "Words to Watch" where they belong in the sentences below.

| affliction | incessantly | resolved | subtle | transcend |

5. I wish Stan didn't talk so _____. It's difficult to get a word into the conversation.

6. The trainer of the circus dogs used _____ signals, which the audience couldn't even see.

7. Meditation helped Philip _____ the stresses of his job.

8. My advisor _____ the conflict in my fall schedule by moving my writing class to a later time.

Reading Check

Central Point and Main Ideas

1. Which sentence best expresses the central point of the selection?
   a. Everybody has problems.
   b. We become stronger by facing and solving the problems of life.
   c. Life is difficult because our problems bring us pain.
   d. People like to complain about their problems.
2. Which sentence best expresses the main idea of paragraph 3?
   a. Most people feel life is easy.
   b. The author feels life is easy.
   c. The author likes to complain about his problems.
   d. Most people complain about how hard their lives are.

Key Supporting Details

3. _____ TRUE OR FALSE? According to the author, life becomes easier once we accept the idea that it is difficult.
4. According to the article, we give school children difficult problems to solve in order to
   a. help them learn to ignore pain.
   b. challenge them to learn.
   c. teach them to fear the pain of solving problems.
   d. teach them respect for authority.

Inferences

5. The quotation from Benjamin Franklin, "Those things that hurt, instruct," (paragraph 7) suggests that
   a. pain cannot be avoided.
   b. pain teaches us important lessons.
   c. we do not learn when we are in pain.
   d. we do not learn from experience.
6. _____ TRUE OR FALSE? The author implies that most people believe life is not supposed to be so difficult.
7. The author implies that people who have no problems
   a. are lucky.
   b. are numerous.
   c. do not become strong.
   d. do not become artists or writers.

The Writer's Craft

8. The author's main purpose is to
   a. entertain readers with his ideas about problems.
   b. inform readers that everyone experiences problems.
   c. persuade readers that it is better to face and solve problems than complain about them.
   d. persuade readers that he has more problems than they do.
9. The author probably used just one short sentence in the first paragraph to
   a. save space.
   b. get readers' attention.
   c. confuse readers.
   d. make readers laugh.
10. If you were selecting a different title for this selection, a good choice would be
    a. "Ignore Your Problems and They'll Go Away."
    b. "How Your Problems Help You Grow."
    c. "My Problems Are Worse Than Your Problems."
    d. "America's Most Serious Problems."

Summarizing Activity

1. Circle the letter of the statement that summarizes the supporting details in paragraphs 1 through 3.
   a. It does not matter how difficult life is.
   b. Accepting the fact that life is difficult actually makes life easier, but instead most people just complain.
   c. People think that they have more problems than anyone else and that life should be easier than it is.
   d. The author has done some complaining himself.
2. Circle the letter of the statement that summarizes the supporting details in paragraphs 4 and 5.
   a. Life is a series of problems.
   b. The many problems in life can be solved through discipline.
   c. People face one problem after another in their lives.
   d. Children should learn to solve their problems instead of moan about them.
3. Circle the letter of the statement that summarizes the supporting details in paragraph 6.
   a. It is painful to confront and solve problems.
   b. Emotional pain can never be as uncomfortable as physical pain.
   c. Some problems make people feel lonely.
   d. Life can be joyous.
4. Circle the letter of the statement that summarizes the supporting details in paragraph 7.
   a. School children are challenged to solve problems.
   b. Some problems cannot be solved.
   c. Benjamin Franklin said, "Those things that hurt, instruct."
   d. Problems should be welcomed because they help people grow.

Discussion Questions

1. Do you agree with Peck's central point? Can you think of instances in your life (or someone else's) in which facing and solving a problem helped you (or the other person) grow?
2. What are some things people do when they're trying to avoid facing their problems?
3. In paragraph 5, Peck claims, "With total discipline we can solve all problems." Do you agree that discipline can solve *all* problems? Can you think of any problems that discipline by itself will not solve?
4. Peck concludes this selection by stating that wise people actually "welcome the pain of problems." What kinds of problems might people welcome? Why?

Paragraph Assignments

1. How old were you when you began to realize that life is difficult and that there are not always easy or obvious solutions to life's problems? Write a paragraph about an experience early in your life that made you realize that things don't always work out the way you would like. Use a topic sentence such as one of the following:

   When I was twelve years old, I realized I would never be a great baseball player.
   My parents' divorce showed me that not all problems have solutions.

2. Think of a problem that could be solved by discipline. You might choose to write about a problem you or someone else has had with school, work, family, or social life. Write a paragraph providing specific step-by-step advice for solving the problem.

Essay Assignments

1. Write an essay that begins, as Peck's does, with one sentence stating a "great truth" about life. Use a sentence such as:

   - Life is unfair.
   - Life is easy.
   - Life is confusing.
   - Life is a party.
   - Life is beautiful.
   - Life is amusing.
   - Life is an opportunity.
   - Life is for the brave.
   - Life is too short.
   - Life is a gift from God.
   - Life is a challenge.
   - Life is a chance to help others.

   Prove your point by writing several paragraphs, each on a different experience that supports your central point.

2. What are your strategies for making life easier? Write an essay about one or more of the ways you cope with life's difficulties. You could write about the ways you organize your time, relax, make decisions, or get other people to help you. Your thesis statement could be something like "Whenever I must make a difficult decision, I _____, _____, and _____." Devote a separate paragraph to each strategy you discuss. Use examples to show what the problems are and how your strategies work.

Partial Answer Key

Note to the Student: The explanations in this section are provided to help you understand how to answer the questions and complete the activities that follow the first selection in each of the last five units. Try to figure out each answer by yourself first. Then check your answer. Study the explanation, especially if your response wasn't correct. If you treat each wrong answer as a learning opportunity, you will gradually improve your scores as you continue to work through this book.

Batter Up—*Bill Cosby*

Vocabulary Check (pages 59-60)

1. The sentence implies that the men on the benches look as if they have lost a battle. Knowing that, you would not assume that they were staring "happily" (*a*) or "hungrily" (*b*). There is nothing to suggest that the men are "proud" (*c*). Instead, looking defeated, they are "pathetically" staring ahead, answer *d*.
2. The passage says that the school claimed credit for the better behavior of Cosby's son. But what is the relation between Cosby's "own parent-student conference in the barn" and "this work by the school"? Cosby's "conference" with his son did not "cause trouble for" (*a*) the school's work. Further, it did not "leave out" (*c*) or "profit on" (*d*) that work. Rather, the effect of the punishment turned out to "add to" (*b*) the work done by the school.
3. The passage suggests that *redirect* has something to do with putting the son "on the road to righteousness." But "civilized ways" of redirecting him had not worked. Knowing this fact, you can reason that Cosby was not trying to "dress" (*b*) or "reward" (*c*) or "pay" (*d*) him. The meaning that makes the most sense, then, is "guide" him (*a*).
4. The sentence suggests that *cruising altitude* occurs after the plane takes off. "Runway" (*a*), then, doesn't make sense. The sentence also says that the plane "uses less fuel" at cruising altitude. Thus, "final destination" (*c*) and "crash landing" (*d*) do not make sense either since the plane would

not be moving or using fuel in those cases. The choice that makes sense, then, is *b*, "normal flying level."
5. If a nine-year-old begins to do babyish things like suck his thumb, he has "reverted" (returned) to earlier behavior.
6. In order to stay on the team, the person must keep or "maintain" a "C" average.
7. If the person spent "several weeks" trying to decide which refrigerator to buy, he or she was thinking carefully or "pondering."
8. The water supply must have been kept in a storage area or "reservoir."

Reading Check (pages 60-61)

CENTRAL POINT AND MAIN IDEAS

1. As the example of Cosby's son proves, raising a child is difficult and children do lie, so choices *a* and *c* are false. Cosby makes no comments about whether most parents do or do not have the courage to punish their children, so choice *d* is wrong. The better behavior of Cosby's son after the punishment suggests that *b* is the correct choice.
2. Sentence *b* is a detail, so it is too narrow to be a main idea. Sentence *c* is not stated or implied anywhere in the paragraph. Sentence *d* might at first seem likely until you realize it is exaggerated and funny. Sentence *a* accurately expresses the main idea.
3. Sentence *a* is too broad and general to state the main idea of this paragraph. Sentence *c* is a supporting detail, and sentence *d* states a point not contained in the paragraph. Sentence *b* correctly expresses the main idea of the paragraph.

KEY SUPPORTING DETAILS

4. Cosby's son did not forget his phone number, nor did he run away from home, so choices *a* and *d* are incorrect. At first, choice *b* might seem correct, but it is only part of the answer. The real reason Cosby punished his son was that he broke "the law of the house" (paragraph 5), which was to do what his parents told him to do. Not doing his chores would have been only one example of his "breaking the law and lying" (paragraph 18), so *c* is the correct choice.
5. TRUE. See paragraph 19.
6. There is no evidence that choices *b, c,* and *d* are true. But you can see in paragraph 26 that *a* is the correct choice.

INFERENCES

7. There is no evidence to show that Cosby wanted to hurt his son; instead, the selection states that Cosby loved his son (paragraph 36), so *a* is incorrect. Paragraphs 28 and 30 suggest that *b* is also incorrect. Paragraph 29 shows that Cosby did not miss the first time, so *c* is incorrect. Paragraphs 30-35 show that *d* is the correct choice.
8. In paragraph 40 Cosby asks his son about school, so you can assume that the son's response is about school. The son's motion "like a plane that

had leveled off" refers to not starting and stopping in his studying, so *b* is the correct answer.

THE WRITER'S CRAFT

9. Cosby does not say anything in the selection about his son's baseball playing, so the answer is FALSE. Actually, the title "Batter Up" is a pun referring to Cosby's decision to hit—in this case, his son. We know this is the correct interpretation because later in the selection, Cosby refers to himself as "a father with absolutely no batting average: I had never before hit him or any of the other children" (paragraph 19).
10. Cosby often lets us know how he feels about his son's and his own actions, so he is not "objective" (*a*). Nor is there any self-pity (*b*). Cosby is angry with his son, but he shows his anger very briefly; it does not last throughout the narrative. Rather, as the title and other humorous statements indicate, Cosby's tone is "amusing," *c*.

Outlining Activity (pages 61-62)

B. The answer is *b*. See paragraphs 5-8.
E. The answer is *c*. See paragraph 33.
G. The answer is *a*. See paragraphs 41-42.

Fun. Oh Boy, Fun. You Could Die From It—Suzanne Britt Jordan

Vocabulary Check (pages 104-105)

1. The key word in this sentence is "fun." The sentence suggests that *puritans* are the opposite of people who "have a little fun every day." Knowing this, you can rule out "people who like to cook" (*c*) and "people who can't make decisions quickly" (*d*). You can also rule out as illogical "shy people who fear strangers" because not having fun doesn't necessarily make people shy or fearful. So the answer is *b*: puritans are "serious people who avoid pleasure."
2. A honeymoon is a "big occasion," so it should be fun. That means you can rule out "worst kind" (*b*), "opposite" (*c*), and "end" (*d*). *Epitome*, then, means "perfect example" (*a*).
3. The sentence suggests that when sailors *scan* the horizon, they do so to find out what lies ahead of them in the sky or on the sea. Thus, they do not "ignore" the horizon (*a*), nor can they "touch" the horizon (*c*). They would not "copy" the horizon unless they were drawing or painting, which doesn't make sense in this sentence. But they would "look at" the horizon to see what was ahead, so the answer is *d*.
4. Since the day Jordan described took place in her childhood and because it was fun, the sentence implies that having to grow up takes fun away. "Happy" and "prayerful" both indicate that the author would be glad to grow up and no longer have as much fun. But that is the opposite of what she means, so *a* and *c* can be ruled out. Jordan may have been

"surprised" by her discovery (choice *b*), but surprised in an unhappy way. The definition of *regretful* that makes most sense is "sorry," *d*.
5. The sentence suggests that certain people like cleanliness so much that they can't stand even the least bit of dirt. They wouldn't "make a 'blasphemy' of cleanliness," so choice *c* can be ruled out. "Horizon" (*c*) doesn't make sense in the sentence, nor does "capacity" (*b*). That means the correct response is "fetish," *a*. The idea is that the people described in the sentence admire cleanliness so much that they seem to worship it.
6. Since the judge mentioned in the sentence urged Ryan to give something up and "live a moral life," the missing word will be opposite to "a moral life." Once you realize this, it's easy to pick out "licentiousness" (*b*) as the correct response since it means "immorality."
7. The word "and" in this sentence suggests that it expresses two similar ideas. So the word that fills the blank will have a meaning similar to that of "respected." Therefore, you can immediately rule out "licentiously" (*a*) and "blasphemously" (*b*) because they are the opposite of "respect." "Mirthfully" (*d*) does not mean "with respect" either, but "reverently" does mean "with great respect." So (*c*) is the correct answer.
8. This sentence implies that by insisting that the party-goers turn the music down, Melvin's father did something that made them want to go somewhere else to have fun. Certainly he did not put a "fetish," "mirth," or "benefit" on the party. What he did seems to have quieted things down and depressed people, so the best response is "damper," *d*.

Reading Check (pages 105-107)
CENTRAL POINT AND MAIN IDEAS

1. Sentences *c* and *d* are too specific to express the central point of the entire selection. Sentence *a* can be eliminated because it expresses the opposite of what Jordan believes (see paragraph 13, for instance). Even though the central point often comes at the beginning of an essay, sometimes an author begins with views contrary to her own and states her central point later. That's what Jordan has done here. The correct response is *b*, as paragraph 13 indicates.
2. Sentences *a* and *b* state details, not main ideas. Sentence *d* states an idea that is opposite to one of the details in the paragraph. Even if you recognize that Jordan is intentionally stating a view opposite to her own, sentence *d* still expresses a detail, not a main idea. Only *c* is general and accurate enough to be the correct answer.
3. Sentences *a* and *d* give details, not main ideas. Sentence *b* is more general, but it is, in fact, too general. It doesn't mention fun, and it is too broad to express the main idea of only one paragraph. Sentence *c*, then, is the correct response.

KEY SUPPORTING DETAILS

4. The key phrase in the sentence is "more thrilling sources of fun." Watching television, celebrating Thanksgiving, and buying candy aren't "thrilling." The correct response, as paragraph 9 shows, is *d*.

5. Jordan says in paragraph 13 that "we ought to treat fun reverently," so she obviously has respect for fun. Thus, the correct choice seems to be *c*. To check, you can immediately rule out choice *a*. If you look at paragraph 10, you'll see that TV commercials can depress us, not provide us with fun, so you can rule out *d* also. And while work is supposed to be fun, that view is one of the false ideas people have about fun (paragraph 6).

INFERENCES

6. At first, choice *a* might seem to be the correct response since Jordan also implies that fun seems to come more easily to children than to adults. But a trip to Disney World (paragraph 8) is not necessarily fun for kids, nor is a honeymoon or Thanksgiving. But then honeymoons and holidays aren't necessarily fun for adults, either (paragraph 11). Jordan never compares other big occasions to going to Disney World, so the correct answer isn't *c*. Paragraphs 8 and 11 indicate that *d* is correct.
7. Knowing Jordan's attitude about fun (which is that people often try too hard to have fun), you might reason that she does not go to "many" parties, so *a* is out. There is nothing to suggest that Jordan had an unhappy childhood. In fact, the example of her afternoon with Pam Davis suggests that her childhood was probably happy, so you can rule out *b*. There is nothing to suggest that Jordan has not been on family outings, so *d* is incorrect. The correct answer is *c*, and Jordan's first thirteen paragraphs provide examples of how people overemphasize fun.
8. Most people believe that fun can come only on weekends, when they expect to have fun. So you might think that *a* is the correct answer. But in the next-to-last sentence of paragraph 13, Jordan says that "When fun comes, . . . you probably won't be expecting it." Thus, the correct response is *d*.

THE WRITER'S CRAFT

9. The only paragraph that uses repetitive phrasing is paragraph 6, choice *a*. Note all the sentences in that paragraph that use the same kind of wording: "Family outings were supposed to be fun. Sex was. . . . Education was. . . . Work was. . . . Walt Disney was. . . . Church was. . . . Staying fit was. . . ."
10. The correct answer is *b*. Jordan ends her essay with a description of her experience walking with Pam Davis to the College Village drug store and her opinion that this everyday experience was fun.

Summarizing Activity (page 107)

Your answers may be slightly different from the answers given here. The important thing, though, is to express the right ideas in your own words.

1. drugs
2. depress
3. lives
4. expecting
5. with a friend when she was twelve

What is Intelligence, Anyway?—Isaac Asimov

Vocabulary Check (pages 144–145)

1. If Asimov had always made high scores, how would he feel about his intelligence? He would not feel "surprised" when he did well, at least not after the first few times. Also, there's no apparent reason for him to feel "uneasy" or "misunderstood." Rather, he would feel "self-satisfied" (*a*) about how smart he was.
2. What would Asimov do with his car when something went wrong? He would *hasten*, or hurry, to his mechanic with it. Therefore, the correct answer is *d*. None of the other choices makes sense.
3. The sentence implies that a small group has acted as an arbiter (judge). A judge usually has a great deal of power. The small group has used its power to force the majority of people to accept its judgments. Therefore, the correct answer is *b*.
4. The auto repairman had just gotten the better of someone, and he was delighted. Certainly he did not laugh "secretly" because Asimov heard him. There is no reason for the mechanic to laugh "immorally" or "late." Rather, he laughed "noisily" (*a*), enjoying himself at Asimov's expense.
5. Since *intricate* means "complicated," you know that the video recorder is difficult to use. Therefore *b* is correct.
6. *Pronouncements* are made by authorities, so Rhonda must think she's an expert. Choose *b*.
7. An arbiter must be objective and fair, so *b* is the correct answer.
8. A *smug* person is self-satisfied. If Steve was a very successful athlete in high school, winning three varsity letters every year, he might well be very satisfied with himself. The answer, therefore, is *a*.

Reading Check (pages 145–146)

CENTRAL POINT AND MAIN IDEAS

1. The central point must be broad and accurate enough to cover all the ideas in the selection. Choice *a* may be an accurate description of Asimov's repairman, but it does not cover the entire selection. Neither does choice *b*, which refers only to the first paragraph. Sentence *d* is not the central point because there's nothing in the selection about what most of us think about smart people. Only sentence *c* states the central idea of the entire article.
2. There is no evidence that Asimov's intelligence was criticized by people in the Army. In fact, they made "a big fuss" over him. Nor is there any evidence to support sentence *c*. Sentence *a* is accurate, but it doesn't cover the whole paragraph. Only sentence *b* expresses the main idea of the entire paragraph.
3. If you read paragraph 4 carefully, you will find it never actually says who should make up the intelligence tests. Therefore, choice *a* is wrong. Sentence *c* says the opposite of what the paragraph says, so it's wrong, too. Even though Asimov admits he is not good with his hands, sentence

d is too narrow to be the main idea. Only sentence *b* is an accurate statement of the paragraph's main idea.

KEY SUPPORTING DETAILS

4. A careful reading of paragraph 2 will show that *d* is correct.
5. The only accurate answer here is *d*. The selection does not mention any of the other choices.

INFERENCES

6. You can tell from reading paragraphs 1 and 2 that *a* is incorrect and from reading paragraphs 4 and 5 that *d* is incorrect. A careful reading of paragraph 4 will tell you that *c* is also wrong. Only *b* is supported by the facts and examples in the selection.
7. The easiest choice to cross off is *b* because the repairman never mentions school. The repairman might believe that being able to fix cars (*a*) indicates intelligence, but he would think there was more to intelligence than that. He would feel that the ability to figure out riddles or jokes, which requires "common sense," was important, too. Thus *c* is the right answer.
8. Asimov says in paragraph 3 that he listened to his auto repairman's pronouncements "as if they were divine oracles" and adds that "he always fixed my car." This suggests he does respect his repairman's skills, so the answer is TRUE.
9. Asimov doesn't try to "puzzle the reader" (*a*) or "show off his intelligence" (*c*), in either his title or his essay. And while Asimov admits that intelligence is hard to define, his essay tries to show us what it is and what it is not. Therefore *d* is the right choice.
10. Asimov mentions his auto repairman as an example or illustration of his idea that there are several kinds of intelligence. The correct answer is *a*.

Summarizing Activity (page 146)

Your answers may be slightly different from the answers given here. The important thing, though, is to express the right ideas in your own words.

1. Army
2. intelligence
3. that would not mean he was not intelligent
4. probably score lower on them
5. his auto repairman's joke.

A Crime of Compassion — *Barbara Huttmann*

Vocabulary Check (pages 189-190)

1. The last sentence implies that because Huttmann did not "resuscitate" Mac again, he died. If she had resuscitated him, he would have been "brought back to life," *c*.

2. The sentence implies that the tests told something about whether Mac had lung cancer. Since Mac died of lung cancer, the tests must have "proved" (*b*) that he had it.
3. The sentence suggests that *haggard* means something similar to "beaten old lady." Knowing that, you should ask yourself if a "beaten old lady" would be "smiling," "singing," "silly," or "worn out." The best answer is *a*, "worn out."
4. The sentence suggests that an *imperative* is similar to a "duty" or an "obligation." Knowing that, you can rule out all the choices except "requirement," *d*.
5. What would bullets do to a saloon door? They would have "riddled" or pierced the door with holes.
6. What would a rescuer's hands do to keep someone from falling over a cliff? They would "clutch" or grab the person.
7. Ghosts are usually thought of as being whitish in color. Since Ruth has "pale bleached hair" and wore a "snowy white gown," she appeared whitish. Ruth also appeared "sickly," which means her face had lost its healthy color. Ruth's face, then, had a "sickly pallor," or paleness.
8. Why would Bill and Annie's children go to school without lunch? One reason would be that their parents should have packed a lunch for them, but did not. If so, Bill and Annie are guilty of "negligence," or failure to do their duty.

Reading Check (pages 190–191)

CENTRAL POINT AND MAIN IDEAS

1. Since Huttmann doesn't tell us what all doctors feel about keeping dying patients alive, *a* isn't correct. Sentence *c* provides only a detail, not the central point. Sentence *d* is true, but it doesn't state what the entire selection is about. Only *b* states Huttmann's central point.
2. Sentences *a*, *b*, and *c* are too specific to cover all the points made in paragraph 5; they present only facts. Only *d* explains how Huttmann and the nurses felt about Mac and Maura and how Mac suffered.
3. Sentence *d* is true, but it's only a vivid detail; it's not the main idea of the paragraph. Sentences *a* and *c* are false. Huttmann pressed the button because she wanted Mac not to suffer any longer, so *b* is correct.

KEY SUPPORTING DETAILS

4. FALSE. Paragraph 4 states that Mac "felt great" except for a cough.
5. The last sentence of paragraph 16 indicates that Maura did not want the code blue team to revive Mac, so the answer is *b*. Other facts in the article show that Maura continued to visit Mac and that she and Nurse Huttmann liked each other.

INFERENCES

6. The first sentence of paragraph 7 states that when Mac stopped breathing, a "code blue" was called and a special team was rushed "to resuscitate the patient." The correct completion, then, is *d*.

7. Paragraph 9 explains that unless a doctor gives a "no code" order, a dying patient has to be revived. Paragraph 18 states that until laws permit dying patients the right not to be kept alive by machines, we all face the same fate as Mac's. Huttmann's actions and her article both show that the statement is TRUE.

THE WRITER'S CRAFT

8. If you look back at the first three paragraphs of the selection, you will see that Huttmann begins her article with direct statements of people on the Phil Donahue show who express anger at her action. The correct answer, then, is *b*.
9. The article focuses on Huttmann's experiences with one patient, Mac. Huttmann reports no statistics or research. The correct completion is *c*.
10. Huttmann's article covers about six months' time, and she notes that the code blue team resuscitated Mac 52 times in a single month (paragraph 3). So *d* is not the correct answer. Nor is *a* or *c* correct, for Huttmann's purpose isn't simply to inform us of problems nor to entertain us. Her purpose, suggested in paragraphs 11 and 18, is to persuade readers that dying patients should have the right not to be kept alive by machines if they do not want to be. The correct choice, then, is *b*.

Summarizing Activity (pages 191-192)

Your answers may be slightly different from the answers given here. The important thing, though, is to express the right ideas in your own words.

1. murderer
2. cop/police officer
3. healthy
4. cancer
5. 52
6. the code blue team resuscitated him
7. die
8. human life had to be extended
9. she was sure that the code blue team could not revive him
10. we need laws that give terminally ill patients like Mac the right not to be resuscitated.

The Smart Way to Buy a New Car—Luella Fern Sanders

Vocabulary Check (pages 245-246)

1. The sentence says that Rick *balked* at the price because it was too high. Knowing that, you can rule out *a*, "accepted." After Rick *balked,* the saleswoman then asked him to give her a price. Thus, Rick couldn't have yet "named" a price, so you can cross out *c*. You can also eliminate "forgot" because the saleswoman wouldn't ask him to name a price he had forgotten. The word that makes sense, then, is *b*, "refused."

2. The sentence says that because Rick's car "was ready to *expire*," he had to make a quick choice of another car. Something must have been so wrong with his car that he had to buy a new one. Thus, you can rule out all the choices except "die," *c*.
3. The sentence says that a customer's source of *leverage* is "a willingness to walk away from the deal." If a customer loses that willingness, he or she might not get the best deal from the salesperson. That willingness, then, gives the buyer some "power" (*d*) in the business deal.
4. The sentence implies that *invaluable* means something similar to "extremely useful." Knowing that, you can immediately strike out "worthless" (*b*). A little more thought will show that choices (*a*), "dangerous," and *d*, "boring," can also be crossed out. The correct choice, then, is *c*, "essential."
5. Since *initial* means "first," you can assume that the payment will be due "next month," (*a*).
6. If the instructor is *pliant*, she would be "flexible" and, thus, "willing to change an exam date if a student asks her to," choice *b*.
7. If a person's education is *subsidized*, he or she receives some help with the payments. Thus, the correct response is *a*.
8. Because Nick is *unscrupulous*, he "lacks morals." This means he would not mind doing something dishonest. Thus, he wouldn't return money, but he might sell a "pet poodle to a lab" (*a*).

Reading Check (pages 246-247)

CENTRAL POINT AND MAIN IDEAS

1. Although the central point of an essay is often given in the first few paragraphs, that isn't the case here. But the title does indicate that the essay is about "The Smart Way to Buy a New Car," so at first glance *b* looks like the right choice. After reading the entire essay and especially the final paragraph, you should be able to see that choices *a*, *c*, and *d* are too narrow. The selection does more than state that "Car dealers often treat buyers unfairly" (*a*), that "Because he had not planned well, Rick bought the wrong car" (*c*), and that "New cars are more expensive than people think" (*d*). So *b* is, in fact, the correct choice.
2. Choice *b* is only vaguely suggested in the final sentence, so it can be eliminated first. Of the remaining sentences, choices *c* and *d* state details, not main ideas. The sentence that expresses the main idea of the entire paragraph is *a*. It covers all the examples of emotional reactions to new cars described in the paragraph—Rick's and other customers'.
3. Choices *a, b,* and *c* are all accurate, but they state details from the paragraph, not main ideas. The general subject of the paragraph is the need to watch out for extra charges added to a sales agreement at the last minute, so the answer is choice *d*.

PARTIAL ANSWER KEY 303

KEY SUPPORTING DETAILS

4. Sanders specifically mentions *Edmund's New Car Prices* (paragraph 12) and *Consumer Reports* (paragraph 13 and 14) as sources consumers should check to find out a dealer's cost. So the statement is FALSE.
5. At first, any of the answers might seem correct. But paragraph 6 points out that Rick made a mistake when he combined negotiating for a new car with trading in his old one. Paragraph 17 states that Rick should talk about a trade-in price after finding the dealer with the lowest new-car price. So the correct answer is *d*.
6. According to paragraph 19, this item is TRUE. Dealers may try to sell service contracts at the last minute, but consumers should buy them only for cars likely to have mechanical problems (high-risk cars).

INFERENCES

7. The author actually implies the opposite of choices *a, c,* and *d*. By reading between the lines, you can see that Sanders believes the car salespeople make money by keeping customers in the dark and pressuring them to accept unfair offers. So only *b* accurately completes the sentence.
8. In the first sentence of paragraph 18, Sanders says that "Car loans are expensive" and in the next-to-last sentence she says that "low-interest dealer-subsidized loans may be tied to a higher price for the car." The statement, then, is TRUE.

THE WRITER'S CRAFT

9. If you reread the first five paragraphs carefully, you will see that the author begins with an anecdote (*a*), a story about Rick's experience buying a car.
10. Glancing over the selection should tell you the answer to this item. Paragraphs 11 and 12 begin with the word "After," and paragraph 13 starts with the word "Second." These are only some of the clues that show that Sanders organizes her suggestions on car buying "in the order they should be performed" (*a*).

Outlining Activity (pages 247–248)

Central point: Information is the key to a good buy on a new car.
A. 2. Don't fall in love with a new car.
B. Do your homework.
C. 1. Call dealers to find out who will offer you the lowest price on a new car.
C. 4. Shop for the least expensive car loan.

Acknowledgments

Asimov, Isaac. "What Is Intelligence, Anyway?" Reprinted by permission.

Brody, Jane. "Owning a Pet Can Have Therapeutic Value." Copyright © 1982 by The New York Times Company. Reprinted by permission.

Consumer Reports Auto Price Service Auto Form. Copyright © 1988 by Consumers Union of United States, Inc., Mount Vernon, NY 10553. Reprinted by permission from *Consumer Reports,* April 1988.

Cosby, Bill. "Batter Up," from *Fatherhood*. Copyright © 1986 by William H. Cosby, Jr. Reprinted by permission of Doubleday, a division of Bantam, Doubleday, Dell Publishing Group, Inc.

DeLeon, Clark. "Bird Girl." *The Philadelphia Inquirer*, 1987. Reprinted by permission.

Easterbrook, Gregg. "Escape Valve." Copyright © 1981 by The New York Times Company. Reprinted by permission.

Fong-Torres, Ben. "When My Brother Was Slain." Reprinted with permission from *Parade*, copyright © 1985.

Heilbroner, Robert. "Don't Let Stereotypes Warp Your Judgments." Reprinted by permission.

Huttman, Barbara. "A Crime of Compassion." Reprinted by permission.

Jordan, Suzanne Britt. "Fun. Oh Boy, Fun. You Could Die From It." Copyright © 1979 by The New York Times Company. Reprinted by permission.

Kellmayer, John. "Students in Shock." Reprinted by permission of Trend Publications, 31 Price's Lane, Moylan, PA 19065.

Landers, Ann. "What Do Children Owe Their Parents?" Reprinted from the September 1, 1978 issue of *Family Circle*. Copyright © 1978 The Family Circle, Inc.

Lamers, William M., Jr. "Funerals Are Good for People." Reprinted by permission.

ACKNOWLEDGMENTS

LeBoeuf, Michael. "Turning On Turned-Off Workers," from *Japan: The Productivity Challenge*. Copyright © 1982 by Michael LeBoeuf. Reprinted by permission of McGraw-Hill Book Company.

Lewis, Carolyn. "Living the Simple Life." Reprinted by permission.

Lester, Julius. "Being a Boy." Reprinted by permission.

Mebane, Mary E. "The Back of the Bus," from *Mary*. Copyright © 1981 by Mary Elizabeth Mebane. Reprinted by permission of Viking Penguin, Inc.

Miller, H. Bruce. "Boxing Is a Barbarism Civilization Can Do Without." Copyright © 1980 by *The San Jose Mercury News*. Reprinted by permission.

Morris, Lois B. "Face Up to Your Fears." Reprinted by permission.

Nizer, Louis. "How About Low-Cost Drugs for Addicts?" Copyright © 1986 by The New York Times Company. Reprinted by permission.

Peck, M. Scott. "Problems and Pain," from *The Road Less Traveled*. Copyright © 1978 by M. Scott Peck, M. D. Reprinted by permission of Simon & Schuster, Inc.

Rathje, William. "Why We Throw Food Away." *The Atlantic*, April, 1986. Reprinted by permission.

Roberts, Robin. "Strike Out Little League." Reprinted by permission.

Rosenfeld, Albert. "'Learning' to Give Up." Copyright © 1977 by *Saturday Review*. Reprinted by permission.

Ruggiero, Vincent Ryan. "The Urge to Conform," from *Beyond Feelings: A Guide to Critical Thinking*. Copyright © 1984 by Mayfield Publishing Company. Reprinted by permission of Mayfield Publishing Company.

Sanders, Luella Fern. "The Smart Way to Buy a New Car." Reprinted by permission of Trend Publications, 31 Price's Lane, Moylan, PA 19065.

Seliger, Susan. "Back from Death?" Reprinted by permission of *The National Observer*, copyright © 1976 by Dow Jones & Company, Inc. All rights reserved.

Skwire, David, and Frances Chitwood. "Specific Details." Reprinted with permission of Macmillan Publishing Company from *The Student's Book of College English*, 3rd edition, by David Skwire and Frances Chitwood. Copyright © 1975, 1978, 1981 by Macmillan Publishing Company.

Teague, Bob. "To Get a Story, I Flimflammed a Dead Man's Mother." Reprinted with permission from *TV Guide* (R) Magazine. Copyright © 1982 by Triangle Publications, Inc., Radnor, Pennsylvania.

Webb, James. "What We Can Learn from Japan's Prisons." Reprinted by permission of Sterling Lord Literistic, Inc. Copyright © 1984 by James Webb; first appeared in *Parade*, January 15, 1984. Also reprinted with permission from *Parade*, copyright © 1984.

White, Clarissa. "Classroom Note-Taking." Reprinted by permission of Trend Publications, 31 Price's Lane, Moylan, PA 19065.

Wine, Bill. "Rudeness at the Movies." Reprinted by permission.

Winn, Marie. "Television Addiction," from *The Plug-In Drug*. Copyright © 1977 by Marie Winn. All rights reserved. Reprinted by permission of Viking Penguin Inc.

Glossary

Note: This Glossary contains up to fifteen "Words to Watch" chosen from each of the thirty-two reading selections. Vocabulary words are defined as they are actually used in the selections.

PRONUNCIATION GUIDE FOR THE WORDS THAT APPEAR BELOW

Next to each vowel sound is a common word that contains the sound.

ā play	ē be	ō go	ŏŏ book
ă pat	ĕ ten	ŏ pot	ŭ cut
ä calm	ī high	ô raw	ûr fur
â dare	ĭ pit	ōō fool	uh about

abhor (ăb-hôr'): hate
abounded (uh-bound'ĭd): was fully supplied
aboveboard (uh-bŭv'bôrd'): honestly
absolute (ăb'suh-lōot): unchanging
academician (ăk'uh-duh-mĭsh'uhn): scholar
accreditation (uh-krĕd'ĭ-tā'shuhn): official approval
actuarial (ăk'chōō-âr'ē-uhl): referring to statistics on how long people live

adept (uh-dĕpt'): skillful
adverse (ăd-vûrs'): harmful
advocates (ăd'vuh-kāts'): favors
affliction (uh-flĭk'shuhn): suffering
alleviate (uh-lē'vē-āt'): relieve
alleviation (uh-lē'vē-ā'shuhn): relief
anorexia (ăh'uh-rĕk'sē-uh): an abnormal lack of appetite which can result in serious illness or death
alternatives (ôl-tûr'nuh-tĭvs): other choices

anachronism (uh-năk′ruh-nĭz′uhm): something left from an earlier age
ancillary (ăn′suh-lĕr′ē): less important
anguished (ăng′gwĭsht): with great suffering
animal husbandry (ăh′uh-muhl hŭz′buhnd-rē): science of breeding and raising animals
antagonist (ăn-tăg′uh-nĭst): opponent
apparatus (ăp′uh-ră′tuhs): equipment
apprehensive (ăp′rĭ-hĕn′sĭv): worried
a priori (ä′prē-ôr′ē): without testing
arbiter (är′bĭ-tuhr): judge
articulate (är-tĭk′yuh-lĭt): clear and expressive
ascribe (uh-shrīb′): credit
assailants (uh-sā′luhnts): attackers
assertion (uh-sûr′shuhn): statement
asset (ăs′et′): useful quality
atrocites (uh-trŏs′ĭ-tēs): shockingly cruel acts
austere (ô-stēr′): severely simple
autistic (ô-tĭs′tĭk): having a mental illness the symptoms of which are withdrawal and uncontrolled behavior
automated (ô′tuh-māt′ĭd): done by machine
autonomous (ô-tŏn′uh-muhs): independent
axioms (ăk′sē-uhms): basic truths
barbaric (bär-bâr′ĭk): uncivilized
barbarism (bär′buh-rĭz-uhm): cruel custom

barter (bär′tuhr): trade
be reconciled to (rĕk′uhn-sīld′): accept
beachhead (bēch′hĕd′): secure position
beneficial (bĕn′uh-fĭsh′uhl): helpful
beneficiaries of (bĕn′uh-fĭsh′ē-ĕr-ēs): people who profit from
bents (bĕnts): talents
bestow (bĭ-stō′): give
blaspheme (blăs-fēm′): speak evil of something holy
boon (boon): benefit
bouts (bouts): attacks
brittle (brĭt′l): easily broken
buck private (bŭk prī′vĭt): the lowest rank in the Army
bulimia (byoo-lĭm′ē-uh): an abnormal craving for food that leads to heavy eating and then intentional vomiting
by Jove (bī jov): an expression of surprise
caches (kăsh′uhs): hidden supplies
capacity (kuh-păs′ĭ-tē): ability to do or hold something
capital (kăp′ĭ-tl): punishable by death
capitalize on (kăp′ĭ-tl-īz′): take advantage of
carnage (kär′nĭj): slaughter
catatonic schizophrenia (kăt′uh-tŏn′ĭk skĭt′suh-frē′nē-uh): a mental illness in which the patient cannot move or speak
celestial (suh-lĕs′chuhl): heavenly
celluloid (sĕl′yuh-loid′): movie film
chastening (chā′suhn-ĭng): humbling

chronic (krŏn′ĭk): continuing over time
circumvent (sûr′kuhm-vĕnt′): get around
clammy (klăm′ē): unpleasantly damp
clutch (klŭch): tight grip
collaborating (kuh-lăb′uh-rāt′ing): cooperating
comestibles (kuh-mĕs′tuh-buhls): food
compassion (kuhm-păsh′uhn): sympathy
complacently (kuhm-plā′suhnt-lē): contentedly
compulsion (kuhm-pŭl′shuhn): irresistible force
conceded (kuhn-sēd′ĭd): admitted
conclusive (kuhn-kloo′sĭv): final
confront (kuhn-frŭnt′): face
contend (kuhn-tĕnd′): struggle
continuum (kuhn-tĭn′yoo-uhm): connected series
convey (kuhn-vā′): communicate
conviction (kuhn-vĭk′shuhn): believability
counterintuitive (koun′tuhr-ĭn-too′ĭ-tĭv): opposite to what people would assume
covertly (kŭv′uhrt-lē): secretly
counterproductive (koun′tuhr-pruh-dŭk′tĭv): interfering with the output of goods or services
crater (krā′tuhrs): hollows
craves (krāvs): strongly desires
cremation (krĭ-mā′shuhn): the burning of a corpse
crimp in (krĭmp ĭn): interference with
crystallized (krĭs′tuh-līzed′): took form

cubicles (kyoo′bĭ-kuhls): small rooms or spaces
cutting edge (kŭt′ĭng ĕj): severe test
damper (dăm′puhr): something that depresses
dank (dăngk): damp
decathlon (dĭ-kăth′luhn): contest made up of ten athletic events
deferred (dĭ-fûrd′): put off
defiant (dĭ-fī′uhnt): bold
degrading (dĭ-grād′ĭng): humiliating
delve (dĕlv): search deeply
demoralization (dĭ-môr′ăl-ĭ-zā′shuhn): loss of hope
denote (dĭ-nōt′): mean
desensitized (dē-sĕn′sĭ-tīzd): weakened the effect of
designated hitter (dĕs′ĭg-nāt-ĭd hĭt′uhr): in baseball, someone who bats instead of the pitcher
despondent (dĭ-spŏn′duhnt): depressed
devastated (dĕv′uh-stāt′ĭd): completely destroyed
devastating (dĕv′uh-stāt′ĭng): very destructive
devised (dĭ-vīzd′): designed
diluted (dĭ-loot′ĭd): watered down
diminish (dĭ-mĭn′ĭsh): decrease
dinned (dĭnd): repeated forcefully
discharge (dĭs-chärj′): get rid of
disenchanted (dĭs′ĕn-chant′ĭd): disillusioned
dismay (dĭs-mā′): disappointment
disputed (dĭ-spyoot′ĭd): argued over
disrepair (dĭs′rĭ-pâr′): neglected condition

disrepute (dĭs′ri-pyōōt′): disgrace
disrupt (dĭs-rŭpt′): break up
dissenting (dĭ-sĕnt′ĭng): disagreeing
disservice (dĭs-sûr′vĭs): harm
dissipate (dĭs′uh-pāt): get rid of
distorted (dĭs-tôrt′ĭd): unnaturally twisted
domestic (duh-mĕs′tĭk): within a country
dominant (dŏm′uh-nuhnt): strongest
dubbed (dŭbd): called
dutifully (dōō′tĭ-fuhl-lē): obediently
dynamics (dī-năm′ĭks): pattern of forces
eccentric (ĭk-sĕn′trĭk): peculiar
edifice (ĕd′uh-fĭs): structure
effecting (ĭ-fĕkt′ĭng): bringing about
eligible (ĕl′ĭ-juh-buhl): qualified
eloquence (ĕl′uh-kwuhns): ability to speak persuasively
eloquent (ĕl′uh-kwĕnt): expressive
eluded (ĭ-lōōd′ĭd): escaped
embedded (ĕm-bĕd′ĭd): firmly placed
emerged (ĭ-mûrjd′): came out
empathy (ĕm′puh-thē): sharing another's thoughts and feelings
encephalitis (ĕn-sĕf′uh-lī′tĭs): a brain disease
encounter (ĕn-koun′tuhr): meeting
endeavor (ĕn-dĕv′uhr): task
endorse (ĕn-dôrs′): support
enervated (ĕn′uhr-vāt′ĭd): weakened
engulfed (ĕn-gŭlfd′): swallowed up

enhance (ĕn-hăns′): increase
ensuing (ĕn-sōō′ĭng): following
enterprising (ĕn′tuhr-prī′zĭng): clever and hard-working
enumeration (ĭ-nōō′muh-rā′shuhn): list
equivalent (ĭ-kwĭv′uh-luhnt): equal
escalate (ĕs′kuh-lāt): make more intense
essence (ĕs′uhns): basic nature
esthetic (ĕs-thĕt′ĭk) (also spelled *aesthetic*): based on a love of beauty
estrangement (ĭ-strānj′mĕnt): being cut off
exacted (ĭg-zăkt′ĭd): demanded
exempt (ĭg-zĕmpt′): free
exodus (ĕk′suh-duhs): departure
exploit (ĕk-sploit′): take advantage of
facilitated (fuh-sĭl′ĭ-tāt′ĭd): helped
farce (färs): ridiculous joke
fascist (făsh′ĭst): a right-wing dictator
feces (fē′sēz): solid bodily waste
fester (fĕs′tuhr): be infected
fetish (fĕt′ĭsh): something that is worshiped
forlorn (fuhr-lôrn′): very unhappy
frieze (frēz): picture
fundamentals (fŭn′duh-mĕn′tls): basics
galling (gô′lĭng): irritating
gaucheries (gō′shuh-rēs): actions in bad taste
goad (gōd): urge
generalizations (jĕn′uhr-uhl-ĭ-zā′shuhns): broad statements
generate (jĕn′uh-rāt′): produce
gerontology (jĕr′uhn-tŏl′uh-jē): study of old people

gladiator (glăd′ē-a′tuhr): trained fighter in ancient Rome
greasers (grē′suhrs): tough, bullying teenagers
gregarious (gri-gâr′ē-uhs): sociable
gross (grōs): very obvious
guerrilla (guh-ril′uh): rebel
gumption (gŭmp′shuhn): boldness
hamper (hăm′puhr): interfere with
hedge (hĕj): protection
hierarchies (hī′uh-rar′kēs): ranks
horizon (huh-rī′zuhn): line where the sky and earth seem to meet
host (hōst): great number
illicit (ĭ-lĭs′ĭt): illegal
implore (ĭm-plôr′): beg
impotence (ĭm′puh-tuhns): powerlessness
impoverish (ĭm-pŏv′uhr-ĭsh): make poor
inadvertently (ĭn′uhd-vŭr′tuhnt-le): unintentionally
incarceration (ĭn-kär′suh-rā′shuhn): imprisonment
incentives (ĭn′sĕn′tĭvs): motivating forces
incessantly (ĭn-cĕs′uhnt-lē): without stopping
incompetent (ĭn-kŏm′pĭ-tuhnt): not capable
incontinent (ĭn-kŏn′tuh-nuhnt): unable to control bodily waste functions
indelible (ĭn-dĕl′uh-buhl): not able to be removed
indiscretions (ĭn′dĭ-skrĕsh′uhns): small sins
induced (ĭn-dōōsd′): caused

indulgently (ĭn-dŭl′juhnt-lē): going along with someone's wishes
industriously (ĭn-dŭs′trē-uhs-lē): busily
inevitably (ĭn-ĕv′ĭ-tuh-blē): unavoidably
infectiousness (ĭn-fĕk′shuhs-nĕs): ability to be spread
inflicted (ĭn-flĭk′tĭd): caused (something harmful)
infusing (ĭn-fyōōz′ĭng): filling
inherent (ĭn-hēr′uhnt): built in
inimitable (ĭn-ĭm′ĭ-tuh-buhl): not able to be copied
initial (ĭ-nĭsh′uhl): first
initiative (ĭ-nĭsh′uh-tĭv): lead
injunction (ĭn-jŭngk′shuhn): command
insouciance (ĭn-sōō′sē-uhns): lack of concern
instigators (ĭn′stĭ-gā′tuhrs): leaders
integrity (ĭn-tĕg′rĭ-tē): high standards
intensified (ĭn-tĕn′suh-fīd): made stronger
interdict (ĭn′tuhr-dĭkt′): forbid
interim (ĭn′tuhr-ĭm): meantime
intractability (ĭn-trăk′tuh-bĭl′ĭ-tē): difficulty
intricate (ĭn′trĭ-kĭt): complicated
intuitive (ĭn-tōō′ĭ-tĭv): understood without thinking
invariably (ĭn-vâr′ē-uh-blē): always
involuntary (ĭn-vŏl′uhn-tĕr′ē): automatic
ironically (ī-rŏn′ĭ-kuhl-lē): in a way opposite to what we expect
irrationally (ĭ-răsh′uh-nuhl-lē): crazily

irrigate (ĭr′ĭ-gāt′): wash out

i.v. (ī vē) (abbreviation for *intravenous*): given by an injection into a vein

juncture (jŭngk′chuhr): place where two things are joined

KP (kā pē): abbrevication for "kitchen police," or cook's assistant in the armed forces

lapse (lăps): end

lest (lĕst): for fear that

licentiousness (lī-sĕn′shuhs-nĕs): immorality

litigation (lĭt′ĭ-gā′shuhn): legal action

longevity (lŏn-jĕv′ĭ-tē): long life

lucid (lōō′sĭd): clear minded

macabre (muh-kä′bruh): gruesome

magnitude (măg′nĭ-tōōd′): great importance

maintaining (mān-tān′ĭng): keeping

malaise (mă-lāz′): discomfort

malicious (muh-lĭsh′uhs): mean

mandatory (măn′dŭh-tôr′ē): required

mania (mā′nē-uh): madness

materialism (muh-tîr′ē-uh-lĭz′uhm): greed

meditation (mĕd′ĭ-tā′shuhn): deep thought

mirth (mûrth): amusement

mitigated (mĭt′uh-gāt′ĭd): reduced

mobile (mō′buhl): movable

muster (mŭs′tuhr): gather up

negligence (nĕg′lĭ-juhns): failure to do one's duty

negotiated (nĭ-gō′shē-āt′ĭd): bargained for

nominal (nŏm′uh-nuhl): very small

nondescript (nŏn′dĭ-skrĭpt′): ordinary

notoriety (nō′tuh-rī′ĭ-tē): being widely known for something unfavorable

nurturing (nûr′chuhr-ĭng): caring

obsolesence (ŏb′suh-lĕs′ĕns): becoming out of date

obstacle to (ŏb′stuh-kuhl): something that is in the way of

oppressors (uh-prĕs′suhrs): tyrants

oracles (ôr′uh-kuhls): messages from the gods

organic (ôr-găn′ĭk): physical

organism (ôr′guh-nĭz′uhm): living creature

oriented (ôr′ē-ĕnt-ĭd): directed

outset (out′sĕt′): beginning

oversedate (ō-vuhr-sĭ-dāt′): give too much calming medicine to

pallor (păl′uhr): paleness

panoramic (păn′uh-răm′ĭk): including everything

paradoxical (păr′uh-dŏks′ĭ-kuhl): apparently contradictory

pathos (pā′thōs′): ability to arouse pity

Paul Bunyanesque (Pol Bŭn′yuhn-ĕsk′): like Paul Bunyan, a fictional giant

perennially (puh-rĕn′ē-uhl-lē): permanently

permeated (pûr′mē-āt′ĭd): completely filled

perpetrated (pûr′pĭ-trāt′ĭd): committed

perpetuate (puhr-pĕch′ōō-āt′): cause to continue

perseverance (pûr'suh-vēr'uhns): not giving up
phenomenon (fĭ-nŏm'uh-nŏn'): unusual event
phobias (fō'bē-uhs): abnormal terrors
pittance (pĭt'ns): very small amount
pliant (plī'uhnt): flexible
plight (plīt): desperate situation
podium (pō'dē-uhm): speaker's platform
pondering (pŏn'duhr-ĭng): thinking carefully about
postulate (pŏs'chuh-luht): principle
potentially (puh-tĕn'shuhl-lē): possibly
preconceptions (prē'kuhn-sĕp'shuhns): judgments made ahead of time
prefabricated (prē-făb'rĭ-kāt'ĭd): put together beforehand
prelude (prĕl'yōōd'): introduction
premise (prĕm'ĭs): underlying idea
preordained (prē'ôr-dānd'): decided in advance
prescient (prē'shē-uhnt): knowing what will happen beforehand
prevailed (prĭ-vāld'): won out
procedure (pruh-sē'juhr): process
productivity (prō'dŭk-tĭv'ĭ-tē): worker output
profound (pruh-found'): far-reaching
pronouncements (pruh-nouns'muhnts): statements by an authority
prospect (prŏs'pĕkt'): something expected
protocols (prō'tuh-kôls'): customs and rules
provocation (prŏv'uh-kā'shuhn): urging
pugilism (pyōō'juh-lĭz'uhm): boxing
pummeling (pŭm'uhl-ĭng): hitting
punitive (pyōō'nĭ-tĭv): punishing
quid pro quo (kwĭd' pro kwō'): something given in exchange for something else
quiescent (kwī-ĕs'uhnt): motionless
raises ... hackles (rāz'ĭs hăk'uhls): angers
raison d'etre (rĕ-zôn'dĕ'tr): a French phrase meaning "reason for being"
reactionaries (rē-ăk'shuh-nĕr'ēs): opponents of change
realms (rĕlms): regions
reason (rē'zuhn): logic
recidivism (rĭ-sĭd'uh-vĭz'uhm): returning to crime
reclusive (rĭ-klōō'sĭv): withdrawn from the world
reconstruct (rē'kuhn-strŭkt'): recreate
reflection (rĭ-flĕk'shuhn): indication
rehabilitative (rē'huh-bĭl'ĭ-tā'tĭv): returning to a useful life
relevant (rĕl'uh-vuhnt): on the topic
relic (rĕl'ĭk): surviving trace
render (rĕn'duhr): make
repertoire (rĕp'uhr-twär'): supply of knowledge

replenished (rĭ-plĕn´ĭsht): resupplied
reservoir (rĕz´uhr-vwär´): storage area
resolving (rĭ-sŏlv´ĭng): working out
restrict (rĭ-strĭkt´): limit
restrictive (rĭ-strĭk´tĭv): limiting
retards (rĭ-tärds´): slows down
reverently (rĕv´uhr-uhnt-lē): with great respect
reverie (rĕv´uhr-ē): daydream
reversion (rĭ-vûr´zhuhn): return
riddled (rĭd´uhld): pierced
righteousness (rī´chuhs-nĕss): moral behavior
ruefully (rōō´fuhl-lē): regretfully
ruse (rōōs): false excuse
sallow (săl´ō): sickly pale yellow
salutary (săl´yuh-tĕr-ē): helpful
semantics (sĭ-măn´tĭks): the study of word meanings
semblance (sĕm´bluhns): appearance
seminal (sĕm´uh-nuhl): original and influential
serenity (suh-rĕn´ĭ-tē): calmness
showmanship (shō´muhn-shĭp): dramatic skill
singular (sĭng´gyuh-luhr): remarkable
skeptical (skĕp´tĭ-kuhl): doubting
slapstick humor (slăp´stĭk hyōō´muhr): rowdy comedy
smugly (smŭg´lē): in a self-satisfied way
spawning (spôn´ĭng): giving birth to
specified (spĕs´uh-fīd´): stated
speculating (spĕk´yuh-lāt´ĭng): guessing

spontaneously (spŏn-tā´nē-uhs-lē): without warning
spritzes (sprĭt´zuhs): sprays
stability (stuh-bĭl´ĭ-tē): steadiness, permanence
stable (stā´buhl): lasting
standardization (stăn´duhrd-ĭ-zā´shuhn): sameness
starkly (stärk´lē): completely
stemming from (stĕm´mĭng): arising out of
stifle (stī´fuhl): hold back
stock (stŏk): typical
strove (strōv): tried hard
subsidized (sŭb´sĭ-dīzd´): helped with payment
substantial (suhb-stăn´shuhl): solid
subtly (sŭt´lē): faintly
superfluous (sōō-pûr´flōō-uhs): unnecessary
supplementary (sŭp´luh-mĕn´tuh-rē): additional
surge (sûrj): sudden increase
sustained (suh-stānd´): received
symptomatic of (sĭm´tuh-măt´ĭk): a sign of
synchronized (sĭng´kruh-nīzd´): occurring at the same time
syphilis (sĭf´uh-lĭs): a disease spread by sexual contact
taboos (tuh-bōōs´): forbidden practices
tacitly (tăs´ĭt-lē): silently
taunts (tônts): insults
technically (tĕk´nĭ-kuhl-lē): by the rules
tedious (tē´dē-uhs): boring
therapeutic (thĕr´uh-pyōō´tĭk): healing
touched a chord in (tŭcht ā kôrd ĭn): sounded familiar to

tract (trăkt): persuasive pamphlet
traipsing (trāps′ĭng): wandering
transcend (trăn-sĕnd′): rise above
transitional (trăn-zĭsh′uhn-uhl): connecting
transmissible (trăns-mĭs′uhb-uhl): spreadable
traumatic (trou-măt′ĭk): psychologically disturbing
trivial (trĭv′ē-uhl): unimportant
truism (trōō′ĭz′uhm): obvious truth
turmoil (tûr′moil′): confusion
ultimately (ŭl′tuh-mĭt-lē): eventually
uncanny (ŭn-kăn′ē): weird
unconditional (ŭn′kuhn-dĭsh′uh-nuhl): unlimited
underground (ŭn′duhr-ground′): secret organization fighting against those in power
unimpeachable (ŭn′ĭm-pē′chuh′buhl): above suspicion
unique (yōō-nēk′): one of a kind
unrelenting (ŭn-ri-lĕn′tĭng): not stopping
unscrupulous (ŭn-skrōō′pyuh-luhs): lacking morals
usurious (yōō-zhŏŏr′ē-uhs): at an overly high rate
vagaries (vā′guh-rēs): chance behavior
vague (vāg): unclear
valiantly (văl′yuhnt-lē): bravely
validation (văl′ĭ-dā′shuhn): proof
vaults (vôlts): jumps over
venture (vĕn′chuhr): risky undertaking
verbal (vûr′buhl): spoken
verbatim (vuhr-bā′tĭm): word for word
vested interests (vĕst′ĕd ĭn′trĭsts): people with something to gain
vicariously (vī-kâr′ē-uhs-lē): as if sharing someone else's experience
vigilante (vĭj′uh-lăn′tē): taking the law into one's own hands
virtually (vûr′chōō-uh-lē): nearly
visited upon (vĭz′ĭt-ĭd uh-pŏn′): forced on
vistas (vĭs′tuhs): views
vital (vīt′l): very important
vitals (vīt′ls): internal organs
vividly (vĭv′ĭd-lē): very strongly
void (void): empty space
vulnerable to (vŭl′nuhr-uh-buhl): likely to be hurt by
warrant (wôr′uhnt): call for
waxing (wăks′ĭng): becoming
wistful (wĭst′fuhl): sadly longing
wrath (răth): anger
wryly (rī′lē): humorously
unwary (ŭn-wâr′ē): not alert
yin-yang (yĭn′yăng′): in traditional Chinese thought, two opposite forces which interact to influence everything
yokels (yō′kuhls): awkward or unsophisticated country people
zeal (zēl): enthusiasm

Index

Activities
    First Impressions, xvi, xxi, xxiv, 6
    Discussion Questions, xxii
    Essay Assignments, xvii, xxii
    Outlining, xvii, xxi
    Paragraph Assignments, xvii, xxii
    Reading Check, xvi, xxi, 8
    Summarizing, xvii, xxi, 11
    Vocabulary Check, xvi, xxi, 6
Anecdotes, xxvi-xxvii
Asimov, Isaac, "What Is Intelligence, Anyway?" 142-148
Audience, xxviii

"Back from Death?" Susan Seliger, 43-53
"Back of the Bus, The," Mary E. Mebane, 21-31
"Batter Up," Bill Cosby, 56-63
"Being a Boy," Julius Lester, 14-20
"Bird Girl," Clark DeLeon, 2-13
Brainstorming, xxxii
Brody, Jane, "Owning a Pet Can Have Therapeutic Value," 254-267
"Boxing Is a Barbarism Civilization Can Do Without," H. Bruce Miller, 132-139

Cause and effect pattern, xxviii, xxxiv
Central point, xxii, xxv-xxvii, xxxiii, 8-9
Chitwood, Frances, and David Skwire, "Specific Details," 278-285
Chronological order. *See* Time order

"Classroom Note-Taking," Clarissa White, 250-258
Comparison and contrast pattern, xxviii, xxxiv
Conclusions, xxvii-xxviii
Context, xxiv-xxv
Cosby, Bill, "Batter Up," 56-63
"Crime of Compassion, A," Barbara Huttmann, 186-193

DeLeon, Clark, "Bird Girl," 2-13
Details, xxii, xxvi, xxxiii, 9
Discussion questions, xxii, xxix
"Don't Let Stereotypes Warp Your Judgments," Robert L. Heilbroner, 176-184
Draft, of an essay, xxxiv-xxxv

Easterbrook, Gregg, "Escape Valve," 210-216
"Escape Valve," Gregg Easterbrook, 210-216
Essay
    assignments, xvii, xxii
    central point of, xxi, xxv, xxxiii, 8-9
    definition of, xx
    thesis statement of, xxv, xxxiii, xxxv
Examples, xxii, xxvi, xxxiv

"Face Up to Your Fears," Lois B. Morris, 268-277

INDEX

Facts, xxvi, xxxiv
First Impressions, xvi, xxiv, 6
Feedback, on writing, xxxv
Fong-Torres, Ben, "When My Brother Was Slain," 83-92
Freewriting, xxxi - xxxv
"Fun. Oh Boy, Fun. You Could Die from It," Suzanne Britt Jordan, 102-108
"Funerals Are Good for People," William M. Lamers, Jr., 149-157

Glossary, xxii, 307-315

Heilbroner, Robert L., "Don't Let Stereotypes Warp Your Judgments," 176-184
"How About Low-Cost Drugs for Addicts?" Louis Nizer, 194-201
Huttmann, Barbara, "A Crime of Compassion," 186-193

Incidents, xxxiv
Inferences, xxvii, 10
Introductions, xxvii-xxviii

Jordan, Suzanne Britt, "Fun. Oh Boy, Fun. You Could Die from It," 102-108

Kellmayer, John, "Students in Shock," 75-82
Key supporting details, xxvi-xxvii, 9

Lamers, Jr., William M., "Funerals Are Good for People," 149-157
Landers, Ann, "What Do Children Owe Their Parents?" 64-74
"'Learning' to Give Up," Albert Rosenfeld, 167-175
LeBoeuf, Michael, "Turning On Turned-Off Workers," 227-238
Lester, Julius, "Being a Boy," 14-20
Lewis, Carolyn, "Living the Simple Life," 93-100

"Living the Simple Life," Carolyn Lewis, 93-100
Location
    see Space order

Main idea
    of a paragraph, xxv, 8-9
Marking a selection, xxiv
Mebane, Mary E., "The Back of the Bus," 21-31
Miller, H. Bruce, "Boxing Is a Barbarism Civilization Can Do Without," 132-139
Morris, Lois B., "Face Up to Your Fears," 268-277

Nizer, Louis, "How About Low-Cost Drugs for Addicts?" 194-201

Order of importance pattern, xxviii, xxxiv
Organization,
    see Patterns of organization
Outlining, xvii, xxi, xxix
"Owning a Pet Can Have Therapeutic Value," Jane Brody, 259-267

Paragraph
    assignments, xvii, xxii
    main idea of, xxv, 8-9
Partial Answer Key, xvii, 293-303
Patterns of Organization
    cause and effect, xxviii, xxxiv
    comparison-contrast, xxviii, xxxiv
    order of importance, xxviii, xxxiv
    space order, xxviii, xxxiv
    time (chronological) order, xxviii, xxxiv
Peck, M. Scott, "Problems and Pain," 286-291
Point
    and support, xv, xx, xxii, xxv, xxx, xxxv
    central, of an essay, xxii, xxv-xxvii, xxxiii, 8-9

Point, *continued*
  making a, xx, xxx-xxxi, xxxv
  supporting a, xx, xxx-xxxi, xxxv
Preview
  as a prereading technique, xxiii
  of an essay/reading selection, xviii, xx, xxiv
Prewriting activities, xxxi-xxxiii
  Brainstorming, xxxii
  Freewriting, xxxi-xxxii
  Questioning, xxxii
"Problems and Pain," M. Scott Peck, 286-291
Purpose, xxviii, 11

Questioning, xxxii
Quotations, xxvi-xxvii

Rathje, William, "Why We Throw Food Away," 202-209
Reading Check, xvi, 8
Reading Performance Chart, 321-322
Reading strategies, xxiii-xxx
Reasons, xxii, xxvi, xxxiv
Repetition, intentional, xxviii
Roberts, Robin, "Strike Out Little League," 117-124
Rosenfeld, Albert, "'Learning' to Give Up," 167-175
"Rudeness at the Movies," Bill Wine, 109-116
Ruggiero, Vincent Ryan, "The Urge to Conform," 158-166

Sanders, Luella Fern, "The Smart Way to Buy a New Car," 240-249
Scratch outline, xxxiv
Seliger, Susan, "Back from Death?" 43-53
Signal words (transitions), xxviii, 11
Skwire, David, and Frances Chitwood, "Specific Details," 278-285
"Smart Way to Buy a New Car, The," Luella Fern Sanders, 240-249
Space order (location) pattern, xxviii, xxxiv

"Specific Details," David Skwire and Frances Chitwood, 278-285
Statistics, xxvi, xxxiv
"Strike Out Little League," Robin Roberts, 117-124
"Students in Shock," John Kellmayer, 75-82
Summarizing, xvii, xxi, 11
Summary, definition of, 11
Support
  for a point, xv, xx, xxii, xxv, xxxiii, 9
  types of, xxii, xxvi-xxvii, xxxiv

Teague, Bob, "To Get a Story, I Flimflammed a Dead Man's Mother," 32-42
"Television Addiction," Marie Winn, 125-131
Thesis statement, xxvi, xxxiii, xxxv
Time (chronological) order pattern, xxviii, xxxiv
Title, of an essay, xxiii, xxix
"To Get a Story, I Flimflammed a Dead Man's Mother," Bob Teague, 32-42
Tone, xxviii, 10
Topic sentence, xxv, xxxiii, xxxv
Transitions, xxviii, 11
"Turning On Turned-Off Workers," Michael LeBoeuf, 227-238

"Urge to Conform, The," Vincent Ryan Ruggiero, 158-166

Vocabulary Check, xvi, 6

Webb, James, "What We Can Learn from Japan's Prisons," 217-226
"What Do Children Owe Their Parents?," Ann Landers, 64-74
"What Is Intelligence, Anyway?" Isaac Asimov, 142-148
"What We Can Learn from Japan's Prisons," James Webb, 217-226

"When My Brother Was Slain," Ben Fong-Torres, 83-92
White, Clarissa, "Classroom Note-Taking," 250-258
"Why We Throw Food Away," William Rathje, 202-209
Wine, Bill, "Rudeness at the Movies," 109-116
Winn, Marie, "Television Addiction," 125-131
Words to Watch, xvi, xxi, xxiv-xxv, 6-7
Writer's Craft, the, xxvii, 10
Writing assignments, xvii, xxii
   essay, xvii, xxii
   paragraph, xvii, xxii
Writing strategies, xxx-xxxv

Reading Performance Chart

Note: To obtain your score, give yourself 5 points for each correct Vocabulary Check or Reading Check item. Divide the number of blanks in the Outlining or Summarizing Activity into 10 to find the point value for the items in this section.

Title of Selection

	Vocabulary Check (40 points)	Reading Check (50 points)	Outlining/ Summarizing (10 points)	TOTAL SCORE
1. Bird Girl				
2. Being a Boy				
3. The Back of the Bus				
4. To Get a Story, I Flimflammed a Dead Man's Mother				
5. Back from Death?				
6. Batter Up				
7. What Do Children Owe Their Parents?				
8. Students in Shock				
9. When My Brother Was Slain				
10. Living the Simple Life				
11. Fun. Oh Boy, Fun. You Could Die from It				
12. Rudeness at the Movies				
13. Strike Out Little League				
14. Television Addiction				
15. Boxing Is a Barbarism Civilization Can Do Without				

Title of Selection

	Vocabulary Check (40 points)	Reading Check (50 points)	Outlining/ Summarizing (10 points)	TOTAL SCORE
16. What Is Intelligence, Anyway?	_____	_____	_____	_____
17. Funerals Are Good for People	_____	_____	_____	_____
18. The Urge to Conform	_____	_____	_____	_____
19. "Learning" to Give Up	_____	_____	_____	_____
20. Don't Let Stereotypes Warp Your Judgments	_____	_____	_____	_____
21. A Crime of Compassion	_____	_____	_____	_____
22. How About Low-Cost Drugs for Addicts?	_____	_____	_____	_____
23. Why We Throw Food Away	_____	_____	_____	_____
24. Escape Valve	_____	_____	_____	_____
25. What We Can Learn from Japan's Prisons	_____	_____	_____	_____
26. Turning On Turned-Off Workers	_____	_____	_____	_____
27. The Smart Way to Buy a New Car	_____	_____	_____	_____
28. Classroom Note-Taking	_____	_____	_____	_____
29. Owning a Pet Can Have Therapeutic Value	_____	_____	_____	_____
30. Face Up to Your Fears	_____	_____	_____	_____
31. Specific Details	_____	_____	_____	_____
32. Problems and Pain	_____	_____	_____	_____